A FORTUNATE LIFE

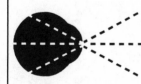

This Large Print Book carries the
Seal of Approval of N.A.V.H.

A Fortunate Life

Robert Vaughn

THORNDIKE PRESS
A part of Gale, Cengage Learning

GALE
CENGAGE Learning™

Detroit • New York • San Francisco • New Haven, Conn • Waterville, Maine • London

GALE
CENGAGE Learning™

Thorndike Press® Large Print Biography.
The text of this Large Print edition is unabridged.
Other aspects of the book may vary from the original edition.
Set in 16 pt. Plantin.
Printed on permanent paper.

LIBRARY OF CONGRESS CATALOGING-IN-PUBLICATION DATA

Vaughn, Robert, 1932–
    A fortunate life / by Robert Vaughn.
       p. cm. — (Thorndike Press large print biography)
    ISBN-13: 978-1-4104-1324-6 (alk. paper)
    ISBN-10: 1-4104-1324-1 (alk. paper)
    1. Vaughn, Robert, 1932– 2. Actors—United
States—Biography. 3. Large type books. I. Title.
PN2287.V38A3 2009
791.4302'8092—dc22
                              2008043170

Published in 2009 by arrangement with St Martin's Press, LLC.

Printed in the United States of America
1 2 3 4 5 6 7 12 11 10 09 08

*To Caitlin, Cassidy, and Linda,
so they might know how it all began*

CONTENTS

7

INTRODUCTION

With a modest amount of looks and talent and more than a modicum of serendipity, I've managed to stretch my fifteen minutes of fame into more than a half century of good fortune. As a performer in almost every entertainment medium, from stage and screen to radio and television, I've enjoyed a lifetime of adventures around the world and worked with an array of remarkably gifted artists. Along the way, I've met many famous and a few infamous people, and in these pages I haven't hesitated to drop some of their names. To paraphrase my colleague and friend the late David Niven, "If you've had lunch with Robert Kennedy, why write about the waiter?"

But I've tried to make this book more than a mere exercise in name-dropping. I hope you'll find it an interesting sketch of a life rich in incident, one rooted in show business but with forays into the larger worlds of politics and international relations. I've been lucky enough to have at least a passing connection or a through-the-window glimpse into some of the great events of my generation, from the blacklisting of Hollywood, the struggle for civil rights, and the anti–Vietnam War movement to the tumultuous presidential campaign of 1968, the crushing of Czech democracy by Soviet tanks, and the still-unsolved mystery of Robert F. Kennedy's assassination. Perhaps the reader of this book will encounter one or two new insights into these epochal events, along with the lighter entertainment to be gleaned from my escapades as an actor.

As you'll see, a running theme of my life has been a continuing fascination with the supreme Shakespearean role, that of the Melancholy Dane — Hamlet. The epigraphs for each chapter are drawn from that greatest of plays, which remains, for me, a fount of apposite wisdom for virtually any occasion. I hope the scholars in my audience will forgive me for decorating my poor edifice with a few garlands borrowed from the master.

ONE:
HAMLET AND ME

Speak the speech, I pray you, as I pronounc'd it to you, trippingly on the tongue; but if you mouth it, as many of your players do, I had as lief the town-crier spoke my lines.

A wise man once remarked, "If you do the thing you love, you'll never have to work a day in your life."

I did, and I haven't.

I am a creature of the theater, in all its forms, from radio and stage to movies and television. The acting bug bit me when I was four or five, living with my mother and her parents on the second floor of a stucco house at 1826 West Broadway in Minneapolis. That was when my mother used some early form of phonics to teach me the most famous dramatic utterance in the English language, the "To be or not to be" soliloquy from *Hamlet,* a meditation on the meaning of life and death by the Bard of Avon, William Shakespeare.

I remember standing facing Mother as she sat almost motionless in my grandfather's wooden rocking chair, repeating the words in a rhythm that locked the soliloquy in my brain forever. When I finally knew all the lines and could recite the speech from beginning to end, she said, "Now you are an actor." And that's when my destiny was forged during a hot summer week three-quarters of a century ago.

I guess the expression we used back then to describe the kind of person I became is "a show-off." But from that summer on, I did everything I could to try to understand what this pretending to be someone else was like, and how to do it so people would pay attention to me. I'm sure a shrink would have much to say about the process (little of it positive). But it all made me mysteriously, completely happy.

Of course, as a child of five, I had no idea what Shakespeare's gorgeous language, so encrusted with metaphor and fraught with feeling, was all about. All I knew was that the words seemed to make people smile and applaud whenever I recited them at my mother's instigation. And recite them I did, in venues that included Fourth of July celebrations, picnics in North Commons Park, firehouse parties, Catholic church socials, Easter and Christmas doings, and family gatherings. No wonder those thirty-five lines remain imprinted in my brain to this day.

I was six in the summer of 1939 when I traveled on my own for the first time, journeying to Chicago on the mighty Twin Cities Hiawatha train with my name, address, and telephone number written on a piece of Captain Marvel stationery pinned to my short-sleeved shirt. I was beside myself with excitement. Mother had sent for me so that I could meet the man who would be her new husband and my step-father, John Ladd Connor. (She and my father, radio actor Walter Vaughn, had separated some six or seven years before.) Mother and John had just finished several seasons acting with the Chicago Federal Theatre, the regional branch of the first and only government-subsidized theater in American history. But the Federal Theatre Project had been abolished that June — alas — mainly because of Congressional umbrage over the alleged Communist sympathies of the writers, actors, and directors it employed.

In that final season of Federal Theatre,

John Connor and Ian Keith had alternated in the Shakespearean roles of Othello and Iago — the noble, misguided hero and the mysteriously malignant villain. This was quite a coup for John. Keith was a nationally acclaimed actor, widely considered the most brilliant American player of Hamlet in the first half of the twentieth century with the sole exception of the great John Barrymore (himself remembered today, if at all, merely as the grandfather of Drew rather than as the towering figure he was). When Keith played the role of the melancholy Dane, John Connor played his uncle Claudius, while my mother played Gertrude. (In an earlier production at the Minneapolis Federal Theatre, she had been Ophelia.)

So *Hamlet* was in the air around me as I was growing up, if not in my blood. But by that summer of '39, with the Federal Theatre a memory, John and Mother were broke, keeping the wolf from the door by tending bar and hostessing a popular dice game called 26 at a bar on Division just off State Street, Chicago's main drag. And that was where I joined them during that steamy late-Depression summer, excited to glimpse the grown-up big-city world of Chicago and the theatrical crowd among whom my mother and her husband-to-be moved.

It so happened that, that same summer, a little opus titled *My Dear Children* was occupying the Selwyn Theatre in Chicago, and starring in that production was none other than Jack Barrymore himself. He'd been on the road for nearly a year with the show, selling out theaters in nearly every burg he played. The play itself was eminently forgettable; the sole attraction was Jack's freewheeling, moderately drunken interpretation of the leading role, which found him sitting on the front apron of the stage, chatting amiably with the audience and telling slightly off-color jokes. Audiences seemingly couldn't get enough of the celebrated movie star's booze-soaked meanderings, and when he finally left the stage he inevitably received a standing ovation.

With Barrymore the play's single great asset, the producers knew that protecting his value called for prudent planning. They'd hired a six-foot-six male nurse named Karl whose job it was to escort the star on his nightly crawl of the near-Northside bars, finally delivering him in the wee hours to his splendid digs at the famed Ambassador East Hotel, where an oxygen tent that Karl was licensed to operate had been installed as a precautionary measure.

The bar on Division Street was one of

Barrymore's favored spots. One particularly warm August night, I accompanied Mother there as she delivered a large bowl of Irish stew — one of the few dishes she could cook — for my stepfather's post-midnight supper. Jack and Karl were holding forth among a crowd of admirers at the bar. Barrymore, seemingly unaffected by the sweltering heat, was wearing his black cloche hat and a black opera cloak and brandishing his FDR-size cigarette holder. It was my first glimpse of the great man whose name I'd heard mentioned so often in tones of hushed reverence.

Fortified by a Tom Collins or two, Mother decided that this would be the night that Jack Barrymore would get to see her little son's *Hamlet* act.

She grabbed me by my tiny shoulders and thrust me forward at the feet of the legendary star. "Go ahead, Robert," she prodded. The circle around Barrymore grew still; the great man himself leaned toward me, an indulgent smile on his face. All eyes were on me. It was a feeling I was already learning to recognize . . . and to like.

Leaning against a bar stool, I struck a dramatic pose and launched into the great speech with all the dignity and pathos a six-year-old could muster:

To be, or not to be: that is the question.
Whether 'tis nobler in the mind to suffer
The slings and arrows of outrageous for-
   tune . . .

And so on, through all those ringing, memorable phrases — "To sleep? Perchance to dream," "The oppressor's wrong, the proud man's contumely," "The undiscover'd country from whose bourn / No traveler returns," and all the rest. When I concluded with the words "And lose the name of action," my small audience burst into applause, and Barrymore himself rose to his feet and, at the top of his mighty lungs, roared, *"More, lad, more!"*

Unfortunately, I was a one-trick pony. But Mother, no doubt tickled by the star's reaction, encouraged me to reprise the great soliloquy . . . which I did, several times.

Before returning to school in Minneapolis in September, I managed to entertain the great man on several other evenings, adding some lines from "Casey at the Bat" to vary the entertainment.

Three years later, Barrymore was dead. He was just sixty years old.

And that was the extent of my acquaintance with either *Hamlet* or John Barrymore for most of my youth. Some time in junior high school, when I was thirteen or fourteen, I came across *Good Night, Sweet Prince,* journalist Gene Fowler's 1944 biography of (and tender tribute to) his friend John Barrymore. And I remember occasionally reading aloud from the play to classmates in my North High School journalism class, to general incredulity (not to say boredom). Otherwise, I did not get involved with the play again until my freshman year at the University of Minnesota.

In the spring of 1952, I was in my final quarter at the U, where I was majoring in journalism, covering boxing and football for the *Minnesota Daily,* and squeezing theater and radio courses into my spare time. The previous summer, I had driven to California with my recently widowed mother. John Ladd Connor had died of the demon drink in March 1951, at the age of thirty-nine. The doctors at Roosevelt Hospital called it the worst case of cirrhosis of the liver they'd ever seen in a man so young. I was brokenhearted.

But before I made my permanent departure for the coast, Chuck La Beaux and I decided to spend spring break at Mardi Gras in New Orleans. (Chuck was my closest childhood friend and became a member of the high-IQ society Mensa, a rare distinction in those days.) It sounded like a pleasant way to squander a little of what was left of the money my father, Walter Vaughn, had willed to me after his death in January 1950. But the day before Chuck and I were to leave, someone told me there was a note for me on the Scott Hall bulletin board from Dr. Frank Whiting, the dean of the drama department. (Whiting was friends with Dr. Tyrone Guthrie, the great Anglo-Irish director, and a little over a decade later the pair would join forces to create the famous Guthrie Theater in Minneapolis. Their opening production would be — of course — *Hamlet*.)

Dr. Whiting's note was to the point: Jim Schroeder, one of the school's leading actors, had had to bow out of the role of Laertes in the department's spring semester production of *Hamlet*. Would I consider playing the role? *Would I?!* I immediately canceled my travel plans and went directly into rehearsal. I was later told that this was the first time in the history of the department that a freshman had been given a principal role in a senior main stage production.

The play went well, and at the end of the run, Dr. Whiting sent me another note. His decision to offer me the role of Laertes, he confessed, had been a hasty one, and he'd worried about it many times since. But now he'd realized it was the single best decision he'd made in casting the show.

When I ran into Dr. Whiting near the end of the school year, he said he'd made tentative plans to do some summer productions on a riverboat on the Mississippi. "Would you consider playing Hamlet if I need you?"

I sure would — after all, I already knew the lines.

For one reason or another, the riverboat production didn't happen. But by now I'd been bitten — but good. In the fall of 1952, I enrolled at Los Angeles City College, where for the next year I would assault my fellow student actors with all the famous soliloquys from *Hamlet* — over and over and over. . . .

Lord Laurence Olivier famously described *Hamlet* as "the story of a man that could not make up his mind." And while that bland description can only hint at the psychological complexity and life-and-death import of the drama, the life goal of practically every post-Elizabethan actor has been to play Hamlet. And there are as many Hamlets as there are men — or women — ready to play him.

I shared the same dream as most other thespians. And at the beginning of the sixties, I thought my moment had come. I was an aspiring young actor immersed in classes, workshops, and small-scale theater productions in Hollywood when I received a call from a man in Minneapolis. The much-discussed Guthrie Theater was preparing to open, and they were checking to see whether I was interested in playing the lead in their first production — *Hamlet.* My answer was an excited yes. I alerted my agent, Stan Kamen of the William Morris office (whom Steve McQueen had introduced me to), to negotiate a deal at *any* price.

Barely an hour had passed before Kamen phoned me back with deflating news. "No deal," he told me. "It has nothing to do with the money. They want you to sign on for an entire season as part of the Guthrie repertory theater. Your career's getting ready to take off, Bob. This is no time to go gallivanting off to fly-over country." (That's how Hollywood types then referred to what today are called the red states.)

I swallowed hard, took Kamen's advice, and notified the Guthrie that I was not available.

But that wasn't to be my only opportunity to play the melancholy prince. In the spring of 1960, I was pursuing an MA in theater arts at Los Angeles State College, the upper division of Los Angeles City College. The school had just built a multimillion-dollar theater, and I was already on campus preparing to direct my friends Tony Carbone and James Coburn in Arthur Miller's *A View from the Bridge.* The school's directors hatched a plan: Why not put on *Hamlet* to inaugurate the new theater, and feature that dashing young fellow Robert Vaughn in the leading role? I jumped at the chance.

I had relatively little time to prepare once my work on the Miller drama was finished. I immersed myself in the abundance of critical literature surrounding *Hamlet.* I learned all I could about the boy/man Hamlet and his inability to satisfy the demands of his murdered father's ghost.

I decided I must get a grip on the crucial *Hamlet* debate dating back to Tudor times: Was the ghost of King Hamlet a mere hallucination resulting from young Hamlet's grief and depression, or, as most Elizabethans believed, a true appearance of the soul of a dead loved one returning to beg for help from the living? Or was there some third explanation?

Most Christian belief consigns the dead either to heaven or to hell. But in Catholic theory, the majority of those who have passed are in a place beneath the earth called purgatory, waiting to be cleansed of their unexpiated sins and then transported to the eternal bliss of heaven. But old Hamlet is not asking for relief from the burden of sin — he seeks revenge for his murder through the killing of Claudius, stepfather of young Hamlet and husband to the recently widowed Gertrude.

Educated in Wittenberg, young Hamlet seems to share the more advanced doctrine of the sixteenth-century Protestant Reformation in Shakespeare's England — that there are no true ghosts, and that all seeming apparitions are delusions or, worse, disguised devils. But by the evidence of the play, his attitude wavers. First, Hamlet says he believes he has seen an "honest ghost." Then he becomes uncertain, saying, "The spirit that I have seen may be the devil." Needing further proof of the ghost's reality, Hamlet asks a troupe of visiting players to the Danish court to stage *The Murder of Gonzaga* before Claudius and Gertrude, but to include a play within the play, written by Hamlet himself. He hopes that when the players replicate the murder as described to him by his father's ghost, Claudius will betray himself and so resolve Hamlet's doubts.

Hamlet, then, is a man torn in several directions — between duty and doubt, certainty and fear, reason and faith, science and superstition. In this ambivalence we see one source of his enduring appeal for the actor.

Then there is the question of Hamlet's "madness." Is it real? Is it feigned? Does he move from sanity to derangement, or does he occupy some halfway zone between the two?

Over the centuries, scholars have argued for all these positions, and actors, including the greatest, have played Hamlet according to every imaginable theory. As for me, I believe that Hamlet crosses the line from sanity to insanity during his first confrontation with his father's ghost, and that he does so not willingly but helplessly. The same thing happens during his next and final contact with his father's spirit, during his visit to his mother's chambers after the play within the play has confirmed to young Hamlet his stepfather's guilt. In between these contacts with the ghost, I believe that Hamlet *simulates* madness when speaking with Ophelia, Polonius, Rosencrantz, Guildenstern, and so on. He does this deliberately, to test them and to provoke a revealing response. Hamlet all but admits his deception when he confides in Guildenstern, "I am but mad north-north-west: when the wind is southerly I know a hawk from a handsaw." "Though this be madness," as Polonius properly observes, "yet there is method in it."

That Hamlet would feign insanity may seem strange or unbelievable, but it's not an unknown phenomenon in the real world. The voluntary production of psychiatric symptoms, known as the Ganser syndrome, nearly always affects men, especially those suffering from depression. In Elizabethan times, what we call today "clinical depression" or "situational depression" (the latter afflicting people suffering from such profoundly disturbing events as a divorce, the death of a loved one, or a serious illness) was called *melancholia.* Hence the epithet "The Melancholy Dane" often used to describe Hamlet.

Many years ago, I dubbed Shakespeare "the first lay analyst of Stratford-upon-Avon." The evidence for this observation was the nonpareil mind of his most famous and oft-performed character. But even licensed psychiatrists find it hard to decide whether Ganser syndrome is a genuine psychiatric disorder or just another all-too-human ploy in the battle for personal survival in a hostile world. So it's not surprising that the debate over Hamlet's madness should persist to this day.

My 1960 performance went well. The *Los Angeles Times* said my performance could be favorably compared to that of the Old Vic's John Neville — heady praise indeed for a young actor.

Hamlet has continued to follow me through life. I've seen some fifty Hamlets, from the British actor George Russell Meade, who was a bit portly, at the Brooklyn Academy of Music (warm and sincere, but not terribly vulnerable, theatrical, or romantic) to Ralph Fiennes, on Broadway in 1995 (the best I've seen). I even recorded an album of *Hamlet* during my stint as television's Man from U.N.C.L.E. — a sincere artistic effort on my part, but a mere money-making gambit on the part of the record producers, I'm afraid, designed to capitalize on my fame among the teeny-boppers of the mid-1960s.

I'm convinced that *Hamlet* will continue to fascinate me until I "shuffle off this mortal coil" and pass to "the undiscovered country from whose bourn, no traveler returns" — if there is such a country after

26

all. And perhaps the final words that escape my lips will include some fragments of those thirty-five lines committed to memory in a Minneapolis summer oh so long ago . . . a show-off to the very end.

Two:
Discovering Life in
a Murphy Bed

This is the very ecstasy of love.

"Frank, I'm only on the third word. I gotta have more coal."

I was standing behind the potbellied stove with the orange isinglass windows that warmed the upper half of the gray stucco duplex in which I grew up in the Minneapolis of the thirties.

Frank was my grandfather, my mother's father, but I always called him Frank. It was the brutal winter of 1941–42, the worst, people said, in over a century. In the next room, on my Mercator projection map over Frank's bed — the one that makes Greenland as large as North America — I followed the war in the Pacific. The Japs were winning everywhere, and I was scared.

To increase the heat where I stood, I repeated my call for more coal. My arms were stretched straight out from my shoulders as I simulated Christ's crucifixion while I spoke his last seven words. Only if the heat were intense enough did I feel I was duplicating, to the best of my nine-year-old imagination's ability, those terrible hours on Golgotha so long ago.

Directly behind my very hot left shoulder was the entrance to Frank's small bedroom, with its wondrous chiffonier containing everything from a Stern's theatrical makeup kit with wigs, noses, putty, and spirit gum to a beaded, bloodied Indian pouch worn, according to Frank, by Sitting Bull at the Battle of Little Big Horn. It was in this room that Frank wrote such playlets as *The Puppy Who Made Bunny Tracks* and *Pigs Whistle More on Sundays.* These playwriting efforts were for me so that I might direct and star in them at the Lowell School in North Minneapolis.

Although I grew up in the American heartland — specifically, in the progressive Minnesota of Hubert Humphrey and Garrison Keillor — my family and I were always set a little apart from the people around us. Our real world wasn't the world of dairy farms, insurance brokers, PTA meetings, and Woolworth's counters that most residents of the Twin Cities seemed to inhabit. Our world was the world of the theater, and without much explicit discussion it was somehow understood from an early age that I would follow in the family tradition by becoming an actor.

In fact, my family had a long heritage of acting. My mother's mother, Marie or Mary Halloran (she was called by both names), was an actress in Glencoe, Minnesota. Frank was the director of the Glencoe Comedy Players acting troupe. (When they later moved to Minneapolis, he made a living as a stage director and paperhanger — though he preferred to describe himself as an "interior decorator.") I've even heard that Frank's father, Sebastian Gaudel, was in the commedia dell'arte in France in the nineteenth century.

As for my father, Gerald Walter Vaughn, he was a well-known radio actor, famous for the raspy voice he deployed effectively in tough-guy roles — gangsters, cattle rustlers, pirates.

My forebears weren't stars occupying the upper stratosphere of the theatrical universe. They were working actors, living from job to job, never too proud to take on a role, however lowly. Looking back at the *very* long list of movies, TV dramas, miniseries, stage shows, and (yes) even radio programs I've done over the past five decades —

including both a handful of recognized classics and quite a few that are blessedly forgotten — one might easily conclude that I inherited their attitude and never abandoned it, even after vaulting with relative swiftness to the airier reaches of Hollywood.

Growing up in a theatrical family carries with it a touch of chaos. In my case, it was pleasant chaos. I lived apart from my parents for much of my childhood, but I don't remember resenting this. And after my mother and father were separated, I saw my dad only twice. Much of the time I was cared for by my grandparents. Yet somehow I knew in my bones that my parents cared about me. From his home in New York, my father sent me twenty dollars a month via my grandparents and sent me cards for my birthday.

He also sent me occasional presents — a watch and, on one memorable occasion, an English racing bike. Apparently no one had ever seen such a bike in Minneapolis, and it was destroyed the first time I brought it to school. Not by me, but by a knot of angry classmates who apparently thought it was time I was brought down a peg or two. As a youngster, I was always a little disliked by my peers because of my actorly attitude. (I suppose it would have been different if I'd

31

grown up in Beverly Hills or Manhattan, but West Broadway in Minneapolis was another matter.) I imagine they thought I was an uppity snot — and I rather imagine I was at that.

But I was always basically happy wherever I was, however, because I could always pretend to be wherever I imagined. For what reason, I know not, but I most often chose to imagine being in England. I would fill my red Radio Flyer with English history books at the public library on Emerson Avenue, then drag it the half mile north to my home at 1826 West Broadway.

The books were very large, with glorious color pictures of Williams I and II and Henry I and Stephen, the Normans whose reigns covered roughly the hundred years from the middle of the tenth to the middle of the eleventh centuries. I returned to the Emerson Library throughout my elementary school years, wagon in tow, replacing big books already consumed with new ones covering the Plantagenets, the House of Lancaster, and the House of York, until finally I came to the Tudors, where I met Elizabeth, the Virgin Queen, and more important, her contemporary, the sire of my Melancholy Dane, Will Shakespeare.

I remember carrying both a first baseman's glove and a catcher's mitt on these library treks. Why I had them I don't know, since I was essentially a pretty good pitcher. But I used the two gloves to carefully cover the English history books during my weekly journey to and from the Emerson Library. I guess I didn't want the local guys to think I was a sissy who read books — let alone books of medieval English history.

Yet the notion of being an actor was always present in the back of my mind.

When I arrived at the age of ten without having acted in a real play, I decided that the next best thing would be a one-man show for my fellow fourth graders at the Lowell School. I also concluded that rather than wait for my grandfather Frank to come up with some material, I would simply borrow George M. Cohan's songs and dances from the Warner Bros. movie *Yankee Doodle Dandy.* I had already acquired an Adolphe Menjou three-piece suit from a local secondhand store (it must have belonged to a midget) along with a big floppy bow tie patterned after the ones Sinatra made famous at the New York Paramount. I found an old derby in one of Frank's theatrical trunks, and I was ready.

I had seen Jimmy Cagney do his strange, butt-out, stiff-legged dancing style as Cohan many times at the Paradise Theater, sometimes spending all afternoon and evening watching his performance. I convinced my favorite teacher, Mrs. Northfoss, to let me entertain the troops. So one day there I was, hoofing and singing, neither of which I did well, to the shock and horror of my classmates.

By January 1943, I figured that since I knew everything there was to know about acting (I was eleven at the time), I might try my hand at directing. I also thought it might be best to select some material other than Frank's and George M. Cohan's efforts. I went down to my beloved Emerson Library and picked out a one-act play titled *The White Birds of Cholula.* It had a starring role for me as Pedro, "a Mexican mystic." This time, I forced my school friends not only to sit through my performance, but to act in the production as well. It was a great success and was held over for a second performance.

In my neighborhood gang at the time, there was Tom next door, Smitty and Ernest Jr. two doors away, and Sally across the alley. Sally and I were the same age, and I gave her a book titled *The Magical Monarch of Mo,* a book that is still in her family today. Arlene, my senior by one year, lived in the other house next to ours and was my walking-to-school friend throughout much of my boyhood. I was always attracted to older women.

A new teacher appeared at the Lowell School for my final year there, the pretty Mary Shattuck. She was fresh out of college, about five feet tall, and appeared to be in her early teens, although in retrospect I am sure she was at least twenty. The boys all fell in love with her, and I decided I would try to kiss her if I could. One day, I was alone with her in the cloakroom, and as I was about to make my move, she sensed something was up and nimbly stepped aside.

Many years later, in the 1960s, when I had become a well-known television personality, I found out that she had married into the Dayton Department Store chain, and I rang her up when I was in Minneapolis on a publicity junket. When I introduced myself by name, she remembered me immediately, not from television, but from the cloakroom. She told me she had retired from teaching at the end of her first year and declined the opportunity to renew our all-too-brief love affair.

After graduating from Lowell in June of '44 and feeling my acting oats, having now directed and starred in a play, I headed off to join Mother and John Connor in Iowa as a resident member of the "Famous Players' Tent Show." I was enlisted by Vincent Dennis, the owner of the company whom John had met in Chicago that winter in a play titled *Unexpected Honeymoon.* My summer job was to be the proverbial "jack of all showbiz trades," meaning I was to serve as the tent setter-upper, the popcorn-maker, the assistant to the magician, the assistant to the chalk-talk artist, the light-board operator, the prop man, and, most important, an actor.

We played a dozen towns in Iowa, moving on each week, striking the tent, hitting the road late at night, and sleeping on top of the canvas as we journeyed to a new venue. There were five plays in our repertoire that summer: *The Stork Laid an Egg, Today's Children, The Shepherd of the Hills, Hollywood Comes to Tildy Ann,* and *Toby Goes to Washington.*

In the last play, I spoke my first line on a professional stage. Standing as straight and tall as a twelve-year-old could, I blasted out, "Telegram for Mr. Edward Mason!" Each night, I came farther and farther onto the stage until I was almost on top of the audience. At long last, I was really in show business, and nothing could stop me from realizing my little boy's dream.

Starting Jordan Junior High School in the fall of '44 as a little seventh-grade "beezer," I strived to hang in there with my friends, all of whom I had known since kindergarten. By then, they had all made peace with my histrionic aspirations. Suddenly, I had to convince a new bunch of twelve-year-olds to get with the program.

My first mistake that autumn was to arrive at my new school in my sixth-grade graduation wardrobe, which consisted of a camel-hair sport coat, a long key chain, rather like the ones zoot-suiters in Detroit wore, and my largest Sinatra bow tie. I was not well-received. In fact, I sensed I was going to be spending a lot of time after school fighting literally for my right to be me — a me who was very different from my new classmates. Basically, a lot of the guys wanted to kick the shit out of me. A modicum of Irish charm coupled with a glib, facile tongue stayed most of my potential tormentors. I avoided all but two punch-ups, one of which I actually won.

During the '44–'45 theatrical season, John and Mother toured in a little production called *Ramshackle Inn,* starring Zasu Pitts and featuring a recent Smith graduate, Nancy Davis — later the First Lady of the

United States, Nancy Reagan. The production played the Lyceum Theatre in Minneapolis, and for the first time, I was able to prove to my nay-saying school friends that Mother was a real actress and not just a product of my fevered theatrical imagination. Luck played a role in her performing in the city of her birth. Although John was a regular member of the cast, Mother had been hired as an understudy for the character lead opposite Pitts. While leaving the train in the city during the company's arrival in Minneapolis, the actress Mother was standing in for fell and sprained her ankle, allowing Marcella to star opposite Zasu in her hometown. Although, to the best of my knowledge, none of my school friends went to see the play, I was secure in the knowledge that had they shown up, Mother would have been up there on the boards for all the world to see.

On rare occasions in my grammar school years, if I had some advance notice of when my father would be on the radio, acting in shows such as *Gang Busters, Crime Doctor,* or *The FBI in Peace and War,* I would gather some of the neighborhood kids and tell them to listen closely to the closing credits. They did, but none of them ever believed Walter Vaughn was related to me. So I eventually gave up that stratagem, figuring I would have to wait for some better proof of my other life in my show business summers with my real family and actor friends.

But I wasn't completely cut off from normal life. I made my share of friends, did well in some classes, skated by in some others, and participated in most of the usual hijinks Midwestern kids would have enjoyed in the years preceding midcentury. I developed an interest in sports, and by the time I reached high school, I was fast and strong enough to be named co-captain of the cross-country team. I also ran the half mile (actually the 880) on the track team and even played basketball for one season.

And I was involved in other activities outside the theatrical world, including some that verged on another later interest of mine — the political. I spent the spring of 1945 (as World War II, the constant backdrop of my boyhood, was finally winding down) setting up chairs at Howie's Beer Hall on Penn and West Broadway in North Minneapolis. Various candidates for mayor stopped by this local bar, a favorite of my mother's, to deliver speeches explaining why each should be the one to lead the larger of the Twin Cities.

One of them was a young fellow with the improbable name of Hubert Horatio Humphrey. Hubert always arrived early at Howie's, and over the clatter of the metal chairs, he would yell, "Can you hear me, Bobby?" I would yell back, suppressing the giggles, "I can hear you, *Hubert!*"

A score of years later, Hubert and I shared an open car at the St. Paul Winter Carnival. He had become Lyndon Johnson's Vice President, and I was television's Napoleon Solo.

I'm sure that, as my teenage years unfolded, the fact that I was a fairly good-looking fellow helped win me social acceptance. I didn't think much about my looks, but I was obsessed with clothing, scraping together spare change from my allowance and the occasional odd job in a vain effort to buy stylish duds like the ones I saw pictured in the glossy magazines of the day.

I wasn't cured of this obsession until my years on *The Man from U.N.C.L.E.,* when I sometimes had to change costumes six or seven times during a single day's shooting. Yes, there can be too much of a good thing.

At the same time, as my chest broadened and my voice deepened, thoughts about more than an acting career began to fill my mind, just as they do with most healthy young guys. ("The Child is Father of the man," as Wordsworth had it.)

When does a young boy become a young man? And how does he know the difference? For me, it was when I stumbled onto a copy of *Esquire* magazine in my beloved Emerson Library in Minneapolis sometime in the early years of World War II — around the time I began to have double digits in my age.

The "Magazine for Men" featured pictures of what were called Varga or Petty girls, named after the talented artists who painted them. In ultra-vivid colors and textures so hyper-real they looked practically three-dimensional, they depicted voluptuous ladies spilling out of whatever they were barely wearing. I didn't quite know why, but somehow those female images — with their lushly welcoming smiles, luxuriant manes, amazingly slender torsos, exploding breasts, and endless silky legs terminating in strappy high heels — made me feel warm and happy. I wanted to see more of them. Occasionally, when I was lucky, I might even find photographs of partially dressed girls. (I never even dreamed of seeing one naked.) But in time, I began to suspect that these newfound emotions had something to

41

do with being a "man" in the sense that the publishers of *Esquire* had in mind.

The summer following this discovery I spent in New York City with my mother and my newly minted stepfather, John Ladd Connor. By that time, he was in his early thirties and to me a very old person like some of my teachers at the Lowell School. It was the first of many summers I spent with them in New York, where we always lived on West Sixty-ninth Street. When Mother and John had a good year in their profession — steady jobs in decent roles in long-run shows — we lived very near Central Park West. (One particularly flush season, we actually had an apartment on Central Park West itself.) But more often we stayed at the Congress Hotel on Sixty-ninth Street; other times, we rented rooms in slightly down-at-heels apartment buildings at 37 and 63 West Sixty-ninth Street near Columbus Avenue.

(Perhaps you are noticing that I have a memory for names and numbers. Addresses, dates, and other figures have somehow always seemed to stick with me. Maybe it's because I am mildly superstitious about them. For example, I assign some significance to the fact that so many important moments in my life have taken place on my birthday, November 22.)

Today, Manhattan's Upper West Side is a trendy community crowded with Starbucks and Zabar's outlets, boutiques offering frocks and suits in styles just a couple months beyond their debuts in Paris and Milan, and restaurants featuring costly versions of whatever ethnic cuisine the foodie brigade is currently embracing — Thai, Peruvian, Zambian, or what have you. Kids are seen, if at all, in the company of nannies or fetching au pairs from Scandinavian finishing schools. In the much more relaxed time of the early forties, I was allowed to play in "the Park" unescorted every day from early morning until after sunset.

With Mother's permission, I hung out after supper in nearby Columbus Circle, then a haven for soapbox oratory, an American version of London's Hyde Park speaker's corner. The crowds standing in the circle included men, women, boys, and girls. The listeners were often jammed next to one another, and it was there that I experienced — in addition to my first uncomprehending exposure to the heady atmosphere of street-level wartime politics of every stripe, from Communist to Syndicalist to Fascist — my first *real* hard-on. "Real" meaning an erection caused by sexual

43

excitement and induced by contact with another person, one-on-one.

I still remember Her. She was dark-skinned, about my height (I must have been twelve or so at the time), and built a bit like today's popular actress and singer Jennifer Lopez, round and firm of butt. (I told you I have a memory for figures.) She was standing in front of me in the densely packed, restlessly jostling crowd. And it was the gentle yet somehow electric pressure of that protruding butt against the front of my trousers, pulled tight across my boyish hips, that elicited my physical reaction.

Feeling a little guilty, though without knowing why, I fleetingly glanced at her face. I caught a glimpse of a faint, distant smile playing about ripe lips. Looking back, I can readily interpret that expression. She knew that she was teasing me and that I was responding.

I knew in a vague way that the inner tumult I was experiencing had some connection to the kinds of feelings I had had at the Paradise movie theater on West Broadway in Minneapolis when I saw Ann Miller dance. Later, Kathryn Grayson, Virginia Mayo, and (best of all) Jane Russell would all make me feel excited, hot, and happy in much the same way.

Of course, nothing came of my fleeting encounter with the girl in Columbus Circle. But it was one of those formative moments that somehow remain with you for decades after the fact. I wonder whatever became of her, and what she would think if she were to learn that her image has remained imprinted in my mind for all these years?

Meanwhile, I was working to try to sort out the significance of all these oddly pleasant new emotions. Thanks to Father Bartholomew's catechism class at St. Anne's church, which I attended every Saturday morning back home in Minneapolis, I knew this feeling must have something to do with one of those ten rules or, as he called them, Commandments, which he harped on in preparing us for the sacraments of Communion and Confirmation. I wasn't exactly sure what was to come next in this newly discovered world, but I was open to anything that might increase my excitement.

I heard that the Catholic Legion of Decency put out a list of movies you were allowed to see, either with or without adult supervision, depending on the moral tendency and contents of each picture. More important, there was a shorter list at the end of each month's approval list that named the pictures rated as "Condemned."

This was the famous Index. If you saw one of those films you would have committed a mortal sin. And as a good Catholic boy, I knew all too well what that meant: If you died without having rid yourself of that Big One, you went to the fires of hell with *no* purgatorial stop along the way.

Well, this was a titillating concept — especially for young Catholic boys who knew, with the customary sangfroid of youth, that they had decades of life ahead of them for leisurely repentance. Word got out that the World movie house on Hennepin Avenue in downtown Minneapolis was showing a Condemned picture titled *Ecstasy,* starring an actress named Hedy Lamarr who was seen swimming bare-assed and bare-boobed. (The picture had actually been produced as long ago as 1933, but I suppose it took a decade or more to make the cross-Atlantic trek from its native Czechoslovakia to the American hinterlands of Minneapolis.)

In my crowd, plans were immediately made to devise a way of getting into the World by a side door from a back alley off Eighth Street. But I didn't go along with the gang. I was seriously determined to catch a glimpse of the delicious Miss Lamarr. Fearing my friends might blow the operation by laughing or horseplay, I decided to try it by myself. I hung out by the theater and noticed that the longest lines were usually on Saturday afternoon, right after Father Bart's catechism class. I took one of my grandpa's hats and fashioned it into a porkpie style (the fashion of the day), and added dark glasses and my longest winter coat, which was maroon and looked to my mind's eye like some sort of military getup. I calculated that, in this disguise, I could pass myself off as age-qualified to buy a ticket.

When the appointed Saturday was at hand, a major Midwest snowstorm shut down my Operation Hedy. I spent the next week feverish with disappointment, counting the hours till the next window of opportunity. The next Saturday, all was clear, the crowds were enormous, and I weaseled in and got an aisle seat near the front. When the nude scene arrived, it was fast and distant and filmed in what I later learned was called "soft focus," so it was over before anything happened — below my waist or anywhere else.

I pulled my hat low, scurried out into the Eighth Street alley, and caught a streetcar going north from Hennepin back to 1826 West Broadway. I knew I had missed something, but I didn't know what.

Then there was the Alvin Burlesque House, formerly the Schubert Theatre, where my mother made her professional acting debut in the late twenties. It was there that I saw (still clad in porkpie hat and dark glasses) such busty female specimens as Lois de Fee, Sally Rand, Tempest Storm (later a "friend" of John F. Kennedy's), and other burly queens of the day. Based on the reactions of the men around me — as well as my own — I began to flesh out my understanding of the strange attraction exerted by the opposite sex.

I looked about at the girls in my neighborhood — Sally across the alley, the Donut sisters next door (they pronounced it DONet) — and wondered if I'd ever know what the mystery was all about.

In Jordan Junior High (called "middle school" in the American Northeast), we began to have boy/girl parties, sleigh rides, hayrides, and much talk about French kissing, touching the girls above the waist (where, in most cases, what we called "titties" had not yet matriculated), and, heaven forfend, touching the dreaded below-the-waist spot where who-knew-what dark secrets were concealed. As we lads hit our early teens, we began to move around during the spring and fall to various girls' front porches, where, it was rumored, some girls would actually kiss more than one boy from the group during our very short stays at each house.

The forms and faces of my first teenage crushes still linger in the brain cells where they were so powerfully imprinted. My early favorite at the house parties (unchaperoned in those days) was Vivian, who, horribly enough, would die in a car crash before high school graduation. Then came Mary Lou, who babysat on Penn Avenue and let me kiss her, close-mouthed, until our lips went raw. I think to this day that I could have gone much further with Mary Lou, but Father Bart's admonitions about sex always scared me off from making the big push to toe-to-head horizontal hugging, hopefully leading to a crack at doing the biggest baddest word. As far as I know, when we graduated from Jordan Junior High in June 1947, all of us in my crowd were still batting zero in the big sex ballgame.

I spent several summers in the late forties with Mother and John in Cragsmoor and Skaneateles, New York, where they were working in summer stock. There I got a good look at professional actresses close up. They were always mysterious and serious, which greatly increased my fascination with them. I did not know at this time that virtually every professional actress I would subsequently meet in Hollywood during my twenties was not only serious but self-absorbed to the point of living on another planet. This is not necessarily bad for the aspiring actress, but it was not much fun for the aspiring actor. And it certainly did me no good as a starstruck teenager admiring these self-styled goddesses from the wings.

Back in the Midwest, in the fall of 1947, in Al Christopherson's biology class, I was moonstruck by a tall, full-figured girl named Margaret Louise Silbert, whom everyone called Peggy. Since, as a high school sophomore, I had not reached my full adult height, I was reluctant at first to try to get anything going with this brownette beauty. But destiny had selected her as the one who would ultimately initiate me into the secrets of love.

We sat at tables alphabetically, and being a Vaughn, I was at the back of the room, while Peggy Silbert was in front of and diagonally across from me. One day, feeling my juices rumbling, I caught her eye and mouthed the words, "I love you." Perhaps this was not the correct ploy, because we didn't start our relationship until the fall of 1949. We connected at a pajama party for her club, the Klover Kids, to which the members of my boys' club, Zenith, were invited. From that point on, through our graduation in June 1950, we were together.

Peggy's stepfather was a traveling man whose work (as I recall) took him up and down the Mississippi, and her mother went to work each morning, leaving their one-bedroom apartment a block from West Broadway empty and available. Why the North High School truant monitors did not notice that Peggy and I were frequently both absent on the same day remains a conundrum to me.

And it was on Thanksgiving Day in 1949 that at long last the great unsolved mystery of youth was revealed to me in all its glory and simplicity . . . by darling Peggy in her mother's apartment.

That evening, she gave me a picture of herself, inscribed "November 20, 1949, 10 P.M. All my love, Peggy." I still have that picture, and Peggy and I are still good friends.

All of this adolescent adventuring took place against a somber backdrop.

The great housing shortage that followed the war reached its nadir in 1948, and

Frank and Grandma were informed that, come the spring, we would have to move from the only home I had ever known. Frank's heart problems had increased, and his breathing could be heard from the street as he returned each day after searching for a rental. He told me to keep a sharp eye out for a place for us to live, but there was nothing to be had.

Finally, my grandma's sister, Ann Kennedy, and her husband, Jack, whom I always called Jocko, took Grandma and me in, while Frank rented a small room near North High School. On the day we left West Broadway, we all boarded the streetcar crying as we started a new life as guests in other people's homes.

Shortly thereafter — a matter of weeks, perhaps — Frank died alone in his rented room of a heart broken physically and emotionally. He had been my father figure for as long as I could remember, and had done everything he could to give me a good little boy's life. I loved him very much.

But always, for me, there was the theater.

Throughout the forties, whenever I was in New York, I either "second-acted" the hottest plays (meaning I slipped back in with the crowd after the first act) or I somehow hustled a ticket that got me in for the opening curtain for a cut-rate price.

I saw all or part of *A Streetcar Named Desire* with Marlon Brando, *Death of a Salesman* with Lee J. Cobb, *Deep Are the Roots* directed by Elia Kazan, *State of the Union* with Ralph Bellamy, *You Touched Me* by Tennessee Williams, with a very young Montgomery Clift, and numerous other productions now forgotten. It was always "magic time" for me: the audience, the lights dimming, the curtain rising, the stage set, and the actors and actresses telling me a story I loved and cherished, even though I did not always fully understand.

In the middle of June 1950 — exactly in the middle of the twentieth century, as it happens — I graduated from North High School in Minneapolis.

Five years later, in Hollywood, in the middle of the fifties, as a twenty-two-year-old senior in college, I starred in my first network television show. The show was *Medic,* and I played Charles Leale, the doctor who cared for Abraham Lincoln from the time he was shot by an actor until he died. (Every so often, *Medic* would run historical shows like that.) From that point forward until today, my fiftieth year in professional show business, I've earned my living playing "dress up" for enough bucks to allow me to do just about anything I desired.

There was no master plan, unless you can call unrelenting focus on an abstract goal — success — a master plan.

In other events that June of 1950, one affected whatever plans I might have had for my future. One Sunday, June 22, North Korea crossed the 38th parallel to invade South Korea. The subsequent war (called a "police action" by Harry S. Truman) lasted until the election of Dwight D. Eisenhower and the cessation of hostilities in 1953.

As of my eighteenth birthday on November 22, 1950, I would be required to register for the draft and would be eligible to kill or be killed by the Communist aggressors.

Another significant event occurred on June 15, 1950. A 213-page paperback book titled *Red Channels: The Report of Communist Influence in Radio and Television* was published. (Notice that the title was "The" report, not "A" report.) The publisher was identified as "Counterattack: The Newsletter of Facts to Combat Communism," located at 55 West 42nd Street, New York, New York. On the last page of the book, Counterattack was further identified as a "private, independent organization founded 3 years ago in May 1947 by a group of former FBI men. It has no affiliation whatsoever with any government agency."

A generation later (in the late sixties), I would write my Ph.D. thesis — later a published book, titled *Only Victims* — about the blacklist era. It detailed how Counterattack and other organizations, both public and private, dealt in ferreting out alleged un-American, Communist, pinko, Soviet-directed members of show business, including stage, screen, radio, and the new media sensation, television.

But at the time, I was only vaguely aware of these and other stirrings on the global political front. More personal matters occupied my attention. My father — that distant and benign figure from my boyhood — had vanished from my life forever. He died in Barbados in the British West Indies in January 1950. That summer, after my father's death, I met his (fourth or fifth?) wife, Margaret Tuts. She was thirty-nine years old and quite attractive. She told me that he'd once drunk a lot — then stopped, because it was too expensive. And that fall, she called me to tell me about my father's will, which was going into probate. My father had left me ten thousand dollars in the form of two war bonds. The rest of his estate, valued at a couple of hundred thousand dollars, was left to Margaret.

(In subsequent years, I maintained a relationship with Margaret. In the early seventies, when I was in Spain to film *The Protectors,* I heard that she was there, too. I tracked her down and she visited our set with her son. She traveled a lot and in fact married a sea captain after my father's death. Later she lived in Manhattan and visited me at the huge house in Connecticut where my wife, Linda, and I lived for seventeen years. I last saw her at the Coach House restaurant in 1992, when she was in her eighties.)

Well, I was sad about my father's death. But I was excited about my inheritance, which seemed like a vast fortune at the time. With an eighteen-year-old's perspicacity about money, I quickly bought a multi-suited and sport-coated wardrobe from Liemandt's department store in downtown Minneapolis (I believe Jack Liemandt was some sort of relative to me) as well as a beautiful maroon '48 Packard four-door sedan. With the remaining funds, I opened a charge account at the East Hennepin Bar.

In June, I graduated from high school and launched my quest for success in the theater or on radio. For the summer, I joined Mother and John Connor for a second season at the Skaneateles Theatre on one of New York's famed Finger Lakes. Once again, I was the Bobby of all trades backstage, out front, and onstage, with duties ranging from sweeping the theater and ushering patrons to their seats to collecting props, painting scenery, working the switchboard with its gigantic handles (no electronic controls for many years to come), and, best of all, playing small roles in the plays presented. If I was not in the play, I watched every performance from out front. I was obsessed with learning how good actors did their work.

Mr. and Mrs. Walter Davis were the operators of the theater. They were actors whom my mother and stepfather had met in the 1949 touring company of Rodgers and Hammerstein's first and only all-dramatic musical, *Allegro.* They also had a son, David Davis, who had worked in New York television. The week after the invasion of South Korea, David became highly distraught about the possibility of his being re-upped into the Army and sent into the new war zone, seven thousand miles from Broadway.

This all meant nothing to me until he asked how old I was. "I'll be eighteen in

November," I said.

"Well, maybe we'll be working together again," he replied. "Only not in the theater — in Korea."

I asked what that meant, and David said, "You're draft bait when you turn eighteen" — which I hadn't fully understood until that moment.

Knowing that I had the promise of a job at WCCO, the 50,000-watt CBS radio outlet in Minneapolis, which had been arranged by my father's friend and former roommate, actor Ralph Bellamy, I thought, "Well, I'll just play it by ear. Maybe the whole shooting match will be over before November." This made sense to me — after all, hadn't we just beaten the Japs and the Nazis? No peanut-size country on the northeast coast of Asia was going to be any match for the Americans.

How wrong I was.

Just after dusk on November 1, 1950, Chinese forces hit an American unit with full force for the first time. Prior to that, General Douglas MacArthur, commanding the combined forces of the Republic of Korea and other United Nations forces, had maintained that the Chinese Communists were not supporting their brethren to the south. There was now evidence of three

Chinese divisions fighting with the North Koreans.

MacArthur remained in Tokyo, refusing to acknowledge that the war had changed from a civil confrontation between North and South Koreans into a proxy war between a Communist superpower and Western liberal capitalism. (The next proxy war, in a little-known corner of Southeast Asia known as Vietnam, was still a decade and a half away.) The Korean War would last more than two more years.

When the fall rolled around, there were amorphous plans to hook up with Peggy. But for no particular reason we drifted apart. I started working at WCCO. Harry Reasoner, later a famous newsman for the CBS and ABC networks, was a morning newswriter there for Cedric Adams, who was a sort of Midwest Arthur Godfrey. My job was a kind of glorified page-boy position, but I was allowed to wear civvies rather than the silly uniforms often sported by studio guides and messengers in those days.

My eighteenth birthday rolled around, and as required by law I registered for the draft. I decided that my show business career, at least professionally, would have to wait. I stayed at CBS and registered for the spring quarter of 1951 at the University of

Minnesota as a journalism major. As long as I carried a full load of course credits and maintained a C-plus average, I wouldn't be shooting at Communists — nor they at me. (I eventually was drafted in December 1956, by which time I had completed my undergraduate college career with a BA in theater arts at Los Angeles State College. But that's getting a little ahead of the story.)

Meanwhile, my home life — never the most stable — fell into a state of complete disorder. My grandmother and my stepfather, the aforementioned John Ladd Connor, both died within a month of each other in the spring of '51, and my mother returned bereft and penniless to Minneapolis in April of that year. John's death was a terrible surprise to me.

In June, she and I drove together to Hollywood — my first glimpse of the city that would loom large in the rest of my life. We made the trip in my '41 DeSoto "businessman's coupe," a strange car with a tiny, two-seater turret for the driver and passenger, and a trunk the same size and length as the hood, into which everything Mother owned was somehow stuffed. (The '41 DeSoto was my first car. I wouldn't buy the '48 Packard until later that year.) The car also had a malfunctioning heater, and for most of the first day, the heat in the cab was well over a hundred degrees — and then it got hotter. We stopped to find out what was causing the problem, and a mechanic told us the radiator would have to be replaced. This was impossible, of course, since there were no discretionary funds available in our highly restricted budget. He then suggested we buy some canvas bags which could be filled with water and hung over the front fenders for our trip across the Mojave Desert. So that's how we traveled west, refilling the bags and the radiator during the unbearably hot days and sleeping in the car at night.

We rolled into Las Vegas a week later, almost dead from dehydration and exhaustion, and slept in front of the Sands Hotel. Finally, a few days later, we chugged into Los Angeles with smoke and steam billowing from the hood of our oddly shaped car. We found our way to an old friend of Mother's, a character actress named Kathryn Card, whom Mother had worked with in Ohio at the Wright Players. Kathryn lived in "Gower Gulch" on El Centro, a stone's throw from Columbia Studios, where one day I would be under contract.

After sleeping for eighteen hours, I walked over to Columbia to get a gander at what a movie-making facility looked like. My first impression never changed. Then and now, it looked like a high-security prison: tall, tan, windowless walls where one was certain movie heavy Barton McLane was keeping a baleful eye on what was going on in the yard below.

After a series of one-night occupancies in crummy hotels and rental rooms off Hollywood Boulevard, we found a room for the summer in an old house on Whitley Avenue just north of the boulevard. Mother got a job at an Orange Julius stand, and I found employment parking cars for Warner's Cinerama on Wilcox. I found out where Schwab's Drug Store was, and one day I was certain I saw Montgomery Clift leaving the fabled spot immortalized by Billy Wilder in *Sunset Boulevard.* When I got closer, I saw that it was not Monty, but I realized a decade later it was a large version of Clift named Vince Edwards (more about him later). Such was my compulsive need to see movie stars.

Mother stayed on in Hollywood, looking for work of whatever kind she could get, while I bussed back to Minnesota in the fall (having junked the DeSoto) to return to school for my second year.

I was majoring in journalism at the U,

figuring that if I didn't make it in the acting game I would have a fallback position as a sports writer and commentator. By the winter quarter of '51, however, I'd had enough of jocks and stinking locker rooms. I reregistered as a theater arts major. At the same time, I auditioned for and was accepted at KUOM, the famed radio voice of the University of Minnesota, broadcasting through five states.

During that artsy school year, from the fall of 1951 through the spring of 1952, where I was never offstage or far away from a microphone, girls had pretty much been put on the back burner — with one exception. During the 1951–52 winter break, Mother called to invite me to come west for the holidays. This time, I didn't make the long drive. Instead I covered my Packard with a tarp and Greyhounded it to L.A. to join my mother in apartment 102 at 1830 North Cherokee, a block and a half north of Hollywood Boulevard. (If you ever happen to be standing on the northeast corner of the intersection of Hollywood and Cherokee, glance down at your feet. You'll spot my star, added to the Hollywood Walk of Fame in 1998.)

Mother and I shared a small room, made even smaller by a Murphy bed that descended from the wall each night. More important, waiting to greet me at Mother's place was her roomie of the time, Patty Wheeler. Patty was the daughter of Bert Wheeler, part of the famous vaudeville team of Wheeler and Woolsey. She was quite the party girl. Among other conquests, she had already been to bed with a young Robert Evans, later to be the head of Paramount Studios. (At least, so Evans claims in his memoir, *The Kid Stays in the Picture*.)

Patty was just the kind of — shall I say, friendly — young lady that a relatively inexperienced but eager young eighteen-year-old dreams of meeting. And Mother, being a liberal showbiz type, allowed Patty and me to share the Murphy bed while she slept on the couch. Since Mother was working days at that time in a hot dog stand on Jefferson and La Brea owned by friends from Minneapolis, Patty and I had all day to play. And she was a player of great imagination and wonderful teaching ability. After a while, I recall, the thought occurred to me: "Patty must be one of those people I've heard about called nymphomaniacs." Her company made the winter vacation exceptionally delightful and highly educational. (What Patty was doing in L.A., other than teaching me about sex and engaging in recreational pharmaceutical experimentation, I really don't know. And at the time I wasn't asking many questions. You know the old saying about a gift horse. . . .)

After capping off the week by spending New Year's Day, 1952, attending the Rose Bowl football game in hundred-degree weather (a friend of my mother's had given me a ticket), I returned to the below-zero cold of a Minnesota winter. I was determined to move to Hollywood permanently once the school year ended.

And so I did.

Three:
From Jew in a Jockstrap to Natalie's Beau

A very riband in the cap of youth.

When I arrived in Hollywood during the last of my teen years, "Rock" and "Rory," "Troy" and "Tab" were the labels pasted on diffident young gentile actors by the sons of Jews whose fathers, at the close of the nineteenth century, had fled the ghettos and pogroms of Eastern Europe and the Cossack terrorists of czarist Russia.

These Jewish refugees came to New York, Boston, and Baltimore with their ethnic names like Fried, Meir, and Goldfish. They labored as glovers, butchers, cobblers, and junkmen. They left behind a culture where the choice was between joining the rise of Marxism, seeking the dream of a Jewish state in Palestine, or embarking on a voyage to the New World. Of the two and a half million Jewish refugees who left Europe, two million opted for freedom in America.

What they found was a watered-down form of freedom — an absence of tyranny but little real chance to better their lot in an economy dominated by an East Coast Anglo-Saxon Protestant hierarchy. And that is where the second generation of refugees from anti-Semitism might have stayed, if it had not been for the invention of a new art form called the movies.

Originally, Thomas Edison, the American credited with developing the technology of the motion picture, considered it only a pastime and amusement for the working class. The earliest moving pictures shown in those first nickelodeons portrayed Jews as petty merchants and blacks as razor-wielding buffoons; the first great blockbuster motion picture was D. W. Griffith's *Birth of a Nation,* a racist apologia for the Ku Klux Klan. Cultural enlightenment and social progress were not on offer here.

But a handful of the Jewish salesmen saw this new hybrid of business and art as an opportunity to make their mark and earn a place in their new homeland. When the WASPs weren't looking, they changed their names to Mayer and Fox and Goldwyn, and headed west to make movies in California, where there was sunshine the year round, and where the legal and economic power of the Edison Trust, which still claimed patent power over the technology of movies, was far weaker. Even more important, there was less social discrimination and religious bigotry to dampen the enthusiasm of the moguls-in-the-making as they set about selling the world their new discovery.

There they built their own motion picture studios, first in a geographical entity bordered on the east by the rapidly expanding city of Los Angeles and on the west by the Pacific Ocean. It would be called Hollywood. If they were not accepted in the Eastern establishment, they would make their own Western establishment and show everyone who had the price of a ticket what America meant to them.

Of course, it meant very different things to the leaders at different studios.

To Louis B. Mayer at MGM, the Tiffany of the studios (where, decades later, a young actor named Robert Vaughn would spend five of his happiest years), America was a mythical kingdom that transcended life's messy economic and social realities. Women in Mayer's movies were "queens" who always had to look right — beautiful, smart, elegant, and *almost* but not quite approachable. Myrna Loy, Jean Harlow, Norma Shearer, and the great, cool Swede, Greta

Garbo, were the kind of ladies L.B. would have had in his real life if he had women other than his wife. And so he exalted their images in silver and black on the magical screen, along with MGM's great male stars: big, handsome, stylish devils with flare and cool, men like Clark Gable, Robert Taylor, Melvyn Douglas, and Walter Pidgeon.

This Mayer fantasy of a glamorous America was coupled with another fantasy of his adopted country. This was the small-town, Norman Rockwell America depicted in middle-class morality tales featuring Mickey Rooney, Judy Garland, and the Hardy Family, which was made up of the wise father, the loving, sweet mother, and the sassy but good-hearted kids, all sharing the immaculate house behind the magnolias and the white picket fence.

This, of course, was not at all what America was like in the thirties, but rather what America should aspire to be according to the L. B. Mayer philosophy. It was this mix of culture and middle-class morality that was the MGM signature style of the prewar years.

Each of the other great Hollywood studios of the era had its own signature style, its own vision of America. Warner Bros. offered a gritty, urban America populated by ruthless gangsters, glamorous dames, and tough-talking working-class street characters embodied by a stable of unforgettable character actors like Edward G. Robinson, James Cagney, Humphrey Bogart, Joan Blondell, Barbara Stanwyck, and Bette Davis. Harry Cohn's Columbia depicted a country of colorful, vivid eccentrics and homespun heroes in comedies directed by the likes of Frank Capra and Howard Hawks and populated by stars like Gary Cooper, Jimmy Stewart, Jean Arthur, and Rita Hayworth.

These images were just as fantastic as the more genteel visions promulgated by MGM. But they all helped shape Americans' image of themselves and their nation during the decades when the USA first rose to prominence on the global stage.

During the ensuing war years, all the studios turned out motion pictures that promoted the fight against the Japanese in the Pacific and the Germans in Europe. The postwar years saw the slow erosion of public interest in movies, as the new talking lamp, television, gradually took control of the American imagination. In the early years of the 1950s, when I turned up in Hollywood, nearly all the major stars had clauses in their contracts forbidding appearances on television. Bob Hope and Bing Crosby were allowed appearances only on "live" programs — even as Paramount president Barney Balaban was quietly telling his fellow executives, "Either we get into the television scam or it will end up burying the lot of us."

He was prescient, of course. In the late sixties, even the mighty MGM fell sway to conglomerates and financial magnates. Eventually, Kirk Kerkorian auctioned off the props and costumes and sold the great studio grounds in Culver City to the highest bidder.

But despite the shifting sands in Hollywood, the modern era of showbiz celebrity was in full swing, and a new generation of stars was grabbing headlines.

Peter Lawford returned from England, where he had sought the hand of Sharman Douglas, daughter of the industrialist and U.S. ambassador to the Court of St. James Lewis Douglas, to which the eminent diplomat reportedly replied, "Not my daughter. Go talk to Mr. Kennedy. He's got one on the market." The very Republican Mr. Douglas was referring to his predecessor as ambassador, the very Democratic Joseph P. Kennedy, whose daughter was the beautiful, witty, and articulate Patricia.

The Ambassador, as he liked to be called,

famously said, "The only person I would despise my daughter marrying more than a Hollywood actor would be a British actor." Nonetheless, on April 24, 1954, the thirty-year-old Patricia Kennedy became Mrs. Peter Lawford, and the Ambassador apparently remained vertical. (A decade later, after Pat's marriage to Peter foundered, she would be romanced by none other than me — but more about that later.)

Darryl F. Zanuck at 20th Century-Fox signed a long-term deal with a young platinum blonde who was being compared with Jean Harlow — Marilyn Monroe. Lucille Ball and Desi Arnaz formed Desilu Productions, and *I Love Lucy* became TV's first megahit.

Former child star, now film goddess Elizabeth Taylor divorced Nicky Hilton, granduncle of Paris. (I would meet Liz ever so briefly in the summer of 1951 when she lived in the same building on Wilshire Boulevard as my mother's bridesmaid, Audrey Totter.) Hungarian bombshell Zsa Zsa Gabor split from George Sanders, and Rita Hayworth ditched Ali Khan. In Las Vegas, Clark Gable and Sylvia Ashley split. Howard Hughes unveiled his latest find, Faith Domergue. Mrs. Henry Fonda, Frances, mother of Jane, committed suicide. One of the greatest playwrights of the twentieth century (and a particular favorite of mine), Eugene O'Neill also died in 1953.

Shirley Temple, the darling of the 1930s, retired from the movies "for good." (In 1968 she would be a luncheon guest of mine in Prague.) Comedian Milton Berle signed an unprecedented thirty-five-year contract for at least five million dollars. (I met his wife Ruth in the 1960s through Pat Lawford.)

Also in that decade, Judy Garland divorced Vincente Minnelli and wed producer Sidney Luft. (She would later marry Mark Herron, my close friend at Los Angeles City College in the fifties.)

And, finally, Ronnie Reagan dumped girlfriend Ruth Roman for his future First Lady, Nancy Davis. They were introduced when Nancy, whom I had met in the forties (when she toured with Mother and Zasu Pitts in *Ramshackle Inn*), went to him to help her get off the blacklist because there was another Nancy Davis in town who was the real object of the blacklisters.

This was the raucous postwar Hollywood that was waiting for me when I arrived in June 1952.

My path to Los Angeles was not without its

mishaps. During my final winter in Minneapolis, I'd totaled my Packard in a collision with a Roman Catholic priest while driving in a snowstorm without windshield wipers. The accident left me in serious debt, since I hadn't known you were supposed to have something called "collision insurance."

Chastened but undeterred, I departed for the West Coast. I hitched a ride with Jack Rebney, a fellow actor at the U., in his new-old car, a 1948 maroon Buick convertible. Accompanying me was Connie Driscoll, whom I'd met when we both worked at KUOM radio and who had become a great friend of mine — occasionally *not* platonic. (The kids of today, I've learned, have an expression for this kind of relationship: "friends with benefits.") Connie planned to pursue a master's degree in drama at UCLA.

My first order of business when I got to L.A. was to get a job and start paying off the debt I'd incurred in the auto accident. Patty Wheeler had been busted for drugs and was no longer sharing my mother's one-room digs on Cherokee Avenue. Though this was disappointing news for me, I moved in. I never did track Patty down, sad to say.

Oddly enough, for someone who as a child had lived long stretches separated from his

74

mother, it so happens that, between the ages of nineteen and twenty-three, I lived in the same room with her. I suppose it would have been an uncomfortable situation for most young men. It worked for me only because of my mother's liberal attitudes and because, as a fellow actor, she completely understood, shared, and supported my goals in life. Things more conventional mothers might have balked at — late hours, questionable companions, impractical job choices, and the peculiar self-absorption of the working actor — she considered normal and unexceptionable.

The only showbiz-related job I had done prior to my arrival in L.A. was my stint at WCCO, CBS's radio station in Minneapolis. Therefore, I went directly to CBS Radio on Sunset Boulevard in search of work. They were not hiring, but the fellow I spoke to at KNX said, "Why don't you go over to CBS-TV on the corner of Vine and Fountain and see if they have any openings?"

They did not, but they were sharing the 1313 North Vine Street building with the independently owned station KHJ-TV (Channel 9). I was sent to speak with the head of guest relations there and met a man named George Hamilton — not the actor later famous for his tan, but a man in his early thirties, dressed in a natty tie and coat and gifted with a wonderful radio actor's voice. Unfortunately for both of us, radio acting was rapidly on its way out, being replaced by the "boob tube," as it was then called. So George was stuck organizing tours and studio audiences for locally produced shows, and I was looking for his help in achieving some kind of foothold on the lowest rung of the showbiz ladder.

George asked me if I had a large wardrobe. Slightly puzzled but game, I answered, "Definitely." That may have contributed to my being hired on the spot.

My job was at the front of the station. Although I was wearing civilian clothes, I was again just a glorified page boy. I would direct people around and lead audiences to *Queen for a Day* with Jack Bailey, which at the time was the number one show in the United States, shown live in California and via "hot kinescope" around the country.

A precursor of today's reality shows, *Queen for a Day* featured down-and-out moms offering competing sob stories — an out-of-work husband, a flood-damaged home, a baby with the croup — in hopes of winning that show's pity prize and, with it, a collection of new appliances, bedroom furniture, and other goodies. (Old-timers recall the time one mom pleaded for a crib for her brand-new baby. Clucking in sympathy, host Jack Bailey asked, "And where is the baby sleeping now?" Without thinking, the mother replied, "In the cardboard box the new TV came in!" She got few votes from the audience that day.) And with no help from me, my friend Connie Driscoll appeared on the program and actually became Queen for a Day. After all, she *was* a good actress.

Also working at the station were such minor notables as Western star Colonel Tim McCoy; former all-American football star from the University of Michigan turned sportscaster Tom Harmon (best remembered today as the father of the erstwhile "sexiest man alive" actor Mark Harmon); Lyn Castile, a nationally syndicated radio interviewer through whom I would meet the young Marilyn Monroe (aptly described at the time in the witticism "Following Marilyn is like watching two small boys having a pillow fight under a blanket"); two television announcers named John — Condon and Carson; and finally, a CBS advertising salesman who one day would be known as the "smiling cobra" when he became head of network programming and president of CBS, Jim Aubrey.

That's the way Hollywood was in the fifties. It was where things were happening, and if you hung around awhile you were almost certain to meet some interesting people, from one-time stars and soon-to-be stars to a gaggle of folks, many of them equally talented, who would never quite break through the ceiling of demi-celebrityhood.

Being a page boy at KHJ-TV was a far cry from stardom. But it was the first rung I'd been seeking, and with the egotism and enthusiasm of youth I was sure I'd soon be climbing higher. Meanwhile, I still needed to maintain my student status so as to avoid the draft, so on my first free weekday from my new job, I went to UCLA to enroll for the fall 1952 semester.

Much to my surprise, I was told by the registrar that the credits I'd acquired during my full year at the University of Minnesota were not transferable. What's more, I hadn't taken the necessary courses in high school to allow me to enter the California higher-education system. When I semi-recovered from that shock, I inquired what I had to take to get into UCLA and where would I have to go to get these courses.

"You need algebra, geometry, biology, and Spanish II," she informed me. (I had taken

Spanish I at North High but apparently that didn't cut the Southern California academic mustard.) "And the place to go is Los Angeles City College."

UCLA, it turned out, had originally been located on Vermont and Santa Monica Boulevard, the current site of LACC. If I took seventeen and a half credits in the fall semester at LACC and passed with an average grade of C+ or better, I could enter UCLA in January 1953.

Well, this was discouraging news, but I took it as just a minor setback. And the price was right: Upon investigation, I discovered that tuition at the Santa Monica–Vermont campus was a mere six bucks per semester. My only other expense would be around thirty-five dollars for books, for which a student loan was available. So I signed up at LACC and prepared to start college all over again.

I hied myself off to Channel 9 and explained to George Hamilton what I had to do. He said, "No problem. We'll put you on the swing shift, three to eleven at night," and I could lead my other life in academia on the day shift, from eight to three. I said, "That's cool," and hopped back into my mother's '41 yellow Packard convertible and drove home to Cherokee Avenue in Hollywood.

My mother and I designed a schedule that allowed me to get to Channel 9 and LACC part of each week by bus. The rest of the time I drove her Packard while she took the bus to her job at a hot dog stand owned by her Minneapolis friends Lylas and Floyd Randall. I usually left home at seven A.M. and got back at around midnight, six days a week. (I had classes on Saturday and had Sundays free.) I shared my salary with my mother, and with the rent for the apartment only sixty dollars a month, everything was fine, except that the other half of my pay was being sent back to Minneapolis each month to repay the priest for the repairs on his Cadillac.

Meanwhile, my friend Connie Driscoll was working full-time waitressing on Hollywood Boulevard at Aldo's Coffee Shop, going to graduate school at UCLA, and living in various rooms in Hollywood and its environs. A big Saturday night for Mother, Connie, and me was settling down in front of our TV to eat popcorn and watch British black-and-white Ealing comedies while Mother and I guzzled Kamchatka vodka mixed with ginger beer (a concoction known as a Moscow Mule).

Other than this, my social life was non-existent, mainly because of my poverty. Mother eventually noticed. Sometime in the fall, she asked me why I didn't use the little time off I had to go somewhere and do something socially. I confessed to her about the accident. She was sympathetic and proud, and she volunteered to cut my half of the living costs so I could have something left over for a bit of social life.

After that, the highlight of my week was to go to the Jester Room, a bar on Vine Street across from the Hollywood Ranch market, on Saturday night, usually with Johnny Carson, and watch Jackie Gleason from eight to nine P.M. on CBS, and Sid Caesar and his gang, Imogene Coca, Howie Morris, and Carl Reiner, on NBC from nine to ten-thirty on Max Liebman's *Your Show of Shows,* written by, among others, Neil Simon, Larry Gelbart, and Woody Allen.

I usually had no duties at KHJ at that time on Saturday night, and no one ever seemed to notice that I was absent from my job. I generally had enough money put away for a couple of beers and a cheeseburger, and on more than one occasion, Johnny popped for the eats and brew. I have no idea what he was pulling down financially, but I do know they gave him a chance to do his own live half-hour show on Sunday afternoons called *Carson's Cellar,* made up of a monologue, sketches, models, and magic. The CBS budget for John's use, to do whatever he wanted, was a hundred dollars per show.

Johnny was very good-looking, very young, and very funny, but also a little reticent, a little withdrawn. He always had a dry wit, but unlike most comedians he had no psychological drive to be "on" all the time — he wouldn't try to take over the conversation.

A decade later, in 1962, after a short time on a game show called *Who Do You Trust?,* where he met Ed McMahon, Johnny would became the host of *The Tonight Show* following Steve Allen, the originator, and Jack Paar, who'd retired. Soon thereafter, a social evening I shared with Johnny ended in a memorable, if slightly scary, confrontation.

I had dinner one night at La Scala with Barbara Stuart, a lovely young actress I'd met when performing in *Under the Yum Yum Tree* at the Las Palmas Theatre in Hollywood. (La Scala was the hot place in town because everyone knew that it was the restaurant that John F. Kennedy ordered take-out dinners from when he stayed at the Beverly Hills Hotel during the 1960 presidential race.) At La Scala, Barbara and

I ran into Johnny Carson and his current date (I forget her name), and the four of us got to chatting. After dinner, we all headed to Barbara's place on Horn Avenue for a nightcap.

Well, the four of us were strolling up the path to her front door — Barbara alongside Johnny, I beside Johnny's date — when suddenly a dark figure leaped from a hiding place behind the shrubbery. He laughingly yelled at Barbara, "STARFUCKER!" Barbara's initial fright gave way to embarrassment and annoyance when she recognized her accuser — it was her fiancé, the actor Dick Gautier. (If you've seen the 1960s TV series *Get Smart,* you'll remember his portrayal of Hymie, the robot-spy. He was also Broadway's original Conrad Birdie in *Bye Bye Birdie.*)

Not long after that, I had the pleasure of giving Barbara away in marriage at the home of her close friend, Ruta Lee. The lucky groom was none other than my longtime friend, Dick Gautier.

Johnny remained America's favorite late-night host for thirty years, and there'll never be another witty, charming, and sexy star quite like him. I'm proud to have been an early friend.

By Thanksgiving of 1952, I was pretty well

set in my dual life as a showbiz hanger-on and a student. For no particular reason other than to avoid having to change my routine, I decided to do my spring semester at LACC, and delay my start at UCLA until the fall of 1953.

Having completed all my required high school work, I took theater and radio courses at LACC, making certain they were transferable to the Westwood campus. Then serendipity struck.

In the winter of 1953, the LACC theater department, headed by a tough-cookie acting teacher named Jerry Blunt, mounted a production of *Stalag 17,* a play about a World War II prisoner-of-war camp. The Broadway version had closed in June 1952, and the movie form would later win my future friend and colleague Bill Holden his only Oscar in the role of J. J. Sefton.

Playing that role in the LACC production was an actor named Tony Carbone. Now, mind you, I am speaking as someone who has seen onstage such monumental figures as Marlon Brando, Montgomery Clift, Paul Muni, Lee J. Cobb, Rex Harrison, and many others. Nonetheless, over a half-century later, Tony Carbone's brilliance in *Stalag 17* stands forever enshrined in my mind as one of the great performances of the American theater.

I saw the production many times, and Tony never let me down. Furthermore, the other young actors — all around my age! — were almost equally wonderful. The staging and direction by a young Persian, Ray Aghayan, was also meticulously professional. (Ray later became, with Bob Mackie, one of television's outstanding wardrobe designers, working with stars like Judy Garland and Carol Burnett.)

I asked myself: If this theater department can do this kind of work, why should I bother going to UCLA?

I didn't. Instead, I stayed on at LACC, where, in addition to Tony Carbone, I met other college artists who became lifelong friends. One of these was James Coburn, with whom I went on to act in *The Magnificent Seven.* Another was Truman Herron (later known as Mark), the star of the department when I arrived from Minnesota. Truman went out of his way to be kind to me when I arrived at LACC. We ended up sharing the school's Best Actor award in 1954. We also did O'Neill's *Great God Brown,* directed by Monte Hellman, soon to become a well-known avant-garde film director.

It was rumored that Truman was bisexual,

and I thought that was just keen, although admittedly I misunderstood the meaning of the word. "Two women at once!" I thought. "He must be quite a guy!"

Things were also progressing well on the job front. By the spring of 1953, I had achieved enough seniority at Channel 9 to more or less dictate my own hours. I managed to set up my work and school schedule so as to leave Monday night free to watch *I Love Lucy.* (So much for the wild life of a young stud in Hollywood.)

I guess the word got around that I was a *Lucy* fan. In the fall of 1953, I heard from Angelo, a midget newspaper seller on the corner of Hollywood Boulevard and Cherokee, that if I wanted to meet Bill Frawley, who played Fred Mertz on the *Lucy* show, I just had to be on that corner at a certain time on a Monday evening. Frawley would be sure to stumble by on his way to Musso & Frank Grill on Hollywood Boulevard. It seems Bill was a lover of the grape and was encouraged by the *Lucy* producers to take this daily walk as a way of getting a little exercise before his nightly tipple. (It also served to keep him out from behind the wheel of a car, which was probably a good idea under the circumstances.)

I was there as scheduled, and sure enough,

Frawley showed up on time. I was introduced to him by Angelo, and he invited me to join him for a splash at Musso's — a Monday-evening ritual that we went on to share for much of the rest of that year.

Several years later, I ran into Bill, greeted him warmly, and reminded him about our Mondays together at Musso's. "What the hell are you talking about?" he growled. In retrospect, I understand the problem — he couldn't remember meeting me because he was sober at the time.

In that long-ago summer of 1952, all the high muckety-mucks of Hollywood's Golden Age were still in place: L. B. Mayer at MGM, Jack Warner at Warner Bros., Harry Cohn at Columbia, Darryl F. Zanuck at Fox, Adolph Zukor at Paramount. Lew Wasserman was a few years away from his rise to power as lord of the MCA/Universal colossus.

The Red Car trolley line ran the length of Hollywood Boulevard, and near the corner of Highland was the all-night Hollywood Theater. A few doors away, you could get breakfast any time of the day at Coffee Dan's or Aldo's. A few yards farther east were the original Egyptian Theater and Grauman's Chinese Theater. At the other end of Hollywood Boulevard on Vine Street

was the famed Brown Derby restaurant —
the one that did *not* look like a hat. On the
corner of Vine and Sunset Boulevard was
NBC Radio, and across the street was
Wallach's Music City, where 78 RPM
records of all the latest big-band hits were
on sale. (Bill Haley and the invention of
rock and roll were still two years in the
future.) And a few blocks north on Vine was
the headquarters of Capitol Records, where
in the 1960s I would meet a young singing
group out of England known as the Beatles.

A few blocks from my place, at Yucca and
Wilcox, another future TV star was en-
sconced, also in a one-room setup (and also,
coincidentally, in apartment 102), with a
Murphy bed that came out of the wall —
and stayed down. The apartment was
humble and it faced the lobby, and the star
in waiting shared the single room with her
grandma rather than her mother. Her name
was Carol Burnett.

A few miles west on Sunset Boulevard was
Googie's, an all-night restaurant where Rod
Steiger and Jimmy Dean parked their Har-
leys every night. Just left of Googie's was
Schwab's Drug Store, where (contrary to
legend) Lana Turner was *not* discovered,
and where I would later meet the beautiful
Judy Campbell, future girlfriend of mobster

Sam Giancana and President John F. Kennedy.

Across the street, on Crescent Heights and Sunset Boulevard, was the Garden of Allah, West Coast haven of such members of the Algonquin Round Table as Robert Benchley and Dorothy Parker. A few minutes' walk farther west on Sunset brought you to the Chateau Marmont, years later the site of John Belushi's death, and the beginning of the Sunset Strip, where the world-famous nightclubs Ciro's and Mocambo's hosted Hollywood's elite in the fifties.

In July of that summer of '52, Ronald Reagan, a former Warner Bros. contract player and president of the Screen Actors Guild who described himself as "the Errol Flynn of the B's," sent a letter on behalf of SAG to MCA granting the agency the blanket right to produce films. Within a few years, MCA, through its television wing Revue Productions, would become the major supplier of television shows in Hollywood.

Although he did not realize it at the time, the SAG president had opened a door that would lead him to the Oval Office. In 1954, Taft Schreiber, head of Revue Productions, told Ronnie about a possible job introducing a new weekly television series, *The G.E.*

Theater. Schreiber owed his job, at least in part, to that 1952 SAG decision. During his eight years as *G.E.* host and his two years as host of Borax's *Death Valley Days,* Ronnie served as a corporate spokesman, polishing a little speech that lauded free enterprise and attacked America's slide toward "democratic socialism."

Thus, in 1964, when Barry Goldwater was unable to appear at a $1,000-a-plate fundraiser at the Ambassador Hotel in Los Angeles, Ronnie was asked to pinch-hit by Holmes Tuttle, a friend of Goldwater's Finance Chairman, Henry Salvatore. Reagan's speech was a nationwide hit. In the spring of 1965, forty-one rich businessmen formed "The Friends of Ronald Reagan," and the following year, Reagan became governor of California.

As for me, my life that year was pretty much work, school, work, school, work, school — along with dreaming about stardom and, whenever I got the chance, sniffing around the edges of the glittering world of show business.

For my twenty-first birthday, November 22, 1953, my LACC buddy Jim Coburn gave a small party for me at his pad on Fountain Avenue. As I arrived, I saw coming down the outside stairs a beautiful

Irisher in a double-breasted blue blazer and plaid skirt, brandishing a long cigarette holder with the aplomb of FDR. Her name was Sheila Ann Noonan.

Sheila was bright as a penny, witty and warm, and had a fierce Irish temper. She was also a brilliant actress who could express more varied emotional colors with the three words "Well, my dear" than Meryl Streep on her best day.

Sheila was working as a buyer at Ohrbach's department store, knocking down a three-figure salary a week, an amount then beyond my comprehension. Shortly after we started seeing each other, she gave up the rag trade and went into waitressing for a good deal less money but a far more flexible work schedule.

At the time, I was without a ride, while Sheila owned a sharp blue-gray 1952 MGTC convertible. We worked out a system of me dropping her at whatever local eatery she was working at, and then picking her up after work when we would repair to Barney's Beanery on Santa Monica Boulevard to hoist as many Pernods as our budgets allowed. (Barney said the Pernod was mixed with absinthe, that reputed aphrodisiac, and I believed him — although frankly at that stage in our lives I doubt that either Sheila or I needed any chemical encouragement.)

One of the first arguments Sheila and I ever had occurred in the hall near the front door of my Cherokee habitat, and it was a memorable one. As our words escalated, her voice got louder and her gestures became more agitated. I said, bluffingly, "Don't hit me, because you'll regret it." In retrospect, it sounds threatening, but it really meant nothing to me — I certainly had no intention of striking Sheila, even if she hit me first. She responded, "Hey, *you* be careful. If I hit you, by the time you come to, the width of your ties will be out of style." It was probably true.

Sheila added, "You know, you're the most well-adjusted psycho I've ever met," and our fight broke up in gales of laughter. That's when I really fell for her — romantically, not literally. Looking back, I can see we were an early version of George and Martha from Albee's *Who's Afraid of Virginia Woolf?* — wild verbal brawlers for whom arguing was a crazy way of making love in public.

Around that same time, I auditioned for the Stage Society, which was the most praised Los Angeles theater group of that period. Its theatrical forebears were the Actors' Lab, which met behind Schwab's Drug

Store in the early years after the war and included many members of the legendary Group Theater. The Lab included an aspiring, not quite bright blonde, who was then going by the name of Norma Jeane Mortenson (later Marilyn Monroe). The Actors' Lab turned into the Arthur Kennedy Group (which included Gary Cooper and Patricia Neal — a gossip-column item at the time — as members), and ultimately, in the early fifties, the Stage Society. Actor Michael Chekhov, a nephew of the great Russian playwright, was its sometime acting mentor.

I had to choose an audition scene for the Stage Society. Though the mid-fifties were the heyday of the Method, with Brando and Dean as the system's great exemplars, I deliberately chose a scene with a very different style and artistic lineage. I picked a scene from *Dial M for Murder* that had been acted on Broadway with great elegance and style by Maurice Evans, the classic actor best known for his so-called *G.I. Hamlet,* a two-hour version of Shakespeare that Evans mounted for armed forces audiences. (There's that play again.)

Despite my against-the-tide stylistic choice, I was accepted by the board.

The Stage Society was a significant stepping-stone in my path toward the status of professional actor. I had my first paid acting role there, performing in Sean O'Casey's *Shadow of a Gunman.* That enabled me to get my first Actor's Equity union card, a minor but significant rite of passage. Later, I appeared in the lead role of Eben in Eugene O'Neill's *Desire Under the Elms* with a young actress named Helen Westcott who had starred opposite Gregory Peck in *The Gunfighter* (1950). That performance won me some favorable notice, including a nod from an agent named Jack Fields, who agreed to represent me — another rite of passage.

Almost equally important, Helen became my newest mentor, both on stage and off. As a sexual adventuress and guide, she ran a close second to Patty Wheeler — very close. The first time Helen and I were together at her small house on Vermont behind the Los Angeles Press Club, she said, "You will remember this night for the rest of your life." In a way she was right. I have no recollection at all of the rest of the evening, but the look on her face when she spoke is vivid in my mind a half-century later.

In the late summer of 1955, I was carrying 17.5 credits at Los Angeles City College. By then, I was also working at the Red

Arrow Bonded Messenger Service located on Cahuenga Boulevard, where the Hollywood Canteen had its home during World War II. (I had plenty of time for this work, since my agent was apparently representing me with minimal zeal, thereby producing minimal results.) Also working at Red Arrow was my LACC school chum Zev Bufman. (Jimmy Coburn worked at Red Arrow, too, but out of the Beverly Hills office — even then he had class.) Zev would later become a successful Broadway producer (*Marat/Sade*) and a partner/producer with Elizabeth Taylor in her two Broadway forays, *The Little Foxes* and *Private Lives,* the latter of which also starred her on-again, off-again husband, Richard Burton.

We were required to wear ugly blue Red Arrow uniforms with an equally ugly kind of stiff-brimmed military cap. Our job was to drive Willy's Overland trucks while picking up and delivering cargo ranging from movie scripts to sets of dentures. At Christmastime, we were given dozens of bottles of spirits to deliver as gifts in office and apartment buildings — not all of which, I'll admit, found their way to their intended recipients. According to Red Arrow lore, once Zev was on a movie lot, he would jump into the back of his truck and change into a tie, jacket, and pants. Thus accoutred, he would go strolling among the soundstages, checking out the productions under way and gleaning whatever he could for future show-business connections.

The contacts Zev made during his unauthorized peregrinations on the movie lots finally paid off for me. One day I got a call at work from Zev asking what color eyes I had. I said, "Brown, I guess."

"Great!" Zev said. "Get your *tuchus* over to Paramount as soon as you can. DeMille is directing *The Ten Commandments.* They're casting Jews for the big golden calf scene with Chuck Heston as Moses, and since you have an Actor's Equity union card, you'll get a hundred bucks a day for five days . . . if they pick you."

I was there in twenty minutes and I was immediately okayed, I think with Zev's help. I was told to have my agent get in touch with Paramount casting. I called Jack Fields immediately.

Jack was his usual caring, supportive self. "What, you're calling me at this hour of the day? Do you have any idea how busy I am? I tell you, I'll call when I have a job for you!"

"No, you don't understand. I already have a job."

"What? I mean, what did I tell you? It was

only a matter of time. Where's the job?" Jack immediately went into his agent two-step mode. "I'll be back to you when I have a deal," he promised.

Of course, I thought there was no deal to be made — an extra is an extra, right? But I was wrong. Jack called later that evening. "I've been battling the powers-that-be at Paramount since we last spoke. I've been able to negotiate a second week for you. You'll play an Arab in the first chariot right behind Yul Brynner."

"Fantastic!" I responded.

"This is what I do for you," Jack replied. "Just be sure to wear your Egyptian helmet low over your eyes in the chariot scene."

"How come?" I was puzzled.

"How come, he asks. So the audience won't say, 'What is the Jew from the golden calf scene doing driving a chariot behind Yul Brynner?'!"

I made a thousand bucks for my ten days' work. By comparison, my average take-home pay from Red Arrow was thirty-five dollars a *week*. Simple math told me I was really an actor, not a truck driver. (Of course, I had never forgotten my mother's declaration to me at the age of four, "Now you are an actor.")

A few words about my initial week's work

as a Jew.

Chico Day was the first assistant director to Mr. DeMille (or C.B., as we intimate friends called him). Chico told me when I met him on my first day on a movie set that the "old man" had a theory that if you put a real actor among a small group of extras, the extras would perform better. Chico said, "That is your responsibility — to make these extras act better." This despite the fact that all of the extras were twice my age and had actual movie experience extending beyond sitting in the audience. But I took Chico's urgings very seriously and promptly began acting up a storm.

In my zeal, I apparently attracted the attention of John Derek, one of the many stars of the film and one of the handsomest young actors in fifties flicks. John pulled Chico aside and, pointing at me, said, "Keep that guy away from me — otherwise the audience will get confused." Presumably he meant that they would get confused over who was the star of the scene. Keep in mind that at six that morning, I had had my entire body sprayed tan while wearing only a jockstrap. (This was the studio's idea of what it would take to make me look Jewish.) I was then fitted with a tan loincloth that barely covered the jockstrap's contents.

John, by contrast, was garbed in flowing multi-colored robes that set off his good looks admirably. Still, John was somehow worried that I would upstage him.

This was my first encounter with the fragility of a star's ego. It would not be my last.

On that last day of that first week, around one P.M., C.B. was up on a high crane. With him were the camera operator and a fellow whose only job it was to anticipate when DeMille wanted to speak to the cast. He would then thrust a slender gold Altec mike in front of the great man, whose stentorian voice would echo throughout the huge stage.

At that moment, DeMille spotted a young girl extra talking when she should have been silent. From high up in the darkened upper regions of the huge stage, he directed Chico to walk over to the girl and point at her. He then said, "Young lady, tell us what you are saying that is so important that you have to talk when we are preparing to shoot?"

Terrified, she could not respond. C.B. asked the same question again. Still no answer. Finally, after he asked her for a third time what she had been saying, she responded, hardly above a whisper, "I was just saying, I wonder when the old bald-headed guy is going to call lunch."

There was a long, quiet, painful pause. Almost all of the hundreds of people working on the scene, including myself, looked downward, riven with fear for the poor girl.

DeMille slowly brought the gold mike to his lips, paused for a very long time, and then barked out simply, "Lunch! One hour."

Cheers and applause erupted, and we all toddled off to our noonday meal.

My movie triumph as the loin-clothed Jew wasn't the only acting experience I was amassing. As I've mentioned, I'd appeared in O'Neill's *Desire Under the Elms* at the Stage Society. After the second (and final) performance, a lovely white-haired gentleman came backstage and introduced himself to me. His name was Dudley Nichols. I later found out that he had been the first screenwriter to decline an Oscar, for his 1935 film *The Informer,* starring Victor McLaglen. (The Screen Writers Guild had been on strike at the time, and Nichols's gesture was an act of protest against the abuse of writing talent by the studios.)

He told me he had been watching me at the Stage Society and also at LACC, where he had seen me do *Laura; Bell, Book and Candle;* Molière's *Tartuffe;* and the lead in *Mr. Roberts*. He said, "With your athletic ability, theatrical flare, and cello voice, if you keep on track in the theater, you could someday be the American Olivier."

I was overwhelmed, to say the least, and thanked him profusely. Mr. Nichols said, "Let me know the next time you're playing on a local stage." As he left, he turned back and said, "But you're a good-looking young fellow — the pictures will probably come calling soon."

A few days later, with my face covered with the beard I had grown for the O'Neill play, I read for and won the role of Judas Iscariot in the 1955 summer production of *The Pilgrimage Play,* performed in a large outdoor theater across from the Hollywood Bowl. (As I recall, I was paid a handsome five hundred dollars per week — not quite on a par with the cool grand earned by the actor playing Christ, but better than the thirty pieces of silver received by the Biblical original.) True to his word, Mr. Nichols saw me in the role and was again very complimentary.

There's an old Hollywood bromide: When in doubt about how a film scene is playing, cut to a dog, a child, or Lincoln. I don't know where the idea comes from and I'm not sure how effective it would be as movie-making strategy, but I did my first TV role opposite Lincoln in the fall of 1955. My agent Jack Fields set up a reading for me at the hit NBC show *Medic,* hosted by Richard Boone. The role was that of Charles Leale, the twenty-two-year-old Army doctor who was at Ford's Theatre the night Lincoln was shot and who cared for him until he died the following day. (As I mentioned earlier, *Medic* used to do historically based dramas like that from time to time.) Virtually every young actor in town wanted the role, and I got it — the first and last time I had to read for a part for several generations. (I'm not counting the screen test I would shortly be asked to make for *The Young Philadelphians,* my breakthrough movie role.)

There were no children or dogs in the episode, just Austin Green, the NBC weatherman, in the role of the comatose Lincoln. I did have to administer the "kiss of life" to Abe, upon which our mucilage-applied mustaches stuck together and peeled off. An even better scene-stealing device than cutting to a cocker spaniel. (It was not used in the film.)

In January 1956, I graduated with my B.A. from Los Angeles State College. I intended to pursue a master's degree at UCLA, thereby retaining my draft deferment and hence my freedom from Uncle Sam's embrace.

Mother was working at that time in the costume jewelry section of Ohrbach's department store on Wilshire Boulevard, a job she had gotten with the help of my favorite lady friend of the time, Sheila Ann Noonan.

One Saturday evening over a few Moscow Mules, I asked Mother why she didn't consider reading for a role in one of the many professional theater companies all over L.A. She offered some sort of demurral, but the truth, I think, was that she'd been rejected so often that she was psychologically bruised and tired of trying. I said, "Well, let me shop around and see what I can scrounge up for you. If I find something, will you promise, in front of Sheila, that you'll try out for the part?"

"Well," she said, "I'll be very nervous, but I'll give it a try."

I made up a CV covering Mother's quarter century as a professional actress, and I began looking and listening for parts for a "mature" female. (At this stage in her career, Mother might have been described as a Tallulah Bankhead type — a *grande dame* best suited to the broad emotional gesture but capable of comedy in a pinch.) In due course, through the connections I'd acquired during two years with the Stage Society, I heard there was a new theater opening on Santa Monica Boulevard and Crescent Heights called the Players' Ring Gallery. I sniffed an opportunity — a new theater meant new stage productions and, probably, an assortment of roles to be had.

The following Monday, I drove our '41 yellow Packard convertible to the theater, where I would encounter another serendipitous moment that would radically change my life.

I approached the girl at the box office. I asked what show they were planning to open with and, as I handed her my mother's CV, whether there were any female character roles for a woman in her late forties with many theatrical credits from back East.

She said promptly, "No, the first show will have an all-male cast. It's set in a military school in the South." She then said, "Are *you* an actor?" and when I answered yes, she said, "Well, why don't you take a look at the script and see if there's anything in it that might be right for you?"

The play was Calder Willingham's *End as a Man*. I later found out it had started as a class exercise at the Actors Studio and launched the career of my future friend, Ben Gazzara. (He also played the lead role in the movie version of the play, retitled *The Strange One*.) A few minutes after I started reading the script, I said out loud, "This is the most perfect role for me that I have ever come across. I must get it."

And I did.

The play opened on Tuesday, March 27, 1956. I played the role of Jocko de Paris, a psychotic, sociopathic upperclassman in the military school (based on Willingham's own experiences at the Citadel) who struck the fear of God in all of those he touched physically or mentally. The *Los Angeles Times* wrote that my performance was "glittering evil." It was just one of many frankly stunning reviews. Many of my later efforts were viewed by a lot more people and have become much more famous, but no single experience in my career has been more gratifying to me than the response I got in *End as a Man*.

Looking back, I can also say that my performance in *End as a Man* required almost no psychological or emotional effort on my part. Maybe I should find it disturbing that a role embodying evil incarnate came so naturally to me. But at the time, I was simply thrilled by the critical and audience reactions. (I actually had audience members gesturing threateningly toward me during curtain calls, as if my real self and the evil character I played had totally merged in their minds.) When that kind of electricity fills a theater — and you are part of it — it's exhilarating.

Once a show-off, always a show-off.

Dudley Nichols — my first fan — wrote a lovely letter to the producers which I have saved to this day. He concluded his comments by saying I was "the only young actor in America I would like to see play *Hamlet*. He's got it."

Max Arnow, my future agent at GAC — the same man who'd brought Ronald Reagan to Hollywood in the thirties — saw me in the play on the Friday of the first week. Max was planning on leaving Columbia Pictures that weekend to join Hecht-Lancaster, then the hottest independent production unit in Hollywood. Built around the partnership of businessman and former agent Harold Hecht and the swaggering leading man Burt Lancaster, the outfit had just won the Oscar in 1955 for best picture — *Marty,* starring Ernest Borgnine, also winner of an Oscar for best male performance.

Max liked what he saw. In fact, he liked it so much that he decided to double-cross his current employer in favor of his future one. He wrote up a report for Columbia saying, "Robert Vaughn is definitely *not* contract material." But then, during the second week of the run, Burt and Harold came to see me in the show at Max's urging. They signed me the following week to a nonexclusive two-picture-a-year deal at $15,000 per picture — a contract that allowed me to do any other television, film, or stage work when I was not working for them.

My first starring role was to be in a film they were developing about a ruthless gossip columnist and a desperate publicity agent, in which the seamy side of showbiz celebrity would be exposed. Ultimately titled *The Sweet Smell of Success,* it has become a noir classic. But don't look for the name of Robert Vaughn in the credits. Marty Milner (later a star of TV's *Route 66*) got "my" role while I was serving my country in the U.S. Army. However, although I missed out on that part, the Hecht-Lancaster contract would ultimately prove a powerful entrée to the world of movies and, eventually, to stardom.

So the opening night of *End as a Man* was a real turning point in my professional life. It was also special for another reason. That evening, I was introduced to the hottest young actress in town at the time — a lovely seventeen-year-old named Natalie Wood.

"Natalia," as I would often call her, had just starred with James Dean in Nicholas Ray's film, *Rebel Without a Cause*. Dean, of course, had been killed the previous September 30 in a car crash on the Pacific Coast Highway. But Natalie's star was on the rise. Already she was slowly elbowing Liz Taylor off the front of all the major movie fan magazines, which played a role in the 1950s comparable to *People* and *Us* today — and arguably were more important in the celebrity culture of the time, since there were then no TV shows like *Entertainment Tonight* to fuel the circulation of gossip.

After the opening performance that evening, there was a cast party, and my friend actor Ben Cooper introduced me to Natalie. If you've seen her in a movie, you know how unforgettably beautiful she was — vulnerable, demure, with enormous brown eyes that somehow suggested a highly combustible blend of innocence and passion. That sense of vulnerability was even greater when Natalie was off-camera; without makeup she looked the picture of childlike innocence, closer to twelve years old than to eighteen.

More than half a century has passed, but the memory remains vivid. There was that moment after we touched hands (it really wasn't a shake) that I knew we would see each other again — a moment confirmed a few minutes later when she asked my mother, "Is your son seeing anyone?" I don't know what my mother said; she was always benumbed in the presence of movie stars. But before the party broke up, I had her telephone number.

We said good-bye, and Natalie said, "If I don't get back to you, don't be discouraged. I may be off to New York to do a live television show with Dennis Hopper." I was actually relieved that she was going to be gone for a while, since I had no money and was sharing a small room and a small car with my mother. (My modest circumstances permitted me to date other girls — but Natalie was a *star.*)

And then everything changed.

Between the time Natalie left and her return, I was signed by Burt Lancaster. I was working back-to-back as a guest star on many hit TV shows. And by June, flush with the cash I was suddenly making as a hot young actor, Mother and I had moved into a three-story penthouse on Orchid Avenue overlooking the lights of Hollywood. So when Natalie came back to Hollywood, sought me out as she'd promised, and promptly put one of her Thunderbirds at my disposal, a ground-level version of my dream of stardom was practically complete. If things could possibly get better for me, I didn't really see how. Suddenly there was light where there had been only shadows, and revelations where there had been only mysteries, and my sweet guide to these formerly unknown experiences was Natalie Wood.

I met Natalie's mother, Maria, who was nicknamed Mud and who referred to Natalie as Natasha. Oddly, in looking back, I remember Mud as a kind of Russian incarnation of the driven stage mother Rose in *Gypsy*, a 1962 film in which Natalie would star, with Rosalind Russell as Rose. But Mud was no Rosalind Russell. Natalie's good looks all came from her handsome father, Nick. I didn't get to know him well because he seemed to be in a perpetual smiling haze. I found out later this state was produced by the demon rum, or in his case (I believe) the demon vodka. Also, he spoke no English — only his native Russian.

Movie studio doors were opened. We went to black-tie world premieres of new motion pictures (I remember Elia Kazan's notorious *Baby Doll,* starring Carroll Baker in the title role). These were events that, before, I had seen only in black-and-white newsreels at Hollywood Boulevard cinemas. I was now on the young A-list for parties where people named Rock and Rory and Tab and Troy were often present — and suddenly my picture was getting snapped along with theirs.

Fan magazines wanted to interview me. "What is Natalie really like? What does she eat? What does she read? Does she always wear makeup? Where does she like to go? Does she drink and, if so, what? Does she go for daiquiris and brandy alexanders, like most kids drink after the prom? Do I care if she dates other people?" The glow of celebrity was mostly reflected off Natalie, but I was basking in it nonetheless.

Natalie was a true acolyte of the god Thespis. She cared deeply about the art of acting, admired fine actors profoundly, and worshiped the great directors (like Kazan) as if they were virtual deities. She was also a deeply generous person. Luckily for me, she believed in my talent and lent me her prestige — an amazingly gracious gift from one young actor to another.

Natalie took me to Warner Bros. to meet Jack Warner, head studio honcho. She escorted me to Columbia Studios for my wardrobe tests for *No Time to Be Young,* a loan-out film from my Hecht-Lancaster deal where my screen credit read, intoxicatingly, INTRODUCING ROBERT VAUGHN.

At Columbia, we ran into the infamous, terrifying studio head, tough guy Harry Cohn. Natalie introduced me to him as a future comer. Harry looked me up and down and snapped, "How big are you?" (Harry himself was on the short side.) I replied, "If you mean how tall am I, I'm as tall as Marlon Brando and Laurence Olivier. Is that big enough?" Natalie blanched, but Harry, unsmiling, said, "He'll do fine," and walked off.

Dressed, courtesy of Western Costume, as Hamlet and Ophelia — that play again! — we attended the Artists and Models Ball, where Mickey Hargitay (Mariska's father) carried his wife, Jayne Mansfield, dressed in a leopard-skin bikini, over his head, supporting the small of her back in his right hand — a photo seen in newspapers round the world the following day.

We road-tested a pink convertible at Casa de Cadillac on Ventura Boulevard in the soon-to-be-infamous San Fernando Valley. We ate hot fudge sundaes at C.C. Brown's on Hollywood Boulevard next to Grauman's Chinese Theater, where cement prints of the stars' hands (and other appendages) decorated the sidewalk. And we drank Chianti and ate pizza at Barone's in Sherman Oaks.

Since we were both still living at home (Natalie with Mud in a house on Valley Vista in Sherman Oaks), our romantic interludes were spent mainly in Malibu after wining and dining at the Point, Tranca's Restaurant, and the Sea Lion, all on the Pacific Coast Highway. Fortunately for us, the local hoteliers were happy to welcome "short-stay" guests and asked no embarrassing questions.

Several nights we dined in Hollywood at the Villa Capri on Yucca, just a block and a half from my former abode on Cherokee Avenue. We met Frank Sinatra there, and Natalie introduced him to me with many nice words about my talent. I had seen him before at the Villa Capri, where, for the price of a beer and if he was sufficiently involved with his friend Jack Daniels, I would hear that glorious voice toot out a few tunes accompanied (as I recall) by their slightly out-of-tune piano.

Oddly enough, Elvis Presley — who was a friend of Natalie's and, in celebrity terms, her nearest male equivalent at the time —

became a kind of presence in our relationship. (By the end of fall 1956, I was told by a Warner Bros. public relations man, that Natalie's fan mail had made her the number one female celebrity in the world.)

One time when Natalie was returning from Memphis after a short visit with Elvis — the kind of trip studio publicists loved to arrange for blazoning across the fan mags and the newsreel screens — I met her at the L.A. airport with a brace of stuffed animals for her bedroom. We rendezvoused at the Santa Ynez Inn in Santa Barbara and were seen together at the opening of the Hilton Hotel in Acapulco.

Natalie and I saw Presley's first movie, *Love Me Tender,* together. I remember remarking how good he was as an actor in the film, and saying, "Now if the old colonel [Elvis's manager, Tom Parker] lets Elvis have his head, he could probably turn into a accomplished film star and actor. But more likely he'll do roles that only require him to sing." And that's what happened.

Another time, we spent an evening at Pacific Ocean Park in Santa Monica as guests of Elvis. He'd bought out the amusement center for a party for many of his new friends. That is where Natalie and I, during a quiet interlude spent looking into the dark swirling ocean waters and sipping wine from paper cups, talked about our mutual fear of drowning. A terribly chilling memory in light of what happened later.

(And my path continued to cross that of Elvis in the odd, serendipitous way such things tend to happen in Hollywood. Ten years later, my four-room suite at MGM would be directly above the offices of Elvis's West Coast Music Publishing Company. Whenever we ran into each other in the hallway or on the path outside, which was often, he was always most courteous and gracious to me, introducing me to his Memphis Mafia high school friends and always addressing me as "Mr. Vaughn.")

There were further dates: a cocktail party for Walter Winchell, seeing the movie *La Strada,* and drinking navy grogs at the Beverly Hills Luau Restaurant owned by Steve Crane, husband of Lana Turner and pal of mobster Johnny Rosselli (who would later claim that he had personally killed JFK by firing a rifle from a sewer in Dealy Plaza).

As you can tell, my friendship with Natalie was one of the most important of my young life. I think of her often.

Of course, we took divergent paths in life. The following year, Natalie became, for the first time, the wife of Robert Wagner ("RJ" to his friends).

In 2006, RJ was the guest star on the fourth season of *Hustle,* a BBC show I did, which was based in London but filmed in Los Angeles and Las Vegas in December that year. Ironically, the segment was shot in part at Marina Del Rey, not far from where Natalie drowned. And the last day Robert worked on *Hustle* was November 29, 2006, the twenty-fifth anniversary of her death.

Natalie occupies a very special place in my memories. Luminous, lovely, exciting, glamorous, she was all those things. But for me she was above all a sweet and generous young woman whose friendship meant — and means — so very much to me.

Thank you again, Natalie.

FOUR:
CHARM SCHOOL

To hold, as 'twere, the mirror up to nature;
to show virtue her own feature, scorn her
own image, and the very age and body of
the time, his form and pressure.

Hollywood in the fall of '54. A Saturday
evening. I was twenty-one years old. I didn't
know that this was to be the night I'd go
mad.

I had spent the past summer as the resident director/leading man at the Summerhouse Theaters in Albuquerque and
Santa Fe, New Mexico. The season's repertoire of plays had included *Mr. Roberts, Stalag 17, The Cocktail Party, I Am a Camera,
Light Up the Sky,* and the Pulitzer Prize–
winning *Hell-Bent fer Heaven,* in which I'd
portrayed Rufe Pryor, a religious psychotic.

As the car I was in moved over the
Cahuenga Pass toward the Valley, the tension and exhaustion of the past summer

were still churning inside me. I was in the backseat of a pre-war convertible, with Ted Markland, a young stand-up comic, on my left, and James Coburn, my Los Angeles City College classmate, on my right.

And then, out of the darkness, Jim said in his *basso profundo* voice, "Hey, man, relax. Have a toke on this."

I had been around pot in Minneapolis back in the forties. On Sunday afternoons, my high school bud John "Yogi" Randall would take me to jazz joints on Olson Highway, where we would split a pint of Guckenheimer Whiskey and listen to the black performers (we called them "Negroes" then) wailing away. Sometimes the guys around us would puff on reefers — marijuana cigarettes. But whenever the weed came my way, I'd point to our bottle and pass.

Now, years later, I still didn't know shit from Shinola about how to smoke a joint. I watched carefully while Jim sucked on the weak-looking cigarette, then I did what he did, and passed it on to Ted. Of course, I, the middle man, took in twice as much smoke as my compadres on either side.

When we arrived at our destination, I told the others that I'd like a few moments alone in the car before going in. They left me alone. . . .

Almost immediately, the sound of waves began to surround me. I had always feared water and now, in my drugged state, I was certain that death by drowning was imminent.

Then another sensation began to permeate my consciousness. I sensed that I was levitating — slowly at first, then more rapidly — while knowing all along that I was still sitting alone in the backseat of the car.

I decided that if I could make it to the front by climbing over the seat and locking my forearms beneath the crossbar of the steering wheel while gripping the wheel's upper half, I'd be grounded and safe. And somehow I became convinced that I'd better do this as quickly as I could. So I dove into the front of the car and locked my hands and arms in place.

But as I adjusted my lower body beneath the wheel, suddenly, like Marley's ghost superimposed on Scrooge's door knocker, a murky, satanic face appeared in the center of the steering circle. It beckoned me with a smile, then looked downward.

I changed what was left of my mind and decided to allow myself to levitate.

As I released my hands from the wheel,

the waves and now the wind began to blow at gale force, buffeting the car. Hail and sleet and snow joined the fray. And at the same time, the image of the devil became clearer to me. He was clutching the tormented body of Judas and shouting above the unbearable din, "Look on him who betrayed the Lord and repented! Can you? Can you?"

I fell back limply on the seat. My thoughts floated back to Father Bartholomew in catechism class at St. Anne's Catholic Church. How I had argued with him about the afterlife, hell, purgatory, sin, heaven, and a host of other subjects. I screamed at the face before me, "I can't repent! I've done nothing wrong! Why am I dying? I'm young. I've got so much to do."

At that moment, the waves began to pour down my throat, stifling my screams as water quenches flames. The thought occurred to me that the face on the wheel was the Antichrist, and that I was living through the Last Judgment with this fellow as my guide to eternal damnation. Whatever was happening, rather than diminishing, it was all growing more overwhelming. Every sensation and sound in and around me intensified until I thought my body and mind might explode.

Was this the hell I had doubted? Was this my punishment for not believing Father Bart's admonitions? Or had he really been another kind of Mephistopheles, tempting me with the mysteries Rome described as truths? All the old questions came floating back, accompanied by new ones. I thought: Since I cannot repent, will I, as in the eyes of the Buddha, remain forever in some kind of limbo? Or is heaven promised me no matter what I've done? What if all the church cant stuffed into my preteen mind at St. Anne's was hogwash?

All I was sure of in that chaotic moment was that I was dying, and that no one was coming to rescue either my body or my alleged soul. So I screamed again, "I can't repent!"

Then, as if to assure me I wasn't in hell yet, the cold came. Freezing, brittle cold, cold beyond anything I had ever experienced in Minneapolis, that coldest of cold cities. My eyes shut, blinded by ice and wind. My limbs cracked like gothic gunshots. My body convulsed and then went rigid as the wind and waves thundered around it. And then there was sudden silence.

Directly before me in the steaming windshield, six faces began to emerge, first vaguely, and then with increasing clarity. I slowly recognized each one. All had died in my late teen years, and they appeared as I had seen them or heard of them dying.

Vivian, her blond schoolgirl beauty mangled in the horror of a car crash.

Richard, his handsome bandaged head rotted from within by brain cancer.

Frank, my grandpa, sitting upright in a wooden chair, alone and dead, with spittle trailing from his mouth to the floor.

Grandma, alone in a hospital room, death rattling in her throat as pneumonia ended her days.

Walter Vaughn, my father, alone in Barbados and dead at forty-seven of a ravaged, rheumatic heart.

And John Connor, my stepfather, whom I worshiped, alone in a charity ward, dying of the drink at thirty-nine.

They were all there with me, but somehow I was still alone.

In that moment of silence and terrible sadness, I was four years old again. I was standing on a bandstand in North Commons Park in Minneapolis. Mother was in front of me, gazing up and smiling at the words I was speaking — the words she had taught me about that "undiscover'd country from whose bourn no traveler returns."

Then I was back in the present, and all the lunacy that had visited me mere moments before began again. I screamed and screamed, and when I thought I could scream no more, I screamed again, "I can't repent." Still frozen in place, I *twisted* in panic to my right and to my left. I was certain I was locked in that car, forever alone.

Then, on my right, a sudden explosion of sound overwhelmed me. It was my name being repeated over and over, yet it was not my name. It was, "Roberto, Roberto! Jesus H. Fucking Christ! Stop! You're going to bring on the fuzz, man."

It was Jim, trying to drag me from the car, pulling, wrestling, cajoling, until finally I was free from the madness that had suffused and surrounded me.

Ted soon appeared, and together they dragged me through the night, still frightened, exhausted, and semi-comatose, to the small apartment where they had gone to relax and get high.

Jim said, "Get inside, man, and don't make a sound. The whole neighborhood is out looking for a maniac." The moment we entered the apartment, I fell on an old, ugly couch, shaken and sweat-drenched from my ordeal. Jim said, "Get in the shower, man, and cool off and relax. We're going to turn off the lights until the neighbors split."

Once the water hit me, the sensation of waves was rekindled, and gradually the earlier mad feelings started again. I thought that if I could focus and concentrate on something, specifically language, perhaps I could fend off another cycle of insanity. I crouched in the corner of the dimly lit shower, and as the warm water cuddled my shoulders, I started to whisper, "To be or not to be . . ." The waves continued, but did not intensify, as I intoned, "that is the question."

I thought that if I could finish that soliloquy without screaming, perhaps the horror would not return. I made it to ". . . that undiscover'd country from whose bourn no traveler returns," and by then all was quiet in my soul.

I was in and out of the shower several times that night, each time repeating my *Hamlet* mantra. Finally, Jim took me back to the Fountain Avenue apartment he shared with Zev Bufman, a future Broadway producer.

I asked if anyone had a taping device, and one of the other fellows living there came up with a wire recorder. I proceeded to describe what I had been through. Later, I transcribed it on paper and kept the written record for years afterward.

For many months after that evening, at unexpected times both day and night, the waves and the fears would return, and each time I would go back to the safety of the soliloquy. By the time I arrived at the phrase "from whose bourn . . ." I was quiet and safe, and all was right with my tormented soul.

Almost a year after the incident, I had occasion to recount this experience to a psychiatrist at a party. He told me, "Robert, it sounds to me as if you had a highly accelerated, drug-induced nervous breakdown, bordering on a psychotic break."

"And what does all that mean?" I wondered.

He responded, "Well, let's just say you were lucky there was no permanent damage. Some people never come back."

Contrary to the doctor's concern, the night's journey into madness changed me for the better. Before then, I had thought about very little outside of me-me-me, I-I-I, and my drive to succeed as an actor. Afterward, I was much more sensitive to the feelings of others.

More important, I started to look at the big world about me. I decided that in the future, I must take the time to learn all I could about why we are here and why, even "against a sea of troubles," we choose to remain moored on this hurtling sphere.

Even now, more than a half century later, some incident will occasionally set off a feeling that touches on the fear I felt that night; then, just as quickly, it passes.

Jim Coburn once told me, "Man, everyone who ever got high is looking for that kind of experience, but not at the price you paid. I've never seen such terror in a face as I did in yours that night."

In her book *The Year of Magical Thinking,* Joan Didion writes about "the shallowness of sanity." I understand what she meant. Needless to say, when the drug culture of the sixties rolled in, it held no allure for me.

In the spring of 1956, after *End as a Man* had closed and the whole wide world of film acting had become my bailiwick, I was asked to become the teacher of the Players' Ring acting class. At that time, the class was being taught by my beloved friend Joe Flynn, whom I'd met in *The Pilgrimage Play,* where he played Jacob Jehosephat, the money changer in the temple. Joe was a master of comedy, both on and off stage and screen, and would later star in the TV series *McHale's Navy* (which ran, for a while, in the time slot opposite another popular program — *The Man from U.N.C.L.E.*). This was a case of my being a sucker for just about anyone who could give me a great laugh. When he wasn't acting, Joe was employed by the State of California, which gave him a free car for his use. He never told me what his job was.

Anyway, Joe taught the Players' Ring class, but he was vacationing and needed a stand-in. Knowing Joe, I realized that, whatever he was teaching the class, it certainly wasn't anyone's "method." Joe's theory of acting was simple: Just do what the script calls for, no matter what it takes. For example, if you need to cry on stage, wear a hat with a freshly cut onion in it. So much for Stanislavski's affective sense memory theory.

But despite the discrepancy between Joe's acting philosophy and mine, I was happy to take over his gig. I loved acting and I enjoyed teaching it.

In fact, I'd done my first teaching at the tender age of eighteen. In the fall quarter of 1951, at the University of Minnesota, Betty Girling, director of the KUOM Minnesota School of the Air, had asked me to teach a Speech 101 class in radio acting. I accepted the invitation with much enthusiasm and confidence.

At that point, I'd already become immersed in the latest thinking about the art of acting. Back in the forties, my stepfather and mother had made me aware of Brando (he was dating a girl named Carmelita Pope, whom my mother knew) and the Actors Studio run by Lee Strasberg, Bobby Lewis, Cheryl Crawford, and later, Elia Kazan, and their use of the Stanislavski system of preparing to act a specific role known as the Method. Constantin Stanislavski and Vladimir Nemirovich-Danchenko had founded the world-famous Moscow Art Theater, whose work I would see during my first visit to Moscow in the winter of 1964.

I had first come across the name of Stanislavski in the summer of 1947 in Chicago when my stepfather, John Connor, was understudying the role of Harry Brock in the national company of Garson Kanin's *Born Yesterday,* starring Jan Sterling in the role of Billie Dawn. (The same role was played on Broadway and in the movie by Judy Holliday, who won an Oscar for her performance.)

Mother and John had subleased Bella and David Itkins's apartment on North Lasalle Street for the summer. The Itkinses were associated with the famous Goodman Theater in Chicago, where my wife, Linda, would one day study. They had gone to the Soviet Union and left behind a library of English translations of Russian books on the theater in general, and acting in particular. Stanislavski's *An Actor Prepares* was my bible for that summer. In 1948, I bought my own copy of Stanislavski's tenth anniversary edition of *An Actor Prepares,* which I still have today.

At the U in that fall of 1951, I tried to tell my students, most of them quite a bit older than I, that after the basic techniques of how to use a microphone as an actor, we were going to explore an unusual way of performing radio plays using what I had learned of the Method as I understood it from the mid-forties in Chicago. It didn't work, whether because of my failings as a fledgling instructor or sheer lack of interest on the part of my students — or perhaps a little of both.

But my fascination with the art of acting continued to incubate. I reveled in the great performances of the era, from Laurence Olivier's 1948 *Hamlet* to Brando's 1952 film of *A Streetcar Named Desire.* In 1954, I met Michael Chekhov, then a lecturer/teacher and an icon at the Stage Society. I was just twenty-one years old and the youngest member of the group.

My college friend Harry Fishbach, now an author and TV director in Toronto, upon hearing I had been accepted in the Stage Society, presented me with a copy of Chekhov's *To the Actor,* personally inscribed by Harry in July 1954, which I also have to this day. I began to imbibe Chekhov's teachings, both directly and through the influence of Jeff Corey, a blacklisted actor and a member of the Stage Society in one of its early postwar incarnations, and Jack Kosslyn, a member of the Society when I was accepted. Both were students of the Chekhov technique of acting.

During the last weeks of *End as a Man,* I had gone to Jeff for tips on how not to go stale in what was, for me, my best work in a play to that date — and probably ever. He and Jack spoke reverently about Michael Chekhov.

I had also sat in on a memorable class of Jeff's in the spring of 1955, when James Dean was invited to join the evening's work. Jeff asked Jimmy to try to convince his acting partner, in an improvisation, to stop drinking. Of the myriad choices Jimmy could have made, he decided that he would be drunk himself and therefore show, but not tell, his fellow player what an ass a drunk can be when others are sober.

His improvised performance was absolutely stunning. Unfortunately, before the end of that year, on September 30, 1955, at the age of twenty-four, James Dean was killed in an auto accident. Coincidentally, a few hours later on that same day, Michael Chekhov, who had been warned to stop smoking, while reaching over to light a cigarette, slumped backward, dead of a heart seizure.

This, then, was the background I brought to the Players' Ring acting class that summer of 1956.

Joe Flynn's class had a normal cross section of aspiring young actors — as well as a few very special individuals. Sally Kellerman, who would rocket to stardom in the motion picture *M*A*S*H,* was a member of the class. Another was Robert Towne, who would win the Oscar for best screenplay for *Chinatown.* Towne didn't really want to be an actor; he just wanted to understand how the acting craft worked, the better to create effective scenes for actors to play.

Then there was Paul Brinegar, a tall, good-looking young fellow who was told by one of the casting people that he was too tall for comedy. He went on to have a very successful run as the jolly cook George

131

Washington Wishbone in the TV series *Rawhide,* starring Clint Eastwood, himself a Chekhov admirer.

My girlfriend that summer often monitored my Sunday-afternoon class but did not attempt to do any improv work or scenes — she was busy being Natalie Wood.

And lastly, there was a handsome young stud from New Jersey with a rather strange accent and a distinctive voice. I remember that Jack tried to do a scene from the play *Bus Stop,* but somehow never quite had the relaxation and confidence to carry it off. Jack's problem with self-confidence proved to be surprisingly long-lasting. I remember him sitting on the floor of my MGM dressing room one afternoon in the early fall of 1967. As he inhaled a brewski, he declared, "Vaughnie, I'm going to give myself two more years in this business. Then I'm going to look for another way to make a living."

"Hang in there, Jack," I told him. "You're too young to quit."

A couple of years later, he figured out how to do this thing called acting and demonstrated to the world his skills in *Easy Rider.* The world still refers to him as Jack, as in Nicholson. He has been nominated for an Oscar more often than any other male actor (twelve times) and has won the award three times (also a record for a male).

As the class began, I knew that I would probably be drafted before the end of the year. Therefore I didn't want to get too complicated in my teaching efforts, lest I leave my students adrift in a sea of acting theories, Russian or Strasbergian. But I did want to emphasize what I had learned from Chekhov.

Apparently I failed. In 1998, when Nicholson received the Golden Globe for best actor in *As Good as It Gets* (a role he almost walked away from), he reflected, "I turned around and imagined I saw my director making fun of my newly acquired Psychological Gesture from Michael Chekhov." I suppose it's a compliment to my unforgettable teaching style that Jack recalled the term from my classes all those years later. (Of course, it's also possible he got his hands on a copy of Chekhov's book.)

Since I've released the Psychological Gesture genie, I'll take this opportunity to explain what I think Chekhov meant by the phrase. To illustrate, I'll focus on portions of the two plays I'm best acquainted with: *Hamlet,* and *A View from the Bridge* by Arthur Miller. I will also address a contemporary comedy that I performed in, Neil Simon's greatest success (financially), *The*

Odd Couple.

When I directed *View* in 1960, I made an agreement with the producers at Los Angeles State College that professional actors would take the principal roles while the supporting roles would be played by undergraduates. I cast Anthony Carbone in the leading role, coincidentally named Eddie Carbone; James Coburn in the pivotal character of the lawyer, Alfieri; and Carolee Campbell, John Hackett, and Minette King in other major parts. This play is the closest Miller ever got to a Greek tragedy, complete with a chorus — Coburn's Alfieri.

More important, the producers agreed to my request to have the set, costumes, and props available from the first day of rehearsal. (This virtually never happens.) To set the stage for Chekhov's Psychological Gesture, we must have an atmosphere in which the actual set of Eddie Carbone's working-class New Jersey apartment is available from the very start of rehearsals. For the actor/artist, the atmosphere created by a set can be compared to a key in music; the cast must sense and embody that atmosphere the way a musician's performance must embody the distinctive qualities of a particular key.

When this happens, the Psychological

Gesture can emerge naturally and convincingly. The expression refers to several things: the visible (actual) gestures of the actor; the invisible (potential) gestures embodied in his words; and the feelings that give rise to both.

All three are intimately connected. We say that a human being or a character in a play "thinks" or "feels" or "wishes" something because those impulses are the prevailing ones at a particular time. But all three functions are present and active in each psychological moment. Thus we use, without thinking, words that describe emotions while implying physical activity: we "draw a conclusion," we "give comfort," we "fall into lethargy" or "jump for joy." The thought precedes and fosters the wish, and the wish fosters the action. And when acting is at its fullest, all three are involved. As Leonardo DaVinci wrote, "The soul desires to dwell with the body because without the members of that body, it can neither act nor feel." (Atheists need read no further.)

Working out the dramatization of *A View from the Bridge* with the complete set visible around us made it easier for the entire cast to find the Psychological Gesture suitable to our purposes — to feel, wish, and then perform the actions that embodied the playwright's vision. (I still have my director's script of *View,* its margins filled with my scrawled notes, including a lot of Chekhovian jargon. It was my best work ever as a director.)

For another example, let's move on to *Hamlet,* Act I, Scene I, where the ghost of Hamlet's father appears for the second time. Horatio speaks:

I'll cross it, though it blast me. Stay, illusion!
If thou hast any sound, or use of voice,
Speak to me:
If there be any good thing to be done,
That may to thee do ease and grace to
  me,
Speak to me:

(Cock crows)

If thou art privy to thy country's fate,
Which, happily, foreknowing may avoid, O,
  speak!

According to Michael Chekhov, the actors' imagination may think of Horatio in a crazed state of mental excitement that flows through the whole speech. Now, what is its main dynamic? Not the nuances. He will surely be facing the ghost, probably reaching upward toward the spectral image (standing upstage in most productions of *Hamlet*). The audience can see the ghost for the first time in all his majestic, eternal form. Probably Horatio's arms and hands are outstretched, facing downward toward the ghost and away from the audience, trying to fix the unknown being by force of the actor's body. Certainly a Psychological Gesture of this kind would be appropriate relative to Shakespeare's words.

"If speech is to be made plastic on the one hand, musical on the other," wrote the Austrian philosopher Rudolf Steiner, "then this is first of all a matter of bringing gesture into the speech." This scene from *Hamlet* is a simple yet vivid example of what he meant and how it can be applied to the stage.

Finally, I'll refer to the passive Psychological Gesture, which is more or less an idea of my own. To shift from the sublime to the ridiculous, I'll use an example from my experience rehearsing *The Odd Couple* in 1969 in St. Louis.

The director was Corey Allen, whom I had first met in the fall of 1952 at UCLA where he was a pre-law major. When I met him, he was playing the principal role in a play called *The Jesus Cop*. Later, in 1955, he appeared in Nicholas Ray's production of *Rebel Without a Cause* as Jimmy Dean's nemesis — he was killed in the film's key scene when the two boys race to see who will be the first to stop his car before reaching the cliff.

In St. Louis, I was playing Oscar Madison (the slob), while my lifelong best friend, Sherwood Price, was playing Felix Unger (the anal one). We had invited a few audiences to watch rehearsals before the opening, and Sherwood and I were getting all the laughs we should. But I was dissatisfied, feeling that we weren't really mining the inner life of Neil Simon's characters.

As the final dress rehearsal neared, I suggested that we do a run-through of the play as if it were a drama — with this addendum: We would make no eye contact with each other in any of the scenes where just the two of us were onstage. In effect, I was suggesting a passive Psychological Gesture. And it worked beautifully. From that point on, through the entire month's run, we had a multilevel Neil Simon comedy that the audiences cheered and understood during all the lengthy curtain calls.

The art of acting is something I find endlessly fascinating. But I must admit that success on the stage or on the screen is often related less to art or even craft than to something a bit more elemental.

In that summer of 1960, when Jim Coburn and I were rehearsing *A View from the Bridge,* we started arguing about some acting point. He said, "Remember what Stella said, Bobby." He was referring to Stella Adler, his acting coach and sometime girlfriend (also Brando's — among others).

"What did she say?"

Jimmy replied that in the late twenties, after studying with Stanislavski in Paris, Stella had told some future members of the Group Theater that the Master had told her one quality was more important for an actor than any other.

"And what quality is that?" I demanded.

With a grin, Jimmy replied, "Charm."

Stella was right.

In the period between March and December of 1956, while I was teaching acting at the Players' Ring — trying, in retrospect, to pass along that elusive but all-important quality of charm — I was also doing a huge amount of acting. I knew this would be my last opportunity to expand my career for a while, with Uncle Sam's call looming in my future. So I crammed in as many starring roles on TV shows and in movies as possible. I'll just mention here a few of the highlights.

On July 4, 1956, live and in color from NBC Studios in Burbank, California, I had second billing to Victor Jory in *Declaration,* about a Tory father and his revolutionary son, a one-hour show written especially for *Matinee Theatre* and directed by Lamont Johnson. *Matinee Theatre* was the only live color show on network TV done every day, Monday through Friday, at noon. The show might be an adaptation of a classic such as *Wuthering Heights* or a contemporary story written for NBC.

My role in *Declaration* was interesting for my mother because people for many years had kidded her that my real father was Victor Jory. It's true that my mother had worked with Victor Jory, an actor best remembered today for his role in *Gone With the Wind.* And some have claimed they see a resemblance between him and me. But the timing was off — my father was, in fact, my father. So there was nothing Oedipal going on in *Declaration* — just another nice role for a young actor honing his chops in the era of live TV.

My first role in a picture where I received star billing was *Hell's Crossroads* starring Stephen McNally and Peggie Castle. I played Bob Ford, the "dirty little varmint" who shot Jesse James in the back while Jesse was hanging a picture. Jesse James was played by an actor named Henry Brandon, who had played opposite Judith Anderson onstage in *Medea.* Henry became a longtime companion of Mark Herron (formerly Truman Herron), another of my friends from LACC.

Mark is now best remembered for having been Judy Garland's fourth (that is, second-to-last) husband — which I guess means he got to do to Judy Garland what every gay man is supposed to want to do to Judy Garland. But he is best remembered by me for the following story.

One evening in the early sixties, I was attending a black-tie dinner at the Beverly Hilton Hotel in Beverly Hills. I arrived alone, which was fairly common for me. The evening was some kind of charity event, and the main draw was to be the appearance of Elizabeth Taylor and Richard Burton, hot off their internationally publicized affair during the filming of *Cleopatra,* while Burton was still married to his first wife, Sybil, and Liz was still married to Eddie Fisher.

As I made my way to my assigned table, I heard a voice calling, "Robert! Robert! Over here!" It was Mark Herron, with Judy

Garland, well oiled with the hooch (and wearing, for some reason, a cast on her right hand). I had met Judy previously. She had been a guest at my home, singing and telling her wonderful stories of her early days at MGM. (Judy was a raconteur *par excellence.*) Now she demanded that Mark ask me to sit with them, which I did.

The world press was there, both print and photographic. They were held away from the main tables by a cordoned-off area that was patrolled by Hilton's security. As we chatted and Judy continued to drink, she grew increasingly boisterous, so by the time Taylor and Burton arrived, she was bubbling over with manic energy. Suddenly upon seeing Taylor, she yelled, "Here she comes, Miss MGM Tits!" followed by, "and look who's with her — that no-talent, nasal-voiced, pockmarked son-of-a-bitch from Wales!"

Every word was loud and clear. Mark and I finally got her seated and calmed her down.

The party proceeded in a little more decorous fashion, and just a few minutes before the speeches and presentations were to begin, the orchestra began playing some fairly slow dance music. Judy got excited. "Robert, Robert, you *must* dance with me!

You simply must!" I tried to decline, for many reasons. But her begging grew more and more rambunctious until finally Mark (by this time sweating like a pig) pleaded, "Please, Robert, maybe she'll calm down — or better yet, pass out."

I took the challenge, and we made our way to the dance floor.

Within less than a minute, I felt an unexpected and slightly frightening pressure in a very delicate spot. Judy had gone for the Vaughn family jewels with her well-wrapped right hand, cast and all. I was deeply embarrassed, and my first thought was, "God! I hope those photographers don't see this!" No such luck. I was suddenly blinded by an explosion of flashbulbs. They continued to go off for several minutes while I wrestled Judy back to our table.

The following week, I searched the papers and magazines anxiously, looking for a photo of that astonishing dance floor exhibition. It never appeared, at least as far as I ever saw. Who knows the reason? I'd like to think it involved some sense of good taste and perhaps a drop of compassion for poor, sweet Judy on the part of the world's editors. It was a gentler time in the industry. Judy herself would be gone before the sixties were over — a possible suicide.

A footnote: Years later, Mark came to my wedding. During the reception, he made the kind of joke only a gay man could get away with. "You know, Robert," he told me, "you ought to do *A Streetcar Named Desire*."

I was flattered, but I demurred. "Oh, I don't know. That role is so totally identified with Marlon Brando. . . ."

"No, no," Herron said, "I mean you ought to play Blanche!"

Turning back to 1956: The second picture I did was for Allied Artists and was titled *Unwed Mother,* a very provocative title for the late fifties. It starred Timothy Carey, an actor who had scored in Stanley Kubrick's *Paths of Glory* alongside Kirk Douglas. In our picture, Timothy played the role of an abortionist (also pretty frisky stuff for that time). When he arrived on the set to do his scene, dressed appropriately in a cheap dark suit, he opened his black medical bag and from it brought out some of the ugliest, vilest-looking knives, tools, hammers, and sundry stuff you'd likely see only in some triple-X horror movie. This bag had not been furnished by the prop department, nor was a bag of that kind mentioned in the script. It was all Timothy's idea, and he had to be talked out of using it in his scene by the director, who threatened to have him fired and, if possible, kicked out of the Screen Actors Guild. He did finally acquiesce, and I heard very little about or from him since then.

The last picture I did prior to my Army service was, ironically enough, the story of a young man who wanted desperately not to go into the Army. As mentioned earlier, it was a loan-out to Columbia Studios from Hecht-Lancaster called *No Time to Be Young.* I'm sure my actual feelings at the time helped to color my performance.

Finally, I did a TV half-hour drama for CBS's *Telephone Time* titled *The Consort,* in which I played Prince Albert of Saxe-Coburg, a German cousin and the youthful lover of Queen Victoria, played by Judy Meredith. Later Judy would become what journalists usually call "a close friend" of John F. Kennedy. (Truth be told, by the time the Massachusetts senator reached the White House, very few young beauties in L.A. couldn't claim at least a heavy flirtation with the cool, handsome fellow in the Oval Office.)

Judy is one of a number of things (including political positions) that I shared with the future president. She'd been introduced to me by Natalie, who had no problem with my spending time with her friend.

Such were the free-and-easy mores of Hollywood, at least among the young crowd I frequented in those days.

Then there was an evening event at the Beverly Hilton that I attended with Joyce Jameson (more about her in a moment). This particular charity gala had enlisted the legendary toastmaster of Hollywood, Georgie Jessel, to serve as emcee.

The ageless Jessel had been part of show business from the beginning of the twentieth century, having been a vaudeville comic, an actor, a singer, a songwriter, and a theater and movie producer. In his later years, when not escorting young lovelies about town, he could be seen hobnobbing at the Friar's Club of New York or L.A., or serving as the roastmaster at almost any imaginable event right down to an Elks convention in Akron, Ohio. Georgie was a man of integrity: He was always available for a price.

This night, the final guest speaker at the Hilton was Jack Warner, the legendary head poobah of Warner Bros. Studio since the thirties, producer of countless classic pictures featuring those great faces from the Warner stable — Humphrey Bogart, Lauren Bacall, James Cagney, Bette Davis, Edward G. Robinson, and many others. He ruled with an iron hand and a stingy purse.

And when not wringing blood from a stone on the studio lot, that hand was often seen shaking from the John Barleycorn, as it was this evening.

Warner went on and on and on telling dumb old stories and jokes that didn't make sense. As the speech continued, the audience, filled with A-listers like Rosalind Russell, Kirk Douglas, Jack Lemmon, and Gregory Peck, grew more and more restless, bored, irritated, and finally angry.

When Warner finally, mercifully, resumed his seat, there was a polite smattering of applause. (After all, this *was* still one of the most powerful men in show business.) Jessel strode to the dais, took a long hard look at Jack seated to his left, and finally remarked, "Tell me, Jack, how the hell did you ever become the head of a major studio?"

There was a momentary silence and an almost audible intake of breath by the entire roomful of dignitaries. Then, as if Jessel had liberated them, the audience exploded. The stars shouted, jeered, laughed, banged their plates with their silverware, waved, stood up and applauded — and Jack, being an insensitive lush, also stood up and took several bows, waving his hand with his cigar clenched in his broadly grinning face.

I imagine that, from Jack's somewhat clouded point of view, his speech and the entire evening were a roaring success.

By the time I was drafted in December 1956, I had actually already served some time in the Army Reserves. Here's how that had happened.

Back on July 27, 1953, an armistice had been signed between the North and South Korean warring factions. A friend of mine who was a colonel in the Army Reserve got in touch with me then and suggested that I join the Reserve for six years.

"Why should I do anything like that?" I demanded.

"Well, if you eventually get drafted and have completed some graduate degrees, I can help you to get a direct commission as a second lieutenant. That way, you might avoid basic training. You can serve your two years with fellows of your intelligence and maturity."

Well, this was rather flattering, and, like getting drunk, it seemed like a good idea at the time. So I joined up, not knowing what was ahead of me.

But now, more than three years later, I could put off active duty service no longer. (Even Elvis ended up getting drafted.) My induction papers listed my civilian occupation as "movie star," which, of course, I was not at that time, and would not be for some time to come. Wearing a black satin motorcycle jacket, black corduroy pants, and black leather boots, I stepped on a Greyhound bus at nine A.M. on December 18, 1956, for the eight-hour drive to Fort Ord, California, near Monterey, to begin my two-year stint in the U.S. Army. Certain that the golden summer of budding stardom that had just passed was gone forever, I was feeling mighty low.

Five:
How I Invented the Bow and Arrow, Directed by Roger Corman

> I have thought some of Nature's journeymen had made men, and not made them well, they imitated humanity so abominably.

Our bus arrived at Fort Ord after dark. We new recruits spent the night locked up in some barracks, sleeping in our underwear, and I was very, very cold in the unfamiliar Northern California climate.

Before dawn, we were hustled out onto the icy parade grounds and pushed about by noncommissioned officers until we formed some semblance of two lines.

A big, mean-looking, heavyset sergeant finally yelled out in a terrifying, growly voice, "Sound off like you gotta pair of nuts." And I assure you, we did. I found out later that morning, after my first chow hall breakfast, that we would not be starting basic training until after the first of the year because the noncoms and officers that would be our trainers were on a Christmas/New Year's break. Sarge said, while we awaited their return, after having been issued our GI uniforms, we would be spending the next fortnight cleaning and polishing the area.

Before I'd left L.A., Beverly Long, one of my lady friends from LACC (and a talented actress who had appeared in *Rebel Without a Cause*), advised me to tell no one at Fort Ord that I was an actor, because it could only bring me grief. I arrived at the Army base with that thought foremost in my mind. And Bev's advice seemed sound enough. The guys I bunked with were a rough-hewn lot most of whom had come in from Montana and were sheepherders in their former lives. I suspected that they wouldn't look kindly on a Hollywood sissy-boy in their midst.

Having some time to kill on my first Sunday at camp, I went over to the canteen to get something to read. I found that, incredibly, the store featured a full display of the current fan magazines. I bought a couple and brought them back to my bunk, figuring I might catch up on a little industry gossip that way. No sooner had I opened one of them than I stumbled across a picture of Natalie and me. She was getting off her flight from Memphis, and I was waiting for her carrying armsful of stuffed animals. I quickly closed the mag and, looking around, tucked it beneath the mattress on my lower bunk. "Jesus," I thought. "That was close."

Lunch was then called. When I returned, much to my horror, I saw a couple of the guys had the magazine and were laughing and riffling through it. I could see that my mattress had obviously been moved. So much for my brilliant college-educated cleverness in hiding something apparently in plain sight.

I lay down on my bed with my hands beneath my head, staring at the upper bunk mattress and fearing I know not what. A couple of the fellows who seemed to be the leaders of the bunch passed the magazine around and, as each one looked at it, he would then look over at me, speculatively. Finally, the leaders came over, scrutinized me, and the more fearsome-looking of the two said in the tiniest voice, pointing at the picture, "Is that you?"

"Yes," I admitted.

They all cheered and patted one another on the back.

We got to talking, and I learned that, with

practically nothing to do on the sheep farm at night, my bunkmates used to watch a little black-and-white TV that had been set up for them with some sort of improvised antenna. They'd seen some of my early TV shows. A 1956 episode of *Gunsmoke* titled "Cooter" was their favorite, and they seemed to remember far more than I did about the story.

One guy asked, "Did you ever fuck Marilyn MONrow?" as he pronounced it. I assured him I had not, but I did so desire to do so. They thought that was wonderful, and we all bonded in a spasm of giggles and laughter. I expected some questions about the manliness of some of the Western stars, but none was forthcoming — I presume because none of them could imagine so heinous a thought as, say, a girlie-man "Duke" Wayne.

Anyway, rather than being thought of as some sort of strange Hollywood type, I was immediately taken in as a respected "bud" by my new friends from the Big Sky country. Meanwhile, I spent the eight weeks of basic training trying to be the best soldier I could be while haunting the base library during my free time. My goal was to find some legitimate method of getting out of the service before my two-year hitch was up.

At the end of the first four weeks, we were all allowed to go home from Saturday noon until five P.M. Sunday — our first time away from training. My happiness at this brief interlude of freedom swiftly gave way to shock. While I'd been gone, my mother had been diagnosed with Berger's disease, or nephropathy, a kidney disorder characterized by blood in the urine. Left untreated, it can require amputation of the legs or cause end-stage kidney failure and death.

I promised Mother we'd get her the best care possible. We spent the weekend commiserating with each other and slowly getting used to this strange, looming new presence in our lives — the idea of death. It was even tougher tearing myself away on Sunday afternoon than it had been to leave home in the first place.

Back at Fort Ord, I began spending every evening after chow conducting research to see whether I qualified for an Honorable Hardship Discharge. After all, I was now the sole support of my mother, who could not work because of the Berger's problem.

At the conclusion of basic training in March 1957, instead of being shipped to Fort Lewis in Washington along with my compadres, I was held over at Ord pending a decision on my appeal for an early out.

Meanwhile, since I had entered the service with an Army Reserve background of three years, I was made a temporary drill instructor, or "cadre," as the Army calls that job. I had also been named as Recruit of the Cycle.

My experience as the psychopathic cadet in *End as a Man* served me well in my new role as a freshly minted drill instructor. Wearing my white helmet, blue ascot, and a perfectly ironed and starched green uniform, and sporting a fake Southern accent, you couldn't tell me from the real McCoy. And being a drill instructor turned out to be laughably easy. It just meant going through eight more weeks of basic training, mostly in reverse: While my recruits ran forward, I was running backward, cheering them on. But my days were long. I had to get up an hour before the lads (four-thirty A.M.) and was still checking rifle racks at ten P.M. My desire to get the hell out of the Army got stronger.

Freedom finally came to me thanks to Joe Flynn. Joe had become friends at USC with Joe Holt who was, at that time, congressman for the Hollywood area. Flynn sought the pol's help in my quest for an early release. I still have the two letters I received from Congressman Holt. The first apologized for being unable to spring me, while the second congratulated me on my release from the Army. "I hope I've been helpful in this matter," he added, angling, I suppose, for a campaign contribution or at least a vote in November. I had no idea what happened between letter one and letter two, and I certainly wasn't going to try to find out for fear someone might change his mind.

Whatever the reason, on May 23, 1957, at ten A.M., I was honorably discharged from the United States Army at Fort Ord, California. I fell to my knees and kissed the Northern California turf. I was headed back to Hollywood, hopefully to restart my truncated career in The Biz.

One last word about my Montana friends. One evening over a blazing fire and some cheap whiskey during a bivouac (sleeping and living outdoors to simulate combat conditions), I heard the sad and sweet tale of how these lonely boys kept themselves from boredom during the cold Montana nights. Yes, the legends are true — sheepherders do indeed have sex with their sheep. In fact, if my fellow soldiers were to be believed, they even named them and swapped ratings as to the, er, charms of each animal.

As Joe E. Brown remarked to Jack Lemmon in the final scene of *Some Like It Hot,* "Nobody's perfect."

After my release from active duty, I finished my six-year reserve responsibility by spending weekends at Fort McArthur, California, and two weeks each summer at Camp Roberts, California, just a hoot and a holler from the Hearst Castle at San Simeon. It was there that I first met Vince Bugliosi, an officer in the Reserve, whom I would later work for in his efforts to become district attorney of Los Angeles. Vince later became famous throughout the world for sending Charles Manson to San Quentin for life, even though Manson had not been present at either of the murder scenes in that summer of '69, when the members of his "family" had slaughtered Sharon Tate, Leno LaBianca, and a collection of other victims.

On the first Saturday after my return, I threw a welcome-home party for myself and invited all the LACC gang to the Orchid Avenue penthouse. Among others, I invited Jackie Joseph, who would later marry Ken Berry of *The Andy Griffith Show* and *Mayberry R.F.D.* Jackie said she would be delighted to join me, but she was performing in a musical at a theater under a bridge on Sunset Boulevard called the Cabaret Concert. The name of the show was *The Billy Barnes Revue,* and it featured a cast that included Ken Berry, Bert Convy, Ann Guilbert, and Billy's former wife, Joyce Jameson.

"You ought to come and see the show," Jackie said. "You'll like it. And Joyce is the woman for you. She's sexy, funny, smart, well-read, and she does a terrific Marilyn Monroe. If you like what you see, we can both come to your party after our late show Saturday night."

I did, and they did, and that was the beginning of my longest relationship as a bachelor. Joyce Jameson was all that Jackie said and more, and she moved in, out, and through my life for the next dozen years.

Joyce Jameson looked like a cross between Dolly Parton and a small Lili St. Cyr, the legendary striptease artist of the 1940s and '50s. Her repertoire of sketch impersonations ranged from Shirley Temple to Marlene Dietrich, with stops along the way as Judy Garland, Aimee Semple McPherson, Debbie Reynolds, and the two Bettes, Midler and Davis.

And those were just the ladies she impersonated onstage. On *The Steve Allen Show,* she created a character that she called her "dummy," as in Charlie McCarthy. Her dummy was the Honee Girl, and she was Joyce's take on a Marilyn Monroe type whom she identified with personally, the Hollywood blonde whose life ended tragically. Critics called Joyce the most versatile sketch comedienne with sex appeal of her era. I agreed.

For as long as I knew her, Joyce was an insomniac, using Miltown as her sedative of choice. She seldom fell asleep until shortly before dawn, arising around noon. In my layman's analysis, she suffered from a mild clinical depression, though she never sought medical help from any doctor, with the exception of an older psychiatrist in Sherman Oaks whom she saw briefly at my insistence, and whom she considered to be a charlatan.

With all this, she was the most fascinating girl I'd ever met. She was warm, articulate, and well-read in the Beat literature of the day. She had a razor-sharp wit, was a wonderful audience for humor, and a delight to be with when she chose to be. Unfortunately, when she chose not to socialize, she would simply turn off the phone and the lights and lock the door, literally and emotionally, until whatever problem was currently plaguing her had passed.

I don't believe she was a woman of multiple personalities as Roseanne Barr claims to be, or the character depicted in Joanne Woodward's Oscar-winning performance in *The Three Faces of Eve.* But I was never quite sure who would be opening the door when I came to pick her up. Most of her personalities were pleasant, provocative, and fun to be with. Her greatest professional shortcoming was her inability to present that same pleasing, warm personality to an audience. This was the fatal flaw that prevented her from enjoying the kind of career she otherwise deserved — hosting a comedy show on television, for example, like the one featuring the well-loved Carol Burnett.

Anyway, this is the charming, contradictory, remarkable Joyce Jameson I met for the first time back in 1957. I also met Tyler, the son she'd had with her former husband, Billy Barnes. Tyler was four at this time and living with a couple behind the house that Joyce lived in on Keith Avenue off Doheny Drive in what is now called West Hollywood. (Tyler is now in his fifties, living in Hawaii, and working as a drug counselor and companion to seniors.)

I was now in superb physical condition, after going through basic training twice, back to back, and I wanted to stay that way. So I joined the Beverly Hills Health Club, located on Santa Monica near Doheny (and not in Beverly Hills). The club membership was made up of three groups. One were young actors, including Dennis Hopper, Nick Adams, and me. A second group were older players like Paul Newman and Rock Hudson (who had become a major star in *Giant* with Elizabeth Taylor and the late James Dean). Sammy Davis Jr. would drop by from time to time to practice his quick-draw talents, bringing his own holster and pistol and hanging out in the locker room that opened onto the street.

The rest of the club was made up of retired Jewish businessmen who lived in the area. They never went into the weight room, choosing instead to take the sun outside near the many phones, where they could be in instant contact with their stockbrokers, just in case something big happened during the East Coast market hours. On occasion they also stripped down to take the sweats in the steam room. Many of them knew little or nothing about the movie business, and the culture clashes between them and the two platoons of actors sometimes led to quirky moments.

A favorite of mine involves two elderly

members of the club — let's call them Abe and Louie. One day they were in the steam room when Rock Hudson came in. Glancing up, Abe remarked, "Look at that nice big boy. He'd make a good basketball player." (Rock was indeed a good six-foot-four.)

Louie replied, "*Putz,* that's Rock Hudson!"

Adjusting his towel, Abe replied, "Rock? That's a good name for a basketball player!"

Ed Feldman told me that tale my first week there. I don't know what Ed's job was other than greeting each arriving member with, "How ya doing, athlete? You look great." Ed seemed to have never learned anyone's name, but he always had a cigar in his hand and a yellowish, toothy smile on his gray face. One day after I had not been in the club for a while I learned that Ed dropped dead in the steam room trying to pick up his unlit cigar from the floor while greeting a club member.

The fifties were now more than halfway through. The post-war era was rapidly giving way to something new, a spirit of youth and innovation that would explode in the sixties. In that summer and fall of 1957, Ike was in his second term at 1600 Pennsylvania Avenue. Senator Joseph McCarthy, who'd been called a true patriot, pugnacious, controversial, and a madman, and who had terrorized much of the political world for the past four years, dropped dead at the age of forty-eight, probably as a result of all his boozing. In Soviet Russia, premier Nikita Khrushchev foiled a plot to replace him. The youthful senator John F. Kennedy made a speech on the Senate floor urging the administration to cease its support of France's colonial repression in Algeria. And in show business, MGM, now in the fading twilight of its glory years as the glamour studio of Hollywood, had one more musical hit in the old tradition with *Silk Stockings,* starring Fred Astaire and Cyd Charisse.

And I was working like crazy, trying to revive the budding career I'd left behind when Uncle Sam had beckoned. In the last seven months of 1957, among many other TV shows, I did *Dragnet,* produced by and starring Jack Webb. It was a TV gig like any other, interesting mainly because of the encounter it led to a few years later.

At that time, Webb was at Warner Bros. with a television production deal. He contacted me personally and rattled off practically all my post-Army television appearances. (Flattering, of course, to see that Webb had tracked my career so closely.) He said he had an idea for a one-hour drama starring a young conservative lawyer and his mother who was a kind of contemporary liberal and famous Clarence Darrow type. He had signed Bette Davis for the role, and she had the final say on who would play her son. She had seen my work and wanted to meet me at her Bel Air home at one P.M. the following day. (Arbitrary and short notice — that's how movie stars operate.)

I arrived promptly, assuming (based on the hour of the day) that we would be lunching at her house or perhaps at the nearby Bel Air Hotel, which had a reputation for a splendid kitchen. This was not to be.

Miss Davis did not rise when I entered the room, but merely extended her hand, which I assumed I should kiss or shake. I opted for the latter, and before I could sit down, she pointed at the bottle of Cutty Sark scotch on the table between us and said, in that famous raspy voice of hers, "Help yourself, Bob." Curiously enough, at that time, I *was* drinking Cutty Sark, but never at one P.M., so I politely declined. We chatted about show business and politics, and, increasingly famished, I gradually ate what must have amounted to a pound of peanuts in a large bowl that sat next to the scotch.

Closing in on two P.M., I was looking about rather desperately for some sign of a house person who would conduct us to a room where we would eat something other than nuts. No such luck. So, with no other options, I decided to join Bette in the Cutty Sark. The glasses were filled once, twice. I had a ways to go to catch up with Bette, but I gave it my best shot.

Around three P.M., after another round of Cutty on the rocks, Bette decided to tell me about her life and times. She still had said nothing about our prospective Warner Bros. project. Thanks to the scotch, however, I no longer gave much of a damn.

Around four P.M., her life story winding down, Bette announced that she had to change to get ready for some sort of formal do for her daughter at the Ambassador Hotel, many miles from Bel Air. As I rose, she remarked, "When I've changed, will you be so kind as to drive me to the hotel?"

I said, "Miss Davis, not only can't I drive you to the hotel, I can barely see you."

For some reason, she thought my remark was the epitome of Noel Coward wit. She laughed heartily and raised her hand graciously as I'd seen her do before in her many film portrayals of royalty. "Not to worry, darling. I'll drive, and you'll come in with me for drinks and canapés. Then we'll go on to Chasen's for dinner and discuss Jack's little project."

This was too little, too late. "I'm terribly sorry, Miss Davis, but I'm not feeling well. We'll have to have our project talk at another time and place." I excused myself and walked, nay staggered, to the Bel Air Hotel, leaving my car behind and calling for a taxi to return me to the serenity of my Hollywood digs. I found out later my car was towed away the moment darkness fell.

The Webb project was never made. Bette Davis and I never saw each other again, but I did meet one of her husbands, Gary Merrill, in the sixties. And Gary was no slacker either when it came to the bottle. More about that later.

During this post-Army period, I did two *Gunsmokes* with Dennis Weaver, a friend from the Stage Society. Before I'd been drafted, Dennis had seen me in *Desire Under the Elms* and had joined me for drinks afterward, praising me, in the Method jargon of the fifties, for having been "in the zone" throughout the play. In the early fifties, rumor had it that Dennis had been living in his car. When he died in 2006, years after stardom in *Gunsmoke* and *McCloud,* he was a millionaire many times over.

Other Westerns followed: *Dick Powell's Zane Grey Theater*'s *A Gun Is for Killing* and *Courage Is a Gun; Frontier*'s *The Return of Jubal Dolan; Frontier Doctor*'s *A Twisted Road; Riverboat,* costarring Darren Mc-Gavin and a very young Burt Reynolds; and *Zorro* for Disney, where I played a Mexican rainmaker with a bad mustache and a worse accent. (This role kept me out of a dismal picture with Natalie and RJ called *All the Fine Young Cannibals.* George Hamilton got my part — the real George Hamilton, not the guy in charge of guest relations at KHJ-TV. It was a Southern gothic potboiler in pseudo–Tennessee Williams style. Natalie later recalled, "We all dripped Southern accents, paraded around in wigs, and tried to look terribly, terribly decadent." Today the movie would probably be utterly forgotten if not for the fact that an eighties British pop group took its name from the title.)

Other Westerns I did in 1959 were *Law of the Plainsmen,* where I played a very young Teddy Roosevelt out West, and *Wagon Train,* starring Robert Horton and Ward Bond. Ward was part of the John Wayne "tough guy" group who worked with the famous hard-drinking director John Ford. And I can assure you that Bond took no backseat to any of the tough guys when it came to holding his liquor.

I did *Wagon Train* twice, and I got to know Ward and his drinking habits fairly well. His days usually started in the makeup room at dawn when he had a little eye-opener called coffee royale, made of coffee and whiskey. Following that, on the set he usually had either a bloody Mary or a screwdriver. He referred to these drinks as his "daily vitamins." At lunch, which I shared with him several times, he was a terrific raconteur, and he usually had both red and white wine. For the post-midday meal, he always had a six-pack of iced beer at the ready.

Then five P.M. would roll around, and Bond would declare, "Goddammit, the sun's going down, it's time to have a *real* drink" — which meant, to Bond, some of the hard stuff. I seem to remember it as rye whiskey or some cheap bourbon, or both.

This is what he had during the day. I can't imagine what went on at night.

To give Ward credit, he was always letter-perfect with his lines and knew exactly what was going on at all times. But most important, he was wonderfully warm and believable as the sagacious wagon master of the

Wagon Train. I really enjoyed working with him and was sorry when he passed away in 1960 (age fifty-seven), dropping dead of a heart attack in his bathroom. That ticker had done yeoman service for the old roustabout. I have worked with no TV actor since then that quite matched his powerful persona.

I did one feature Western during this time with Fred MacMurray called *Good Day for a Hanging,* where I played, as usual, the young varmint who was almost hanged for his misdeeds. Fred was the frugal type. For lunch, he always brought a sandwich from home in a brown paper bag. It certainly wasn't out of need, since it was rumored that he owned much of Wilshire Boulevard.

One day, he asked me where I had gotten my gators (low-top boots) and what they soaked me for them. I told him I didn't know what they cost, but I bought them at the Mayfair Riding Shop on Hollywood Boulevard.

The following day, Fred arrived carrying a pair of battered, ancient gators. He said, "I found them in my basement. Saved myself a nifty little sum, I bet." He was a great villain, a very gifted comedic actor, and also a very savvy businessman.

All of these TV and movie roles were fun,

reasonably lucrative, and helped spread awareness of me and my talents (such as they were) among the Hollywood community. But at the time I could never have guessed that my most notable job from this phase of my life would turn out to be the schlockiest picture I've ever been associated with.

Virtually every time I'm interviewed about my fifty years in motion pictures and television, after being asked about *The Magnificent Seven, Bullitt, The Towering Inferno,* and especially *The Man from U.N.C.L.E.,* the questioner invariably, with some reluctance and with downcast eyes, asks, "How did you happen to get involved with *Teenage Cave Man?*" And this is how it happened.

In the summer of 1958, I had helped my *inamorata* Joyce Jameson move out of her tiny apartment on Keith Avenue, just off Doheny Drive, to a new two-bedroom place on Clark Street in West Hollywood. At Keith Avenue, Joyce had more or less consigned the raising of her and Billy Barnes's son, Tyler, to an older couple who lived to the rear of Joyce's space but on the same property. This enabled her to work evenings and weekends in *The Billy Barnes Revue,* her chief source of income at the time.

One afternoon, I dropped by Clark Street to do a little painting in Joyce's new home. On the way, I picked up a script from my agent. He said it was fascinating and thought it would appeal to me politically. The title on the cover was *Prehistoric World.* It was written in a kind of weird blank verse and it was not entirely clear to me what it was about — until the final scene. There it was revealed that I, the "Symbol Maker's Son" (as the nameless character was known) was part of a tiny remnant of mankind that had survived a nuclear holocaust. In other words, the people in the script represented the beginning of a new world after Armageddon. (I know, this sounds like a hokey and predictable idea, and it was, even then — though not quite as hokey and predictable as it would be today.)

The director was Roger Corman. We had a couple of faint personal connections. Corman had seen me in *End as a Man,* and he would later marry Julie Halloran, my second cousin on my mother's Irish side of the family. Later still, he would become an internationally famous maker of future stars and directors (Jack Nicholson, Martin Scorsese, Francis Coppola). Most important, he had made a fortune as a producer of small-budget pictures that cleaned up financially throughout the world. After *Prehistoric World* was released under its final title, *Teenage Cave Man,* Roger rarely directed again, and his wife, Julie, became a very successful producer in her own right.

The author of the movie's weird script actually had an interesting track record. He had been nominated the year before for an Oscar for best screenplay for his work on *Man of a Thousand Faces,* starring James Cagney as Lon Chaney. His name was R. Wright Campbell, brother of Bill Campbell, who at that time was married to the soon-to-be-famous Judy Campbell, one of JFK's ladies. And finally, just to square the circle, Bob Campbell (as he was called) had gone out with Joyce Jameson for several years prior to the time I met her in the summer of 1957. Small world, Hollywood.

I mentioned the script for what was then called *Prehistoric World* to Joyce, and she told me that, in addition to his screen work, Bob was also a gifted novelist and sometime poet. Having not read *Prehistoric World,* she thought I should do it because Bobby Campbell, as she called him, was hot (as a screenwriter, that is). There was also some rumor that Jack Nicholson, whom I knew from 1956 when he had been my student in an acting class at the Players' Ring Gallery

Theater, was also going to be in the picture. However, that meant nothing to me at the time because Jack was a decade away from becoming *Jack*.

Anyway, looking back a half century, I guess I convinced myself at twenty-five years of age that I could use the picture to make some sort of protest about the abolition of nuclear weapons. At least, that's my story and I'm sticking to it.

The upshot was that I joined the cast of *Prehistoric World*.

It was to be a ten-day shoot, a ninety-minute picture, shot in Los Angeles's Griffith Park, standing in for what was left of planet Earth. Wardrobe for the film's entire cast must have come in at around a C note. We all wore Dorothy Lamour sarongs covering whatever was necessary to cover in 1958.

My friend, Beach Dickerson, who when he wasn't moving furniture for a living was buying up property in Laurel Canyon, was also working for Roger as an actor. In this film, he played a bear and a boy in the sinking earth, and helped out running sound for the flick. In the ten-day shoot, I managed to be hospitalized twice and knocked out once by a tree that was supposed to be moved as I fell against it.

I also (I mention this for the benefit of

film historians) invented the bow and arrow after stalking a deer and finding myself in Griffith Park trees with no means of subduing the antlered animal. In the film, you will see me walking alone through a modestly forested part of the park when I bump against a tree branch. I break it off and think for a moment. I then miraculously find a string somewhere in my sarong and tie it to each end of the broken tree limb. Then I have another thought, and I fit a sharp-edged stick to my stringed branch. Bingo, I've invented the bow and arrow.

You've got to see it to not believe it.

The next shot is of me carrying a very stiff, obviously badly stuffed small deer over both of my shoulders. Apparently rigor mortis had already set in. And that's how the Symbol Maker's Son rediscovered the first blood sport after the big boom.

Santa Anita racetrack is near Griffith Park, and there was a stream there with a large log projecting into the water. My job in one scene was to walk out onto the log and then jump into the creek. I asked Roger if anyone had tested the water to see if there was anything that might be harmful to my feet. He said Beach Dickerson had done that job and nothing was found under the water that could be deemed dangerous. Beach, you'll remember, was the boy/bear/part-time soundman — but not an underwater plumber.

Well, I jumped off the log, and the water was icy cold, but other than that I didn't notice anything untoward. Roger decided he wanted another take, which in itself was unusual. I climbed back onto the log, "Action" was called, and I began to walk out to the end of the log a second time when suddenly, I started slipping and sliding and losing my balance. I looked down. The log was covered with blood, and I fell into the stream again. Exactly where I had dropped to before was a mass of broken glass and jagged metal pipes.

I was taken immediately to the nearest emergency room where many stitches were made post haste. Needless to say, I didn't work for the rest of the day. The following day, I was back at work with flesh-colored bandages covering my heavily taped and sutured feet.

Friday was the last day of the first week's shooting. My scene was to fend off a ferocious dog that attacked me near my campfire. (As it happens, I did not invent fire.) I asked Roger if this dog was a movie-trained dog, and he introduced me to the dog trainer, who looked to me like he was half in the bag. Nevertheless, he vouched for the giant dog's docility, saying he had worked with him for years and never had a problem.

So once again, "Action" was called and as I turned around, supposedly because I heard the animal barking as he approached me, the dog took a mighty leap, his head aiming for my face. At the last moment, I raised my left arm and the monster dog bit right into my forearm and held on like a hungry tiger. The trainer rushed over and disengaged the beast from my person. I was covered with blood, and the nurse who was required to be on the set at all times by the Screen Actors Guild ran to me with a tourniquet that she had improvised. Once again, I was sent to the nearest surgery.

That was week one.

Week two found me unbandaged and sans the gauze wrapped around my forearm. My feet remained covered with flesh-colored bandages, and I completed the final five days without injury, mainly because I refused to do anything that smacked of possible danger or violence. A stunt double was brought in for me, and I didn't watch any of his work. I felt by that time I had done the best I could on behalf of world peace.

With my smallish salary for my lead role, I bought a 1955 black Cadillac convertible, my first almost-new car. (I didn't get my first *real* new car until November 22, 1961, when I bought myself a 1962 black-cherry Lincoln Continental convertible as a birthday present. At the time, it was the most expensive American car at seven thousand dollars. I still own and drive it today.)

Teenage Cave Man was also the last time I wore a sarong. When the picture finally opened at the Hawaii Theater on Hollywood Boulevard, it was on a double bill with *Teenage Werewolf* starring Michael Landon. Yes, *that* Michael Landon, the actor who went on to great success in *Bonanza* and *Little House on the Prairie.*

Don't tell me we actors don't sweat blood for our art — and our cars.

But I can't really complain. In 2008 dollars, I managed to accrue a quarter of a million bucks in 1958, my first completely uninterrupted year in the biz. And little by little, I was building up a résumé, a track record, and a reputation — *Teenage Cave Man* and all.

My first motion picture filmed in a foreign location was *The Big Show.* It was the second remake of a 20th Century-Fox story of a domineering father and his rebellious sons. In its first incarnation, it had been an early gangster film starring Edward G.

Robinson; the second version was a Western starring Spencer Tracy. The third time around, it had a character actor and friend of mine named Nicky Persoff in the role of the father. Cliff Robertson, David Nelson (Ricky's brother and the son of Harriet and Ozzie Nelson), and I were cast as the difficult sons. Filming would take place in Germany.

In the strange ways of Hollywood thinking, the picture still had no "star," although there was $70,000 in the budget to pay for one. Fox, spinning through its corporate Rolodex, was looking for a star that qualified at a ten-grand-a-week salary.

The lucky star who met those requirements was everyone's all-time swimming beauty/star favorite, Esther Williams. But since there was no role in the script for her, she was simply written in as Cliff's girlfriend. This decision allowed Cliff, Esther, and me to get to know each other very well over many jars and meals at Munich *brauhäuser*.

I took a Lufthansa flight to Munich. On the way, I was reading the then brand-new book by William L. Shirer, *The Rise and Fall of the Third Reich.* Wearing for the first time my snappy velvet-collared Brooks Brothers black overcoat and a black Homburg hat, I came down the stairs from my flight (no interior tunnels in those days), and was greeted by the Fox production team. As soon as we got inside the terminal, they mentioned that perhaps it would be best that I put my book someplace other than in my hand. The reason was that there was a swastika on the dust cover. I quickly complied.

I was then chauffeured to the new Park Hotel where my acting colleagues were already booked. When I got to my suite, I was delighted to find a small fridge stuffed with booze, snacks, candy, and other goodies. I naturally assumed the studio had furnished this thoughtful amenity and proceeded, after unpacking, to sample the fully stocked bar — believing, of course, that the contents were a gift from Fox. I was young (twenty-six), dumb, and wrong, and eventually I had to pay for everything. It was my first encounter with what we now call a minibar.

Less than a decade and a half had passed since the German defeat in World War II, and Dachau, the first German concentration camp, was just outside Munich. Cliff, Esther, and I visited there before we started filming. It was then very much as it had been when the Allied troops had entered the camp for the first time: crematoria, shower rooms plumbed to release killing gas, ditches for blood that spilled after firing squads had murdered inmates. It had not yet become the shrine it was later to be — a reminder of what happened there and in so many other camps throughout Europe and a horrific lesson in man's capacity for brutality toward his fellow man. The images remained with me for many years after my visit.

On many film locations, strong friendships are created while working all day and eating together after the day's filming. Our star, the very witty, vivacious Esther, was in top physical condition and could drink a Volga boatman under the table, and she proceeded to do just that with her costars, Cliff and me. Cliff usually retired first; I hung in there, but just barely.

One evening, when it was snowing heavily and Cliff had departed, claiming exhaustion, I mentioned to Esther that I had heard there was a stadium very near our hotel where Hitler had made many speeches during the Nazi reign. Esther said, "Let's check that out." We hailed a taxi and explained to the driver where we wanted to go. He said he knew exactly what we meant and said it was still in use for sporting events. We had no trouble gaining access to the great outdoor arena which was lighted by a very full, bright moon. It was now snowing even more heavily.

After the initial moments when we both tried to imagine what it was like to see this gigantic stadium filled with thousands of cheering Germans paying homage to their Führer, we started, for no particular reason, to run up and down the slippery cement seats, laughing and having a fun, liquid-inspired outing. I was holding Esther's hand for safety purposes (I'm sure Esther would have been more help to me than I to her).

She was at that time seeing Fernando Lamas, whom she later married, so there was no room for hanky-panky between the kid from Minneapolis and the world's aquatic love goddess. However, the thought did cross my drink-sodden libido more than once. Boy, would the guys back at North High School wish they had taken up movie acting for a living.

Finally, our multilingual script girl, Ingrid, a German beauty in the Elke Sommer mold, joined me after the shoot in a terrific tour of Rome, Naples, Capri, Paris, and London. It was a wonderful introduction to location filming. I loved it then and love it just as much now — with a few exceptions that I'll get to later.

After the holidays spent in Europe, I returned weighing about ten pounds more than my normal weight of 165. The principal cause was my time spent in Italy, France, and Germany, where I ate two or three large meals a day as opposed to my normal diet: no breakfast, a grilled cheese sandwich in the middle of the afternoon, and then a no-holds-barred dinner around eight P.M.

The problem was easily solved by going back to my old routine, plus spending about twice as much time in the gym at the Beverly Hills Health Club. By early spring, I was back in better shape than I had been since my departure from Fort Ord in 1957.

By now, I was focused on how to get my career out of guest-starring roles on all the major TV shows and costarring in not-quite-A movies. The image of what I was aiming for was very clear in my mind. Here is a story that encapsulates it. Manny Dwork, the tailor my agent had sent me to, had his shop almost directly across the street from the gym. Leaving Manny's place one day, I passed the parking lot of the very respected photographer John Engstead, where, in the fall of '56 before I went into the Army, I had seen Tony Curtis parking his new gray Silver Cloud Rolls Royce

convertible with smashing red leather uphol-
stery. That day I said to myself, "Someday,
someday."

I didn't buy my first magnolia-colored
1974 Silver Shadow until almost a generation later — but it did happen, someday.

Another big step toward that consumma-
tion took place one spring day in 1959.

My agent Sid Gold (Jack Fields's boss)
called me at the gym. "Get out to Warner
Bros.," he said. "Hoyt Bowers will be waiting. He's got a script and a role he thinks
you'll be perfect for."

The picture would be called *The Young
Philadelphians.* And it would be an A picture, exactly what I had been looking for.
Two facts clinched it. First, my friend from
the health club, the thirty-three-year-old rising star Paul Newman, would be playing
the lead role. Second, the movie was to be
directed by Vincent Sherman, one of Warner
Bros.'s famous directors of stars, who had
made pictures with stars like Bette Davis
and then was partially blacklisted in the
early fifties.

However, there was one fly in the oint-
ment. For the first time in my two-year film
and TV career, I was being asked to do a
screen test. I'd have to do a scene selected
by the studio with the lines of the other

actor's character read by a script girl somewhere in the darkness at the side of, or in back of, the camera. The test was scheduled for the following week.

I hit the gym the next morning. Paul was there practicing his fast draw left-handed (quite a challenge for Paul, who was right-handed).

Paul said, "Hey, man, that Warner's picture, *The Young Philadelphians* — I have to do it because that was the deal my agent MCA made to get me out of my studio contract."

Paul had never forgiven Jack Warner for putting him in a costume turkey called *The Silver Chalice,* and the studio further infuriated him by making him up to look like Brando, even darkening his hair. He'd been so furious that he'd taken out an ad in the *Daily Variety,* the number one Hollywood trade paper, disassociating himself from the movie.

Anyway, Paul said *The Young Philadelphians* was kind of a potboiler, a soap opera. But my role of Chet Gwynn, a Main Line alcoholic who loses his arm in Korea and winds up wrongly accused of murder, was by far the best role in the picture. This was news to me, because I had not yet read the entire script.

Paul's description excited me, but I was still concerned about the screen test hurdle. I explained my dilemma, and Paul said, "Don't worry, man. I'll test with you, but I'll be off-camera."

We discussed the story and the key test scene, in which Paul's character comes to see me in jail after I've been charged with murder. Paul's character was that of a corporate Philadelphia lawyer who has never tried a criminal case before. Of course, he takes Chet as his client and gets him off by proving another person guilty.

I went in for the day's shoot early. Paul was already there, and we had a chance to talk further about the critical test.

As good as his word, Paul worked with me off-camera, acting up a storm, applying as much gusto and passion as if it were *his* test. I was told the following day that I'd gotten the role.

It was very clear to me that this was a huge opportunity — one I couldn't afford to blow. I tackled the job in that spirit. I spent a day on skid row researching the part (trailed by a photographer who captured it all for the fanzines, as suggested by my press agent, Jerry Pam). I talked with down-and-out winos, studied their gestures and behavior, and worked on getting inside their

185

personalities. I also rehearsed with Paul the night before my big jail scene was filmed, creating a real opportunity for me to do my best work.

It all came together for me. The picture was released in 1959, and I was nominated for an Oscar for best supporting actor.

Good acting was only part of this success story. My nomination came about in part because of an advertising campaign that I paid for at the suggestion of Jerry Pam. It was one of the first such campaigns, which today are commonplace. I remember that a full page in *The Hollywood Reporter* cost only about $750 back then.

In the late fifties, traditional Hollywood public relations was still the norm. Young actors were expected to be seen in public at Hollywood happenings, generally arranged by press agents. I played along as expected. Jerry introduced me to my "dates" during this period — photogenic starlets like the former Miss America Mary Ann Mobley, Connie Stevens, and Fay Spain, all of whom were just as eager to keep their names and faces in the limelight as I was.

Another of these arranged dates was Stella Stevens, whom I took to the Academy Awards in 1960, the year I was nominated. I also took my mother, who, though I did not know it at the time, had just over a year to live.

Somehow I had been given misinformation about what to wear to the Oscar ceremony, and I arrived at the Pantages Theater on Hollywood Boulevard in white tie and tails. The only other member of the industry wearing tails was the evening's host, Bob Hope.

Mixed in with all my strictly-for-publicity fictitious dates were quite a few real ones. It was during this time that I began to be aware of the early benefits of my growing popularity on TV and in motion pictures. In that era, virtually every curvaceous young eighteen- to twenty-year-old girl in America came to Hollywood to be a star. Ninety-nine percent failed and returned home to become moms and homemakers and office workers. But every year brought a fresh crop to the streets of Los Angeles, and young men with a modicum of success, like me, took full advantage of the lush pickings.

Maybe you remember the old play and movie *The Tender Trap.* (It's one that will always occupy a special place in my heart. In 1970, I met my future wife, Linda, during a production of *The Tender Trap* in Chicago.) In the movie, there's a scene where a character named Charlie Reader, a bachelor played on-screen by Frank Sinatra, is asked by his old married friend, played by David Wayne, "What's it like to be single in this town [New York], with no responsibilities and plenty of money?"

Charlie answers, "It's having died and gone to heaven."

Well, Hollywood in the late fifties and early sixties was indeed heaven. As a matter of fact, someone once said (it may have been George Burns, a considerable roamer in his day), "Hollywood is high school with money." I agree. And as my roles got bigger and bigger, and my paychecks followed suit, I found myself becoming one of the Big Men on Campus, with my choice of the prettiest cheerleaders.

Yet while I was enjoying the fruits of my swelling stardom, my mother was beginning her terrible decline toward death. And even as she became more and more ill, she was doing her best to follow my career and participate in it as best she could.

Here's a story that captures a bit of that bittersweet time. In the late spring of 1961, I did a TV show called *The Asphalt Jungle* starring Emmy Award–winning actor Jack Warden. I played a character named Warren W. Scott, who was head of a Nazi-type political party in the United States. The character very closely resembled George Lincoln Rockwell, the real leader of the American Nazi party.

My mother visited the set the day we were filming a scene in which my character gives a Hitler-style speech to an auditorium filled with cheering admirers. My mother rarely visited any show I was working on, but I thought she'd enjoy this bit of high-level melodramatic acting.

Her reaction stunned me. "You scared me, Robert. You really scared me."

Her words reminded me of an early experience when she and I had acted together. In 1954, we had done *I Am a Camera* by Christopher Isherwood onstage. (It's the same story that later became the musical *Cabaret.*) Mother played the German housekeeper, and I played the character based on Isherwood, the young, gay English writer in decadent 1930s Berlin.

In the final dress rehearsal, when I did my full-out anger rant, Mother simply stopped. The scene came to a complete halt. I said, "What's the problem?"

"I can't remember my lines," Mother told me. Her lower lip was trembling a little.

"What?!" the director interjected. "You never forget a line. What's going on?"

189

Mother pointed to me and said, "That's exactly how your father acted when he got angry at me."

Now, seven years later, my acting apparently still scared my mother.

Jack Warden came over after my harangue and said, "You scared the shit out of me, man." Then, knowing nothing about my mother's health and finding her attractive, Jack said, "When we wrap, Warren" (calling me by my character's name), I want to take you and your mother to the Swiss Café in Beverly Hills for dinner."

I said, "Fine with us," knowing my mother would love it. And we had a hell of a good, long Swiss-wined evening with much laughter from Jack's wonderful off-color stories. Many years later, I ran into Jack and he asked after my mother. When I told him she had died later that same year, he was very warm and sympathetic.

However, there is one more leg to my remembrance of Jack Warden — one that ends the story on a little more comical note.

During the mid-sixties, when my friend Ben Gazzara was doing a TV series at Universal called *Run for Your Life,* Benny had a kind of open house most Sunday afternoons, serving drinks and Italian food in his Cheviot Hills home quite near the

20th Century-Fox studios. The party usually extended well into the late evening, and even into the following morning.

The story I was told was as follows. Jack Warden, having been drinking at Ben's place for about twelve hours, left shortly after midnight, and after getting into his car, fell fast asleep. He was awakened by a cop shaking him as his flashlight startled him into consciousness. He was taken to the nearest pokey and left there to sober up.

At dawn, Jack woke up and found himself behind bars along with some other reprobates who had been tossed into the clink to sleep off their boozed brains. One guy near Jack dimly recognized him and asked, "Are you that guy in the movies and on TV?"

Jack nodded hazily and then his questioner asked, "Do you know Peggy Ann Garner?" (Garner was a charming child actress of the forties whose career petered out when she reached adulthood.) And Jack, not quite knowing where this was going said, yes, he knew her.

The guy then announced, with more than a touch of pride, *"I fucked her maid!"*

It just goes to demonstrate the truth of the old adage, "Everybody wants to be in showbiz" — no matter how tenuous the connection.

SIX:
NOT SO
MAGNIFICENT

There are more things in heaven and
    earth, Horatio,
Than are dreamt of in your philosophy.

Every motion picture, even the biggest flop,
is launched in an atmosphere of hopeful
expectation. From the executive producer
and the above-the-title star down to the
lowliest gaffer, on the first day of shooting
everyone dreams that *this* will be the picture
of pictures, the one that will sweep the
Oscars, generate quarter-mile lines at the
box office, and elevate cast and crew to a
new level of professional grandeur. Which
suggests the question: Why can't experienced Hollywood folk tell in advance which
movies are going to work and which ones
aren't? The difference is certainly obvious
in retrospect.

The only honest answer is, I have no idea.
All I know is that it's apparently impossible

for anyone associated with the movies to pick winners and losers with any consistency. When I played Casca in "Chuckles" Heston's ill-fated production of *Julius Caesar,* I had no idea it would be a fiasco. You couldn't tell by the cast. Heston played Marc Antony, Jason Robards played Brutus, Sir John Gielgud played Caesar, Richard Chamberlain played Octavius, and Diana Rigg played Portia, all backed up by a fine collection of British theater actors in lesser roles. Only Robards sensed disaster. Just as he feared, *Julius Caesar* proved to be an ignominious footnote to motion picture history. (More on this later.)

On the other hand, I was convinced that *The Magnificent Seven* would be a failure. Instead, of course, it became a box-office hit, a star-making vehicle for several in the cast, including Steve McQueen, James Coburn, and Charles Bronson, and a classic Western drama still enjoyed today almost half a century after it was made. It's the second-most frequently played movie on American TV (trailing only *Casablanca*).

So what the hell do I know?

The way the picture was cast certainly didn't portend success. The Screen Actors Guild had called a strike for spring 1960, which meant an ax was hanging over every movie project in Hollywood. Unless the casting for a picture was completed by noon on a particular Friday, production couldn't begin. This put United Artists and director John Sturges in quite a bind. They'd been working for a while on the idea of a Western based on Akira Kurosawa's famous movie *The Seven Samurai,* and they'd already had sets constructed in Cuernavaca, Mexico. But only two actors had been cast — Yul Brynner, who'd won an Oscar for *The King and I,* and Steve McQueen, a young actor widely perceived as being on the verge of stardom. Either the rest of the cast had to be signed up fast, or the picture would be dead.

Sturges started scrambling. He'd seen me playing a drunken socialite in *The Young Philadelphians,* my first A picture, a role for which I'd soon receive an Oscar nomination. He decided I'd be perfect for the part of Lee, a professional gunfighter spooked by the thought that his reflexes and skill might be eroding. Through my agent he called me. "We don't have a script," he warned me, "just Kurosawa's picture to work from. You'll have to go on faith. But we'll be filming in Cuernavaca. Never been there? You'll love it — it's the Palm Springs of Mexico."

If I'd known that I would spend my three months in Cuernavaca with a stomach-churning case of the Aztec two-step, I might have demurred. But I was willing to take Sturges at his word. He'd directed two great pictures, *Bad Day at Black Rock* and *Somebody Up There Likes Me,* which was good enough for me. "I'm in," I told him.

"Good decision, young man," Sturges said. "And do you know any other good young actors? I've got four other slots to fill."

"What sort of fellows do you have in mind?"

"I need a Gary Cooper type — tall, tough, quiet."

"I went to college with a guy named Jimmy Coburn. Big lanky fellow with a great voice."

"Sounds like he might do. Where is he?"

"I haven't spoken with him in five years. Last I heard he was shacked up with a colored chick in Greenwich Village, smoking dope." (In the interests of historical accuracy, I am re-creating the jargon I would have used at the time.)

Sturges was pretty desperate. "Do you think you can find him?"

"I'll try."

After half a dozen phone calls, I tracked

Jimmy down. "You gotta get out here — fast," I told him. He managed to borrow some money, flew out to L.A., and met Sturges. He got a career out of it. Britt in *The Magnificent Seven* was Coburn's breakthrough role. (Actually, I'd forgotten about how Coburn's involvement had come about. Not too long before his untimely death in 2002, Jimmy reminded me about it at dinner one night at the Dome on Sunset Boulevard. Jim picked up that dinner tab, saying he would be on the lookout for a good role for me in one of his upcoming flicks. But the grim reaper interceded, and I said good-bye to him at his memorial service at Paramount Studios arranged beautifully by his lovely young wife, Paula, who herself died shortly thereafter.)

The rest of our hastily assembled cast included Charles Bronson, German star Horst Buchholz, and an actor named Brad Dexter who is the "Bashful" of *The Magnificent Seven* — the actor in the group who most people fail to name, just as most people forget Bashful when naming the Seven Dwarfs. Many movie buffs will mention Eli Wallach as one of the Seven, which is wrong: He was great in the picture as Calvera, the leader of the bandit gang that is terrorizing the Mexican villagers we come to rescue.

It's a sobering thought to realize that I'm the last of the Seven still alive. (Eli is still going strong.)

Coburn used his first big paycheck from the picture to buy a brand-new sports car, and in the middle of filming, his then-wife Beverly and a girlfriend of hers drove the car down from L.A. to Cuernavaca, a pretty dangerous stunt considering that there were *banditos* on the roads back then who wouldn't hesitate to rob you (and slit your throat if need be). To celebrate Bev's safe arrival, the four of us went to a local dive called *Las Mañanitas* — the only place in town where you wouldn't get the runs. (They served *unopened* bottled water, unlike the other dives, which filled the bottles with stuff from local wells, then recapped them so they could charge full price.)

At the door of the restaurant, a red-vested valet, all bows and smiles, took Jimmy's car away. I was nervous about this — we weren't in L.A., after all, but in semi-lawless Cuernavaca. Jimmy laughed at me, and all seemed well when we came back out after an evening of merrymaking. Jimmy handed over five hundred pesos, and the valet scurried off into the midnight darkness to fetch the car. In a few moments, we saw headlights rushing toward us. "Isn't he going awfully fast?" I exclaimed. As we scrambled for safety, the car roared past us and smashed into the wall of the restaurant, not twenty feet away. The women screamed, the car's front end imploded in a tangle of crushed and broken metal and glass, and the valet fell headfirst out of the driver's-side door. Apparently he'd been doing some merrymaking of his own.

Jimmy just looked at his watch, clapped me on the shoulder, and said, "I tell you what, Roberto — we're *never* gonna get a taxi at this time of night."

Jimmy always was the quintessence of cool.

Our three months in Cuernavaca were filled with such antics. There were long periods when we didn't work because the script was still being written. We'd be told one evening, "Tomorrow we'll be doing scene so-and-so," and that night carbon copies of the script on onion-skin paper would be slid under our doors to learn for the next day. During our idle hours, we drank, played poker, commiserated with one another over our stomach ailments, and complained about working on this rotten picture.

Yul Brynner was by far the biggest star in

the cast, and he comported himself accordingly. He was aloof and distant. However, he did take part in our regular games of five-card draw, along with Steve McQueen, Brad Dexter, and me. I didn't fare well financially, but I hung in there because I wanted to study the implacable Mr. Brynner.

After several weeks, one late afternoon when the others had left and before predinner margaritas were served, Yul and I got to talking about the Russian theater, particularly Stanislavski's Moscow Art Theater, and its American offshoots. It was an interest the two of us shared. Names like Meyerhold, Boleslavski, Rapoport, Danchenko, Vaktangov, Pudovkin, and particularly Michael Chekhov rolled easily off my lips, much to Yul's delight and amazement. There had been no plan of mine to chat about the Method. It just happened, and it created a bond between Yul and me.

I recently reread Yul Brynner's preface to Michael Chekhov's 1955 book, *To The Actor.* It was written in New York at the St. James Theatre on July 23, 1952, as Yul's hit play *The King and I* was beginning its second year. The preface took the form of a letter to Chekhov, and among other things, Yul wrote: "To my mind your book, *To the Actor,* is so far the best book of its kind that it can't even begin to be compared to anything that has ever appeared in the field. And, in my opinion, it reads as well as any good fiction I've ever come across."

It's quite a tribute to the magnetic power that Chekhov had over a whole generation of American actors — including me.

The artistic bond between me and Yul did not prevent me from joining with the other actors in *The Magnificent Seven* in mocking him — which we enjoyed doing mainly because of the lofty professional position he occupied in relation to us. Yes, ego has been known to rear its head in show business on occasion.

At some point, the rest of us in the cast — arrogant young bastards that we were — decided that Yul looked liked a pig. (Actually, I confess that I was the first one to point out the resemblance.) A very attractive pig, mind you, but a pig nonetheless. So this became Yul's code name, used only behind his back: "Is the pig working today? Anyone seen the pig?" and so on.

Yul seemed oblivious to our sniping, although it was hard to tell what he was and wasn't aware of. He had a favorite story — he told it over and over again, actually — about working in a musical called *Lute Song* back in 1946. (Making her Broadway debut in that show was Nancy Davis, who later married Ronald Reagan and ultimately became the First Lady of the land.) In Yul's account, one of the character actors in *Lute Song* used to warm up his voice every night by declaiming the words *waffle* and *baseball* — VERY LOUD. And, of course, Yul demonstrated, booming out *"Waffle! Baseball!"* in that famous, stentorian voice of his — VERY LOUD.

The story was reasonably amusing the first time we heard it. By the fourth time, however, it was getting on our nerves. The next time he told it, the group of us were sitting on our horses, waiting to shoot a scene (we spent a lot of time sitting on our horses). When Yul roared out, *"Waffle! Baseball!"* I couldn't resist. Under my breath, just barely audible, I added a third word: *"Oink!"*

The others almost fell off their horses laughing.

Maybe Yul had a better sense of humor than I gave him credit for. A few days later, he told the same story yet again. This time, he roared, *"Waffle! Baseball! Oink!"*

If Yul Brynner was the number one star on *The Magnificent Seven,* number two was the young Steve McQueen. And Steve was determined that he would steal the picture

201

out from under Yul. Damned if he didn't do it.

I first saw Steve at Columbia Studios sometime shortly after James Dean's death on September 30, 1955. Natalie Wood and I were at Columbia for a wardrobe test for a film introducing me titled *No Time to Be Young.*

Like all of the other young actors in their mid-twenties in Hollywood in the mid-fifties, we were both trying to be recognized as Jimmy's logical successor. (I still have a picture of me taken by my good friend Will Sage in downtown Los Angeles in the first week of October 1955. It's a fine example of how I looked in my own James Dean period — brooding expression, lock of hair carelessly drooping, the epitome of soulful youth.)

Steve was sitting in the corner of an office staring fixedly at nothing with his Deanish-colored hair, loosely coiffed about his sullen face. I remarked to Natalie when we left the office, "There's another Jimmy Dean waiting in the bullpen to be called to the mound." In the following decade, Natalie and Steve would, of course, star together in *Love with a Proper Stranger.*

Steve was always intensely competitive, even to the point of being paranoid. It wasn't enough for him to be successful — true satisfaction required that he be *more* successful than anyone he perceived as a rival. I remember Steve from these early years vowing that someday he would be billed *above* Paul Newman in a picture. Sure enough, by 1974, in *The Towering Inferno,* he was — sort of. Actually it was what people in the business call "an X billing," with McQueen listed on the posters and in the screen credits first, furthest to the left, and Newman listed second — but just slightly *higher.* With an X billing, both actors can legitimately claim top billing status.

(For my role in that same multi-star picture, I was listed in the second tier of actors, placed alphabetically just before Robert Wagner and just behind somebody named O. J. Simpson. I wonder what ever happened to him?)

Anyway, when we were filming *The Magnificent Seven,* Yul stayed in a private house while the rest of us stayed in adjacent rooms in a local motel. I had Charlie Bronson and Steve McQueen on either side of me, which meant many long hours listening to them compete with stories about their childhood deprivations. (Steve grew up in a home for orphaned boys while Charlie worked in an open-face coal mine. I guess my vote goes to Charlie.)

Once Steve decided to focus his competitiveness on Yul, he started knocking on my door around six-thirty in the morning, an hour or so before we were due to show up on the set. Naturally, I'd invite him in, and our conversations were always much the same.

"Man," he would say in that husky whisper of his, "did you see Brynner's gun on the set yesterday?"

"I can't say I noticed it, Steve."

"You didn't *notice* it? It has a fucking *pearl handle,* for God's sake. He shouldn't have a gun like that. It's too fucking fancy. Nobody's gonna look at anything else with that goddamn gun in the picture." (Of course, Steve meant that nobody would be looking at Steve McQueen.)

What could I say? "Maybe you should talk to the director," I'd suggest. Steve just shook his head — obviously I was too naive to comprehend the depth and villainy of the conspiracy against him — and left the room.

A couple of days later, there'd be another early-morning knock on the door. "Did you see the size of Brynner's horse? It's goddamn gigantic."

This time I *had* noticed. "Actually, Steve, I've got the biggest horse of the seven." I called him Señor Jumbo.

McQueen shook his head. "I don't give a fuck about your horse," he replied. Evidently he didn't regard me as serious competition. "It's Brynner's horse I'm worried about."

Steve did more than just complain. In one scene, several of us, including Yul and Steve, were sitting on our horses next to a stream and debating our strategy for retaking the village from the *banditos.* In the midst of the scene, Brynner suddenly doffed his black Stetson, revealing his famous bald pate glistening in the afternoon sun.

Between takes, McQueen drew me aside. "Did you see what that bastard Brynner did?" he hissed. He couldn't take this act of scene-stealing lying down. A few minutes later, we shot another take. Once again, Brynner doffed his hat. This time, McQueen took off *his* hat, leaned way over from his perch in the saddle, lowered his hat into the stream, and filled it with water. Then, without missing a beat, he replaced it on his head. Water cascaded down his head and shoulders, soaking him thoroughly.

He looked like a fool — but at least no one was looking at Yul Brynner.

In later years, Steve's paranoia continued to expand, even as he was becoming the highest-paid star in the world. But not all the members of the Magnificent Seven went on to careers of Hollywood stardom.

Horst Buchholz returned to Germany and rarely did any acting in the States. Brad Dexter hardly ever acted again at all. He spent the rest of his life as a professional buddy of Frank Sinatra's, having saved the singer from drowning in the waves off Malibu. Till the day Sinatra died, Brad was always on Sinatra's payroll, listed in movie credits as a producer.

Dexter's main contribution to the filming of *The Magnificent Seven* was due to his intimate knowledge of Mexico City, where we shot the interiors after filming in Cuernavaca was completed. He seemed to know every bar, nightclub, and restaurant, and could also recommend excellent establishments for sensual pedicures, steam rooms, and massages. He even escorted us to the home of Delores Del Rio, the legendary film star and beauty of the 1930s and 40s.

On Good Friday, 1960, work shut down in Mexico, that most Catholic of countries — including filmmaking. Brad suggested that Steve and I join him in a visit to what he called "one of the finest brothels in North America." Having spent nearly a decade wandering L.A.'s Sunset Strip, I'd met many ladies of the evening in such places as the Melody Room (now called the Viper Room, the place where River Phoenix died), the Body Shop, and the Raincheck Room. I considered many of them friends, and had made it a rule not to do business with them. But I decided to tag along.

Brad directed the taxi driver to a lavish high-walled hacienda in a quiet residential district of the city. The blond madam instantly recognized Brad and welcomed us like visiting dignitaries at an embassy cocktail party. (In fact, Brad told us that this cathouse had once actually *been* an embassy.) Rounds of margaritas began appearing, along with many beautifully coiffed and gowned ladies, any of whom could have passed for a finalist in the Miss Universe pageant. Brad left with a pair of dark-haired beauties as still more margaritas arrived.

With the light slowly dimming in the room and in my head, the madam announced that the moment to make a selection was at hand. There were seven ladies in the room. In stumbling Spanish, Steve told the madam that all seven women should stay, "Because we are the Magnificent Seven." It seemed to me that we were just two very loaded Americans (and I wasn't feeling very magnificent). But I didn't object to Steve's gluttonous suggestion. I was flush with both pesos and dollars, having been too sick in Cuernavaca to spend my per diem money. So Steve and I adjourned to a lanai with many large pillows and the seven women.

If you've never experienced sex for seven, you're undoubtedly interested in hearing the salacious details. I can only say that, due to the effects of the tequila, we did a hell of a lot more laughing than humping.

Near midnight, I recalled that filming was scheduled for the next day. I said to Steve, "Let's pay our bill and get out of here."

I hadn't yet heard about Steve's famous habit of *not* carrying money. He replied, "Hey, man, could you loan me some *dinero?*"

The bill came to something like seven hundred dollars — pretty big money in the 1960s. I had about four hundred dollars with me, along with several hundred pesos, and I offered the whole wad to the madam. "I'm paying for three and a half *señoritas,* including tip," I said, hoping to get a laugh.

The madam didn't even smile. Instead, she snapped her fingers and a huge *hombre* entered the room. Fixing a hostile glare on me and Steve, he reached out, grabbed my money, and asked, "How you plan to pay the rest?"

I smiled at Steve. He smiled at the *hom-*

bre. The *hombre* . . . he no smile back.

Suddenly a light seemed to dawn in the midst of Steve's alcoholic haze. Pulling out his wallet, he produced a Diners Club booklet containing coupons for use at restaurants. "How about these?" he asked, pathetically enough. The *hombre* moved toward us, and several more mean-looking Mexicans seemed to materialize at the same moment.

On cue, Steve and I spun around and pushed through the swinging doors behind us. Steve dashed toward the right, while I ran left down a long hall ending in French doors that opened onto a small balcony. Footsteps pounding behind me, I flung open the doors and stepped out onto the balcony. The choice was clear: Wait to see what would happen, or vault the balcony railing. I vaulted.

I landed on moist grass, sprang up, and ran to the high wall surrounding the villa grounds. Here was a break — there was some kind of trellis alongside the wall that would give me a foothold. I scrambled up the trellis and flung my body over the edge of the wall. Eyeing the twelve-foot drop to the street below, I saw two bulky Mexicans standing there as if on guard. I was too weak to pull myself back up, so I dropped to the ground, expecting to be apprehended if not beaten to a pulp.

I stood up and smiled wanly at the two men. They merely smiled, remarked, *"Buenos noches,"* and strolled away.

I caught a cab and fifteen minutes later hit my hotel bed with relief, wondering what had befallen Steve.

The next morning, he arrived on the set forty-five minutes late and badly hung over. He'd somehow talked his way out of the brothel by promising to pay the balance in full and tip generously all around. Steve's years on the street had evidently served him well. But for the remainder of our stay in Mexico City, our new friendship was decidedly cool.

Happily, that didn't discourage Steve from badgering me repeatedly until I finally agreed to costar with him in *Bullitt* several years later. But that's another story. . . .

In March 1961, my mother discovered she had pancreatic cancer and began chemotherapy. Her doctors knew she probably had less than six months to live, and they told me so — but in accordance with the custom of the time, we didn't share the whole truth with her, at least not explicitly. How much did she discern on her own? That's impossible to say, but I'd guess it was more than she let on.

Thankfully, the success I'd been enjoying gave me the ability to give her some special times during those final months. I was able to take her on an airplane for the first time. We did one last grand tour of her life, traveling to see *The Billy Barnes Revue* at the Golden Theatre in New York, visiting Chicago, where she had a good friend, Mary Best, who also was a friend of my future wife, Linda, and finally stopping in Minneapolis, where she had started her acting career in the late twenties. We then returned to L.A., where she continued her chemotherapy and was briefly hospitalized in July. As a result of the new round of chemo, she began wearing the wig that she had worn intermittently on our trip.

In 1958, I had moved one block away from the Orchid apartment to a street called Pinehurst Road, where, for the first time in my life, I lived completely alone in a charming one-bedroom Swiss chalet–type dwelling surrounded by greenery and the distinctly Los Angeles aroma of bougainvillea. It also boasted a working fireplace, which rarely went unused. Now, however, I began staying almost full-time in the second bedroom of Mother's three-story Orchid

Avenue penthouse, where we had moved in June 1956 after I signed my Hecht-Lancaster movie deal.

Like most cancer sufferers, Mother had good days and bad. I remember the time she called me to say she had walked from Hollywood and Vine all the way home to Orchid Avenue, a distance of several miles. However, that was the high point of her bout with the inoperable cancer. Between then and her final one-month stay at California Hospital, I carried her countless times up and down the steep stairs to the penthouse for her biweekly chemo treatments and the draining of the ever-accumulating fluid in the middle of her body. Patty Regan, the uniquely funny high-kicking redhead of *The Billy Barnes Revue,* even volunteered to move in and help with Mother's care, but I turned down the generous offer.

About this time, Bob Reese, a sometime stage producer connected with the Las Palmas Theater off Hollywood Boulevard, asked if I would be interested in playing one of the male leads in a new comedy making its West Coast premiere in Hollywood. The name of the play was *Under the Yum Yum Tree.* It had been done on Broadway with Gig Young and would become a film with

Jack Lemmon and Dean Jones. Richard Long, later to have great success in TV's *The Big Valley* and *Nanny and the Professor,* would be my costar.

I was given the star dressing room at the theater, formerly occupied by Joyce Jameson during the run of *The Billy Barnes Revue* at the Las Palmas. Bob Reese was particularly sensitive to my family situation, allowing me to schedule my rehearsals around daily visits to my mother at the hospital. During her last months, she held court with a martini cocktail party every afternoon at five. Many of my friends visited her, and though she had lost weight and suffered a little nausea, she experienced little pain and was always alert and wonderfully funny with our gang. No one seemed to realize she had less than a month to live.

On September 6, 1961, I was making an appearance on a local live game show when the hospital notified me that Mother's condition had taken a turn for the worse. The TV show released me immediately, but by the time I arrived at the hospital, she was gone.

As I entered her room, I saw a body bag on the bed. I said good-bye and left the room. I remember the last thing she had said to me the night before: "People expected so much from me." It was a sad final note, I thought — not one that captured accurately the pleasure she had brought to so many friends and fans.

Her funeral was September 8, 1961, at the Blessed Sacrament Church on Sunset Boulevard. Many of my friends who had known her for almost a decade were there, and the trip to the cemetery was a mixture of funny Marcella stories and just a few tears. She was buried in the Grotto section of Holy Cross Cemetery where many actors are interred, including her good friend and acting colleague the silent film star and comedienne Zasu Pitts. (It wasn't until a later visit to the Grotto that I realized that buried closest to her was one of her *least* favorite film stars, Gary Cooper, who had died of cancer earlier that year. Mother considered Cooper monotonous, sexless, and boring — especially by comparison with firebrands like Cagney and Bogart.)

The afternoon of the funeral was filled with much chat at the Orchid penthouse about the many laughs we'd all shared with Marcella. We also were much filled with the drink, and that night I went through a dress rehearsal of *Yum Yum* with very little memory of the event. On Sunday night, September 10, we opened the play with great success, the audience standing, applauding, and cheering at the final curtain. In the theater were my friends and many from the Billy Barnes shows, including Joyce, who had also been at the funeral — though we were not speaking at the time. (Why? I have no idea. We'd had a spat of some sort. We were in the habit of fighting, feuding, and making up repeatedly. It seemed to be a natural part of our relationship.)

Under the Yum Yum Tree ran almost a year, with Bill Bixby stepping into my role starting around Christmastime.

Also in the audience that opening night was a beautiful young actress who would be a part of my life until the mid-sixties, Joan O'Brien. We met only briefly that night; she was a friend of one of the other two ladies in the cast, Barbara Stuart (who is still my dear friend of almost a half century as I write this).

Joan was off to New York, and several weeks went by before we finally reconnected. She started as a band singer while still in Ontario High School, a suburb of Los Angeles. Someone had told Tennessee Ernie Ford's manager, Cliffie Stone, about a beautiful fifteen-year-old girl at Ontario High that looked like an angel and sang like a lark. He listened to her and signed her to a contract. She then went on to sing with Bob Crosby's band for four years on CBS TV. She also starred in many movies, appearing opposite Cary Grant, Tony Curtis, John Wayne, Richard Widmark, Jerry Lewis, and Elvis Presley in *It Happened at the World's Fair.*

Joan had two small children from two previous marriages, Missy and Randy. Joyce's son Tyler was four in the summer of 1957. So I had some experience with being a proxy father figure in a young child's life. Even when Joyce and I were not involved, I often took Tyler fishing in the Pacific Ocean (while knowing nothing about fishing myself). Tyler and I also spent time at the children's amusement park on La Cienega Boulevard and hiking in Griffith Park.

Joan was a young lady with a vast capacity to give of herself to her man of the moment. And my moment lasted for nearly half a decade. She also had the singing voice of an angel and the laugh of a well-fortified Irish drinker — though she drank only modestly. She was the ideal girl for me during the first years after my mother's death. When not on foreign film locations, she was there for me round the clock, and her tenderness, compassion, and friendship helped me through many a bad night.

Of course, there was a downside to her personality. And that was her (not unreasonable) expectation that I would always be there for her. In retrospect, I was mostly there, but not often enough for blissful romantic harmony.

And then on January 31, 1965, she almost died at my Mulholland Drive home. I had invited a few friends over for a belated Merry Christmas and Happy New Year drinks party. (As I'll explain later, I'd been in Russia over the holidays.) Sally Kellerman, my neighbor on Woodrow Wilson Drive, just off Mulholland, was one of my guests, as was Bill Tynan, who a year later would be the instrumental person in getting me involved with the anti-Vietnam protest movement. Also there by invitation was Joan O'Brien. I had last seen her in July 1964, when she had guest starred with Carroll O'Connor in *The Green Opal Affair* on *The Man from U.N.C.L.E.*

There had been publicity in the Hollywood trade papers over the holidays that I was planning to do *Hamlet* at the famed Pasadena Playhouse during my 1965 spring break from *U.N.C.L.E.* Joanie had read this and had contacted me about the possibility of her playing Ophelia. I said something to

217

the effect that, "You'd be the best singer ever to attempt the role." (At least at that time. Four years later, I saw Marianne Faithfull play Ophelia opposite Nicol Williamson at London's Roundabout Theatre.)

Joan understood my indirect answer. She sensed I had some reservations about having her make her Shakespearean debut as my Ophelia. She said she had recorded some poems and asked whether I would let her come to my house and play them for me. I agreed. I was very fond of her and I also thought that maybe — just maybe — she could pull it off.

She did come over, and I listened to her poetry readings and was mightily impressed and told her so.

It was nearing midnight, and I was ready to turn in. As was my custom, I instructed my guests to stay as long as they wanted, but to remember to turn off the Christmas tree lights and close the front door.

Around four A.M. I awakened and went to the bathroom. Before leaving London after a recent trip to England, I had purchased some sedatives for the long flight to Los Angeles. I knew I had used only a few of them before regaining my lost equilibrium occasioned by the thirteen-hour flight. Now, on the marble-topped washbasin, I spied the pill box — empty — and an empty glass.

I raced around the dark house and found nothing in my library, living room, or kitchen. I looked down the hall that you could see as you entered the front door, and the guest room door was ajar. Inside, sprawled on the four-poster bed, was Joan. I called her name and shook her over and over, trying to find a pulse or breath in her limp body with no success.

Keeping an eye on her, I called Bill Tynan, who lived just south of Sunset Boulevard, about a fifteen-minute drive at that time of the morning. He said he would be right there, and he was. Instead of taking my large four-door Lincoln Continental, for some inexplicable reason, we carried her to Bill's Volkswagen and somehow got her into the backseat and headed for the Hollywood emergency hospital.

I don't know how long the trip took, but as soon as we arrived, a young intern was at the emergency door. I explained as quickly as I could while they got Joan's inert body on a stretcher. The young doctor, using a stethoscope, began examining her back, lungs, all the while shaking his head grimly.

Finally, he said there was nothing he could do. I said, "Put her in an ambulance and take her downtown now!" And for some reason, unknown to this day, that's what he did.

I spoke briefly with a sheriff's deputy, and suddenly an ambulance appeared. I told Bill to go home, and I rode in the back with Joan's still lifeless body stretched out beside me while an EMT kept checking her vital signs. There seemed to be none.

When we arrived at the downtown Los Angeles hospital, the experienced emergency team met us at the ambulance entrance and quickly put her on a gurney. The moment we arrived inside, a formidable middle-aged doctor was waiting. He held a huge syringe in his hand and proceeded to plunge it into her chest area. Immediately, her body seemed to levitate and then fall back on the gurney. She was then wheeled off to I knew not where.

I'd already given a statement to the sheriff's officer at the Hollywood hospital. No one seemed to have any further interest in me. So I asked for the attending doctor's name and phone number and left.

By now it was around seven A.M. I knew I'd done all I could for Joan, and I hoped it would be enough. But now another aspect of the situation began to dawn on me — the fact that, as a public personality, what had happened would probably be considered a news story. And with our show *The Man from U.N.C.L.E.* at the height of its success, I had some responsibility to other people to handle it properly.

I showered and drove the thirty-minute trip to MGM from Mulholland. As soon as I arrived there, I got in touch with Chuck Painter, the MGM publicist for *U.N.C.L.E.* and *Dr. Kildare.* I explained quickly what had happened and strongly suggested that he get to his office as soon as possible. After he arrived, we discussed all the possible ramifications of Joan's "event," as we then called it.

The Hollywood press could have played the story many ways. It's easy to imagine the kind of lurid saga an unscrupulous editor could have conjured up. Fortunately, when the presses rolled, the gist of the coverage was, "TV star saves dying actress." And that was the end of what could have been a catastrophe for me and all the hard-working people connected with *U.N.C.L.E.*

Within a few days, Joan had recovered. I heard that shortly thereafter she hosted a dinner party for a dozen people.

And against the advice of all my friends, professional and private, I cast Joan as Ophelia. Also in the original cast of *Hamlet* was my friend Carroll O'Connor as King

221

Claudius and Everett Sloan, that distinguished actor from the Orson Welles Mercury Theater and *Citizen Kane,* as Polonius.

At the urging of my then agent, Max Arnow, I hired Leon Askin to direct. He was appearing at that time as a comical German officer on TV's *Hogan's Heroes.* After the first read-through, Carroll and Everett bowed out (I later learned they weren't happy with Askin's direction). I replaced them in the roles of the king and Polonius with two friends of mine from the Stage Society, Will Sage and Peter Brocco. They were both outstanding.

Finally opening night arrived. The Pasadena Playhouse had been closed for several years, and my *Hamlet* was to be their big reopening. I had had five years to think about how I could improve my time in the role of the "story of a man who could not make up his mind."

I had sent out personal invitations to all and sundry, from President Johnson's daughters on the East Coast (they declined) to my close friends on the West Coast. I was ready to knock 'em dead.

On opening night, I scheduled a strong rubdown around one P.M. half a block from the theater. At about one-thirty, it started to rain, and it rained, and it rained. It rained nonstop all afternoon and into the early evening. Traffic was stalled all over Los Angeles and at all the entrances to Pasadena.

At curtain time, only half of the capacity audience had been seated. Then the management decided the theater was too cold, and the elderly, long-unused heating system was turned on. Those ancient pipes began to bang and bing, making a horrific cacophony of loud, ugly sounds.

We had not done a dress rehearsal for an audience. This was the first time that all the theater seats had been used in years. They crunched and squeaked, adding more noise to the already deafening melee. We finally raised the curtain an hour late at nine P.M. People were still arriving, and the rain was now mixed with thunder and lightning. (Actually, this was very effective for the opening scene, which is the first appearance of the ghost of Hamlet's father, set outside at night on the Elsinore castle ramparts.)

In any case, the show must go on. In the second scene, inside the royal court of Denmark, we meet Hamlet, King Claudius and Queen Gertrude, and Laertes and Ophelia with Polonius, their father. After a long self-serving monologue, Claudius finally turns to his stepson Hamlet and says,

"But now my cousin Hamlet and my son." Under the horrible circumstances that had unfolded that evening, I wanted to say, very loudly, "I want out of here." Instead, I responded with Shakespeare's words, "A little more than kin and less than kind."

To the extent that we could, we delivered a two-and-a-half-hour *Hamlet,* cut by me, so that, with one intermission, the curtain finally came down at midnight. The audience shuffled out, relieved to have survived but not terribly entertained, enlightened, or uplifted.

The reviews were unusually kind to me and the performances in general. But I knew it was a disaster, and that's what really hurt me terribly. My friends were equally kind, suggesting that all would be well in the remaining performances. And perhaps it was: A very reputable reviewer for a distinguished Hebrew weekly saw the production in the second week and loved it.

For me, though, the high point of the whole production were the matinees we did chiefly for students from all over Southern California who were bussed in — many never having seen a Shakespearean play before. I had a Q&A session after each matinee and was amazed at their understanding of the story, which, for most of them, must have been difficult to follow.

And finally, Joan O'Brien was a great success as Ophelia, her performance garnering adjectives such as "touching," "vulnerable," "enchanting," "haunting," and "brilliant." And she did sing her last scene with great sadness and madness — beautifully.

Sometime in my late twenties, before my first Hamlet and my direction of *A View from the Bridge,* I was having a drink at the Melody Room with my old friend from LACC, John Hackett. At that time, John was living on the ground level of my Pinehurst Road chalet. During the evening, John turned to me with a thoughtful air and remarked, "I've known you for almost a decade, and yet I've never seen you angry or depressed."

I was amused by the observation. What he was describing sounded, on the surface, like a good thing. But John clearly didn't think so. I said, "What do you think I should do about that?"

He said, "You're either a saint or insensitive. Do you know anything about Krishnamurti?"

I said, "What's that?"

John said, "I'm going to give you something tomorrow. Read it and tell me what you think." We downed a few more drinks, and I forgot all about the exchange.

The following day, I found a copy of *The First and Last Freedom* by J. Krishnamurti stuck inside my screen door. Curious, I glanced at the first page. Then the second. Then the third. Utterly engrossed, I finished the book before noon and was greatly impressed by the Indian mystic. But I was also confused as to how the blissful state he described was to be achieved by the terribly fragile creatures known as humans.

Somehow, Krishnamurti's philosophy reminded me of a book I'd read in the early fifties titled *Escape from Freedom* by Dr. Erich Fromm. It had been published before World War II, and I made reference to it in my book on the Hollywood blacklist era, *Only Victims,* because Fromm's startling theory was that what man has been trying to achieve for millennia — freedom — can actually be frightening. This is why totalitarianism can be such a powerful temptation. For example, many Nazis, after 1945, found solace and security in Communism.

Man has a horror of aloneness. Is this not why a God was created by the first man or woman?

The need to be one with others is not a mysterious quality. In any conceivable culture, man needs to cooperate with others if he wants to survive. And even earlier there is the need of the human child to cooperate with those who are raising him. The baby stops crying when another comforts him and he no longer feels alone. And as the child grows, he begins to be aware of himself as distinct not only from nature but from other people. Ultimately, as he learns about illness, dying, and death, he becomes aware of how unimportant he is in his smallness in comparison with the universe and all the other people around him.

For Krishnamurti, to understand what "is" is requires great intelligence and great awareness. (I suspect that Bill Clinton's use of the same formulation — "It depends on what the meaning of 'is' is" — may have been dredged up from an early reading of Krishnamurti.) It is not merely to accept or give yourself over to an idea. To understand what is requires an effort; an effort is a form of distraction; and to really grasp what is, you cannot be distracted.

For me, this concept of trying to understand what someone is or what someone is trying to tell you while freeing oneself not only from the distractions of the moment — noise, music, people's voices — but also from the distractions of a lifetime of prejudice requires a kind of divinity that few possess.

I have tried to attain this state of mind but only with much effort and with little practical result.

According to Krishnamurti, the understanding of what is, being aware of what is, reveals extraordinary depths, in which lie reality, happiness, and joy.

In other words, it is not a question of *accepting* what is; you do not *accept* what is, you do not accept that you are brown or white, because it is a fact. Only when you are trying to become something else do you have to accept. The moment you recognize a fact, it ceases to have any significance. I believe he means that a mind that is trained to think of the past or the future, trained to run away in multifarious directions — such a mind is incapable of understanding what *is*.

For Krishnamurti, without understanding what is, you cannot find what is real, and without that understanding life has no significance. (I'm not sure about that observation.) Life is a constant battle wherein pain and suffering continue. (I'm sure of that.)

The polar opposite of what Krishnamurti is trying to explain — that state of extraordinary individualism — is what Eric Hoffer describes in his seminal work, *The True Believer,* first published in 1951.

Writing in the years just after World War II, in the wake of the totalitarian movements of Nazism, Fascism, and Communism, Hoffer focuses on the peculiarities common to all mass movements, be they social revolutions, nationalist movements, or religious movements. All share certain essential characteristics which give them a family likeness.

Today, of course, we are faced with a new manifestation of the Hofferesque mass movement: radical jihad as exemplified by the suicide bomber who is ready to die to further his or her cause. The true believer is at the opposite pole from Krishnamurti's seeker of enlightenment. Rather than finding peace in total understanding of all that is, he flees from the terror of loneliness by obliterating his personality in the communal cult.

Krishnamurti and Hoffer, each in his different way, have played pivotal roles in my thinking over the decades. To be an actor, you really don't need a philosophy of life, but you do need to be a complete human being. And that is something I've aspired to be, at the same time that I was disporting myself in front of the footlights or before the cameras.

As Krishnamurti noted, self-knowledge is the beginning of wisdom and therefore the beginning of transformation.

Thought is action, and ideas are not truth. Truth is something that must be experienced directly from moment to moment. It is not an experience that you *want,* which is merely sensation. Only when one can go beyond the bundle of ideas, when thought is completely silent, is there a state of experiencing. Then one knows what truth is.

What about belief or knowledge? The true believer (as Hoffer says) accepts belief out of fear. If we had no belief, what would happen? We'd be very frightened. If we have no pattern of action, based on belief either in God or in Communism or in Socialism or in Imperialism, or in some kind of religious formula — some dogma to which we are conditioned — we feel lost. To escape that feeling of lost-ness is one of the reasons we accept beliefs so eagerly. But beliefs lead to a process of isolation.

Some beliefs, the Christian doctrine for instance, translate into the golden rule of brotherly love, doing unto each other, and so on. Others, such as those that make up the current doctrine of Islamic jihad, translate into murder and mayhem directed against the nonbelieving Western liberal democracies. So beliefs that isolate negativity allow no freedom to think and believe and receive knowledge into a pure and uncontaminated mind or system of beliefs. The goal of our adversaries, following 9/11, is the mass murder/annihilation of all infidels, including even Muslims who are nonbelievers in Osama bin Laden's jihad.

As with the case with Stalin in the late forties and fifties, Osama bin Laden's "secret weapon" in his war on the Western liberal democracies is his ability to generate enthusiasm and self-sacrifice in all manner of people by casting the United States in the role of devil leader of his infidel adversaries. And the chief targets of bin Laden's propaganda efforts consist of dissatisfied, "embarrassed" people as described by the French philosopher Blaise Pascal in his *Pensées:*

Man would fain be great and sees that he is little; would fain be happy and sees that he is miserable; would fain be perfect and sees that he is full of imperfections; would fain to be the object of the love and esteem of men, and sees that his faults

231

merit only their aversion and contempt.

The embarrassment wherein he finds himself produces in him the most unjust and criminal passions imaginable, for he conceives a mortal hatred against that truth which blames him and convinces him of his faults.

Leaving aside the question of truth, the same qualities that make Christian doctrine so emotionally attractive are the qualities that make Communism, Nazism, nationalism, Fascism, and international Islamic jihad attractive. In the words of our autodidact philosopher of mass movements Eric Hoffer:

However different the holy causes people die for, they perhaps basically die for the same thing. . . . [The true believer] multiplied by thousands [is] a shaper of the world to his image. A guilt-ridden hitchhiker on every cause from religion to politics. He's a fanatic needing a fanatic to die for. . . . He's the mortal enemy of things-as-they-are, and he insists on sacrificing himself for a dream impossible to attain.

Writing in 1951, Hoffer presciently described the Islam terrorists' violent deeds that would lead to September 11, 2001, and throw the world into an unrelenting, never-ending defense of democracy against seventh-century Muslim extremist, militant, suicidal terrorism.

Eric Hoffer pointed out that "the chief preoccupation of an active mass movement is to instill in its followers a facility for united action and self-sacrifice," and that it achieves this facility "by stripping each human entity of its distinctness and autonomy and turning it into an anonymous particle with no will or judgment of its own."

In my view, the precondition for conversion is always estrangement from self and almost always is fused in an atmosphere of intense passion. In 1972, I wrote in *Only Victims,* "The man who has achieved inner balance is not a candidate for the fanatical movement. So the fanatic, seeking followers, must first attempt to throw off any inner balance in his potential followers. Such fanatical leaders do this through those precise methods that inflame the passions." I concluded with the observation, "And where fanatical passion rules, reason is a stranger."

This doomsday/Armageddon scenario, currently playing out on the world stage, has been extensively examined by other scholars, from Hanna Arendt and Daniel Bell to David Reisman and (as mentioned earlier) Eric Fromm.

If man cannot stand freedom, he will probably seek the simplicity of totalitarian leadership in one of its many forms, political (dictatorial, authoritarian regimes), military, or religious.

Though Fromm is not a psychoanalyst, he applies the psychoanalytical method to the illness of our civilization, which often expresses itself in an abject submission to dictatorship.

I believe it is true that the rise of democracy set (most) people free and brought to an end the authority of the medieval church and the medieval state. Thus it created a society where a man feels isolated from his fellows, where relationships are impersonal, and where insecurity replaces a sense of belonging.

This sense of isolation may drive an individual to one of various forms of escape. It may drive people to seek escape in blind devotion to a leader (Hitler, Stalin, Mao), in utter submission to a barbarous and sadistic program of aggression against minority groups or neighboring nations (as in twentieth-century Africa after the European colonizers set them free).

In such a world, the position of the artist is highly vulnerable. Generally, the artist can be defined as an individual who can express himself spontaneously. But it is really only the successful artist whose individuality or spontaneity is respected; if he does not succeed in selling his art, painting, acting, dancing, singing, medical, scientific or philosophical breakthroughs, he remains to his nonartistic contemporaries a crank or a neurotic. Witness the packed Soviet mental institutions whose clientele in America might reside in Greenwich Village and be revered by their fellow artists.

The artist in this matter is in a similar position to that of the revolutionary throughout history. The successful revolutionary is a statesman (Jefferson); the unsuccessful, a demonic criminal (Pol Pot).

Escape from political authoritarianism only works if you can handle the isolation that democratic freedom offers its newly arrived immigrants.

What is the meaning of life, then, when we, the objects of the madness, have virtually no control over our destinies?

Philosophers through the ages — as well as bartenders and their customers — have been curious about the purpose and meaning of life. A man living richly, physically and emotionally, who sees things as they are and is content with what he has, is not confused about this question. For him, the very fact of living is the beginning and the end. But as Krishnamurti points out, if the purpose of your life is to find God, surely that desire to find God is an escape from life, and your God is merely a thing that is known. You can only make your way toward an object that you know; if you build a staircase to the thing you call God, surely that is not God. "Reality can be understood only in living, not escape."

If we begin to understand action, which is our relationship with people, with property, with beliefs and ideas, then we find that relationship itself brings its own rewards. This question about the purpose of life is put only by those who do not love. Love can be found only in action that is relationship.

Eminent psychiatrist Rollo May says of Krishnamurti, "These calm searching thoughts of an Eastern thinker pierce to the roots of our Western problems of conformity and loss of personal value. I think many people will get from this book a profound and fresh approach to self-understanding and deeper insights into the meaning of personal freedom and mature love."

Although as I mentioned earlier, I don't pretend to grasp a great deal of Krishnamurti's writing, I have gleaned sufficient insight to his philosophy to slightly expand the way I should live my life. There is an old Irish theory my beloved grandmother told me early on that said, basically, the past is done, the future is yet to be known. So, "Live for today, for tomorrow may be as yesterday."

Maybe Krishnamurti would have gone along with that bush-league version of his philosophy. I hope so anyway, because that's the way I've tried to live my life.

"Nothing then," as Jefferson wrote, "is unchangeable but the inherent and inalienable rights of man." And that's enough philosophy for this book.

SEVEN:
GOING SOLO

A hit, a very palpable hit.

The vagaries of show business can be curious. In the late 1950s and early 1960s, I did literally hundreds of guest-starring roles on one TV series after another, playing cowboys, doctors, lawyers, soldiers, cops, crooks, politicians — you name it. The work was fun and lucrative. And like most young actors I hoped that a role on a hit series might prove to be my springboard to the first rank of stardom. Instead, it was a gig on a major floparoo that ended up transforming my career — and my life.

The linchpin in the story is a TV producer named Norman Felton, perhaps forgotten by all except the most avid show-business history buffs, but someone who in his own way helped shape the industry in its early days. I'd played a couple of very strong guest-starring roles for Norman in MGM

TV shows created under his Arena Productions banner (*The Eleventh Hour, Dr. Kildare*): a zealous prosecutor modeled after Robert F. Kennedy and a confused husband whose wife (Inger Stevens) is suffering a postpartum mental breakdown.

In 1963, Norman asked me to play a continuing costarring role in Gene Roddenberry's TV series *The Lieutenant,* for which Norman was executive producer. Shot largely at Camp Pendleton south of Los Angeles, the series dealt with life in the Marine Corps and starred Gary Lockwood. I'd play Gary's commanding officer, Captain Raymond Rambridge. I agreed to take on the role with the understanding that Norman would use me "subject to availability." That meant I'd be free to do movies and other guest-starring roles on TV.

The Lieutenant died a quick and painless death. Its Nielsen ratings were abysmal, and the show was canceled at the end of the 1963–64 television season. Nobody's career seemed to suffer as a result. Gary Lockwood went on to costar with Keir Dullea in Stanley Kubrick's classic picture *2001: A Space Odyssey* (as well as marrying the beautiful and sexy Stefanie Powers, the one-time "Girl from U.N.C.L.E."). Gene Roddenberry created the *Star Trek* franchise and became obscenely wealthy. As for me — well, Norman Felton said he felt bad that the gig on *The Lieutenant* hadn't worked out, and he promised to find something else that would make me happy.

Did he ever.

While shooting one of the last episodes of *The Lieutenant* at Camp Pendleton, I got a call from Norman around six P.M. one Thursday afternoon. "I'm leaving you a script at the main MGM gate," Norman said. "Meet me tomorrow morning in my office and let know what you think."

"What's it called?" I asked.

"*Solo.* That's the name of the lead character — your part."

We had a long day of shooting. It was eleven P.M. by the time Gary Lockwood and I swung by the studio to pick up the script. But being young and single, we decided to hit the Sunset Boulevard bars before going home. Gary and I picked up a couple of floozies at the Melody Room. We took them to his pad in Laurel Canyon, and I didn't get back to my Hollywood Pinehurst faux Swiss chalet rental till about four A.M. I glanced at Norman's script, muttered, "Fuck this," and staggered off to bed. I was due at Norman's office on the MGM lot in Culver City at nine o'clock.

That Friday morning wasn't the first time I'd had to manage on minimal sleep. (Like I said, I was young and single.) Knowing that the drive to Culver City would take me exactly thirty minutes, I rose at eight A.M., showered quickly, and tossed the *Solo* script into my car. I read a couple of pages at every red light between Hollywood and Culver City. There weren't enough red lights for me to finish the whole script, but even in my hungover state I got the gist of it — James Bond for television.

At the time, I hadn't even seen a James Bond movie. Of course, I knew that Sean Connery had been enjoying international success in the first two films in the series (*Dr. No* and *From Russia with Love*), and that the Ian Fleming spy novels were reputedly President Kennedy's favorite reading matter. That was plenty of background information for me to fake an informed response.

I was ushered quickly into Norman's office in the Thalberg Building at MGM. "So what do you think?" Norman asked.

Woozy as I was from too much hooch and too little sleep, I had enough mother wit to reply, "It's James Bond in your living room. As opposed to his favorite room, the bedroom."

Norman nodded knowingly and gave me

a cryptic smile. "Would you be interested in doing it?"

I said, "An unqualified yes."

Switching into classic mogul mode, Norman barked into the intercom on his desk, "Shirley, put me through to New York." His phone rang almost immediately. "Vaughn wants to do it," he announced into the phone. Then he hung up, turned back to me, and said, "Have your agent give me a call."

Today it can take weeks or months to be cast in the leading role in a one-hour television series, starting with an audition (a "cold reading") for half a dozen Ivy League MBAs — wet-behind-the-ears kids who know nothing about show business except the bottom line, yet somehow have the power to make or break acting careers. But in 1963, business was done mano a mano. All it took was a ten-second conversation between the West Coast and the East Coast to change my life forever.

As I returned to the lot to get my car, the guard at the gate — his name was, believe it or not, Ken Hollywood — asked me, "What's new?"

I said, "Well, Ken, you're looking at TV's James Bond . . . I think."

Later, as I was driving down Sunset

Boulevard with the top down on my new black-cherry Lincoln convertible, a ravishing blonde passed me on my left in her top-down, middle-age Ford convertible. There was a sticker on her rear bumper reading, MAKE LOVE, NOT WAR

At the next intersection, we pulled up at the same time. I said, "When?" And she said, "What do you mean?" And I said, "Your bumper sticker." And she said, kiddingly I think, "How about now?"

And I said, "Sorry, I have an appointment," which was true. And she said, laughingly, before she gunned her motor and shot out of the intersection, "That's why we have wars."

I never forgot that morning. It put a period and a new paragraph on the exciting next chapter in my thirty-year-old showbiz life.

I was represented at the time by Max Arnow. Max made the deal for me to do the pilot for a TV drama called *Solo*. Don Medford (I'd never heard of him) was set to direct. The pilot would be two hours long and in color, and therefore hopefully suitable for release as a feature film if it wasn't picked up by NBC for the 1964–65 season.

I later learned more about the background of what became *The Man from U.N.CL.E.* In

1962, the author of the James Bond novels, Ian Fleming himself, had spent some time in New York with Norman generating ideas for a TV series about a secret agent. Most of Fleming's character concepts didn't make it into *U.N.C.L.E.* — for example, he described the hero as Canadian, the owner of a pet bird with whom he talked, and friends with a local librarian whose encyclopedic knowledge helped solve cases. None of these ideas ended up appearing in the series.

Troubled by a heart ailment and distracted by his work on the burgeoning Bond movie franchise, Fleming ultimately dropped out of the picture and signed any rights in the series over to Felton. However, the use of the name "Napoleon Solo" almost precipitated legal trouble between MGM and Eon Productions, the company producing the Bond pictures. Fleming had coined the name, apparently forgetting that he'd used a similar one in *Goldfinger* (one of the American mobsters who assists Goldfinger in his plot to rob Fort Knox is named simply "Mr. Solo"). MGM and Eon agreed that the TV series could proceed only if the title *Solo* was changed. That's how *The Man from U.N.C.L.E.* was born.

Actually, Norman later commented that the James Bond craze wasn't the sole source of inspiration for *U.N.C.L.E.* In generating the idea for the series, Norman was also influenced by the thrillers of Alfred Hitchcock, especially his 1959 classic *North by Northwest,* starring Cary Grant. In fact, when writer Sam Rolfe, at Norman's invitation, drew up a detailed prospectus for the series, he indicated that the leading role should be played by a "Cary Grant type" — dark-haired, athletic, suave, witty, well-dressed.

I guess they thought I fit the bill. So did another young actor, Robert Culp, who was seriously considered for the role by Norman. But Napoleon Solo turned out to be *my* ticket to the top. Bob got his a year later — the role of Kelly Robinson in the TV series *I Spy,* costarring Bill Cosby.

Once I was cast, the machinery of a major studio and TV network went into overdrive. The role of Mr. Allison, head of the fictitious U.N.C.L.E. organization for which Solo worked, was to be played by a gruff, serious actor with a number of TV credits named Will Kuluva. (As every TV trivia buff knows, the acronym stands for United Network Command for Law and Enforcement.) And making a small appearance in the pilot would be a young Scottish/British actor I knew from George Stevens's movie *The Greatest Story Ever Told,* where he had played Judas Iscariot. His name was David McCallum. In the original script, his role was described as that of "an armed Slavic man." Of course, this was transmogrified over time into Russian agent Illya Kuryakin. With his blond Beatle-like bangs and slender good looks, David would ride the role into stardom, especially among the preteenaged girls of the world.

We were scheduled to start shooting the pilot on Wednesday, November 20, 1963, just two days before my thirty-first birthday. It was also two days before the defining moment of the decade — the assassination of President John F. Kennedy in Dallas, Texas.

That Friday afternoon was a weird and distressing one for cast and crew alike. We were shooting at the Lever Brothers plant an hour south of Los Angeles. The plot of the pilot — like most of the *U.N.C.L.E.* plots, a gimcrack affair — involved the corrupt CEO of a chemical corporation, espionage and intrigue surrounding diplomats from an imaginary African nation, an assassination plot, a super-network of worldwide criminals known as T.H.R.U.S.H., and various other shenanigans. The Lever Brothers plant was used as the setting for Vulcan Chemical Company. (It was renamed Global

Company in the final version, which was released throughout the world as an MGM feature film.) With its vast steel towers, silos, vents, and catwalks, it made a suitable backdrop for a climactic chase scene with the usual ambushes, gunplay, falls, and explosions.

My good friend George Lehr, who was the associate producer on the show for its entire run, and would subsequently become an instructor in the cinema department of my alma mater, USC, had been assigned the job of assessing the possibility of filming from dusk to dawn at the soap plant. He reported back that using the latest Eastman Kodak color film with available light, it could be done. The MGM camera department said that it wouldn't work. It did work. I was there.

To play the leading lady's role in the MGM/NBC pilot, the producers had decided on Janice Rule, at that time married to my friend, actor Ben Gazzara. Quite by accident, I found out that Janice's deal stipulated that she be photographed from her left side.

Since my early films made after I returned from the Army, I had, after viewing "dailies," asked whenever possible to be photographed from the left, and since so many scenes were between only Janice and me, I used my newly acquired power and Janice did not get the job.

I suggested that the leading girl in the pilot who was taken out of her humdrum Midwestern existence and thrown into the world of spies, fast cars, beautiful jewelry and clothes, exotic locations, and me be played by Patricia Crowley.

Pat had portrayed my wife in *The Lieutenant* and had she not been happily married to an acquaintance of mine, Ed Hookstraten, an important Beverly Hills lawyer, I would have made a move on her. She was available and we had great fun and an exciting time working together.

Three days into the shoot, on my thirty-first birthday, the world was stunned by the murder of the thirty-fifth President of the United States, John F. Kennedy.

I was driving down to the Lever Brothers location with my car radio set on CBS, listening to *The Arthur Godfrey Show,* when the program was interrupted at ten-thirty A.M. Pacific time with the announcement that three shots had been fired at the presidential motorcade in Dallas, Texas. I stopped at my friend Bill Tynan's house to pick him up. Bill was starting his job as dialogue director on the show.

We sat in his apartment just south of Sunset Boulevard listening to the breaking news. One half hour after the first shots were reported, Walter Cronkite announced to the country and the world that JFK was dead. It was two P.M. in Washington, D.C., and McLean, Virginia, where the attorney general of the United States, Robert F. Kennedy, heard the news of his older brother's death.

Bill drove my car for the ninety-minute drive to the soap factory. I remember nothing of the trip. We had to wait until dark, which came early in November. After a few attempts at doing the scheduled scene, the director, Don Medford, and Pat Crowley and the newly minted Mr. Solo agreed that we could barely remember our names, let alone the lines in the script.

We all went home to our black-and-white TV sets to watch the unthinkable unfold: the swearing-in of Lyndon B. Johnson as president on *Air Force One* flanked by his wife, Lady Bird, and Jacqueline Kennedy, still wearing the pink suit stained with her husband's blood; the murder of the suspected assassin Lee Harvey Oswald on Sunday morning, November 24, by an unknown bar owner named Jack Ruby; the silent, somber funeral in Washington; two-year-old John-John Kennedy's salute as his father's casket passed before him; and, finally, the lighting of the eternal flame at the young President's grave in Arlington Cemetery.

We still had several weeks of shooting for the *U.N.C.L.E.* pilot. I worried that my melancholy about the President's murder might affect my performance as the dashing, romantic Napoleon Solo in my first shot at TV stardom. I didn't think it had, but I was probably not equipped to make an objective evaluation, and others involved in the production were not going to tell me I was off the mark. So I just kept working and hoped for the best.

We resumed filming on Tuesday, November 26, on the scene previously scheduled for Friday, November 22, which was Patricia and me hanging from a steam pipe with the heat increasing rapidly.

Two days later was Thanksgiving, and Joan O'Brien, whom I had been seeing regularly since my mother died in 1961, offered to cook the traditional dinner. She suggested I invite, among others, my good Irish friends, John Hackett and Bill Tynan, whom she also knew. A kind of Irish wake was improvised for the slain President, involving much boozing and telling of tall tales about JFK romances that were well known even then.

I had never met David McCallum before we filmed his two brief scenes on the pilot. I had seen him in *Freud,* directed by John Huston, where he photographed beautifully and acted superbly, and, as mentioned earlier, he had gotten the role of Judas in George Stevens's production of *The Greatest Story Ever Told,* a part every young actor in town had been up for.

Meanwhile, my move to the next level of show business (from costar to star) had already begun to affect my life. I used the big paycheck from the *U.N.C.L.E.* pilot to buy my first home, a house on Mulholland Drive overlooking the San Fernando Valley that I named Tolemac. (Spell it backward — a little inside joke.)

I moved into Tolemac on November 30. Not much of a move: After I was done, the house contained nothing but a desk, a desk chair, lots of books, a brand-new king-size bed, and a half-empty bottle of low-cal salad dressing in the refrigerator. It was furnished well enough for me to crash there after a day of filming and occasionally to induce some young lady to spend the night. (I'd always had my share of successes with the opposite sex. Thanks to *U.N.C.L.E.,* my rate was about to skyrocket.)

The pilot was called "The Vulcan Affair." If you watch it today (though I can't imagine why you would), you'll see a somewhat creaky vehicle of the early 1960s. By comparison to TV dramas or motion pictures of today, the pace is slow, the special effects are rudimentary, and the story is simplistic. The pilot also used an implausible plot device — having an average housewife and mom (played by actress Patricia Crowley) get drawn into a spy caper, helping Solo conquer evil before being returned safe and sound to her life in suburbia. This gimmick (originally inspired by Hitchcock's *North by Northwest,* where Madison Avenue ad exec Cary Grant is mistaken for a spy) was supposed to be a regular feature of the show, giving viewers a different character every week with whom they could identify. Thankfully, it was dropped after a few episodes.

But however dated and clunky "The Vulcan Affair" might appear today, in its own day it worked. NBC tested the pilot in small theaters around Los Angeles, administering questionnaires about the show and even monitoring audience reactions live via fingertip sensor devices that measured pulse and skin responses, lie-detector style. The feedback was good. Thirty-four percent rated the pilot "excellent," with females showing the highest interest. A respectable 29 percent of those surveyed said they'd watch the show rather than its two expected prime-time competitors, *The Red Skelton Hour* and *McHale's Navy,* and a full 59 percent said *U.N.C.L.E.* could become their favorite TV show. Not bad for an unknown quantity up against two established hits.[*] NBC gave *U.N.C.L.E.* the green light, and we began shooting the series on June 1, 1964.

Before we did, though, a major change in the cast took place. It's another story that illustrates the weird vagaries of life in Hollywood.

Shortly after the pilot had been completed, Norman Felton got a call from an NBC executive. The executive told Norman, "The pilot's good. But you gotta get rid of one of the actors. What's his name . . . ? Ahh, I can't remember. Something with a K, I think."

Norman pondered. "You mean Kuluva?" he asked, referring to Will Kuluva in the role of Mr. Allison, head of U.N.C.L.E.

* I knew none of the above until a young Iowa fan of the show named Jon Heitland published *The Man from U.N.C.L.E.* book in 1987.

"Yeah, that's the guy. We don't like him. Find somebody else."

Felton dutifully canned poor Will and seized the opportunity to add a genuinely classy Hollywood star to the cast — Leo G. Carroll, who'd appeared on the stage in London and New York and acted in pictures since the 1930s. Leo had played a role not unlike the head of U.N.C.L.E. in *North by Northwest,* that of the FBI agent who masterminds the plot in which Cary Grant becomes enmeshed. Now he was hired to replace Will Kuluva in the newly named role of Mr. Waverly.

The irony is that Will Kuluva was never supposed to be fired at all. The NBC executive was actually trying to recall the name of David McCallum's character, Kuryakin. It was that "Russian guy with the long hair" that NBC wanted canned, not Kuluva.

Which explains the NBC executive's surprise when Norman later informed him that he'd hired the seventy-one-year-old Leo G. Carroll to fill the role. "Geez, isn't he too old for the part?" was the understandable response. The confusion was cleared up, but by now it was too late. The *U.N.C.L.E.* cast would include both David McCallum and Leo G. Carroll.

And a damned good thing, too.

Me, aged six, at a Chicago train station on the same trip in the summer of 1939 when I performed for John Barrymore.

Author Collection

My mother played Lucy Seward in Dracula *when it debuted at Broadway's Royale Theatre on April 13, 1931.*

Author Collection

My father, Walter Vaughn, and me at age twelve, taken at Brooks Brothers, New York, in 1944.

Author Collection

My stepfather, John Ladd Connor, in the mid-forties.

Author Collection

In 1945 my mother and stepfather both had roles in the play Ramshackle Inn, *which starred Zasu Pitts (second from left), John Ladd Connor (third from left), and our future first lady, Nancy Davis Reagan (far right).*

Author Collection

Peggy Silbert and me at our senior prom in June 1950, North High, Minneapolis, Minnesota.

Author Collection

This photo was taken the week after the fatal car accident that took James Dean's life on September 30, 1955. Like many young actors who respected his work, I hoped to fill the place suddenly left open by his death.

Author Collection

Appearing as Hamlet at Los Angeles State College in the fall of 1960. The Los Angeles Times *compared me favorably with the Old Vic's John Neville. I also paid homage to John Barrymore's stunningly acclaimed Hamlet in 1922 on Broadway.*

Courtesy of Stuart Nisbet, Author Collection

U.N.C.L.E.'s *popularity helped to put me on the cov-*
ers of more than a few magazines, which often
compared my role as Napoleon Solo to Sean Con-
nery's James Bond.
Author Collection

The episodes of the first season established the elements of the series: Solo, often accompanied by Illya, would be sent by Alexander Waverly to deal with a problem somewhere in the world. I would be helped by an ordinary person who would play a crucial role in the resolution of the problem. Villains were unique, the plots were clever, bordering on brilliantly imaginative. Our first year guest stars were or about to be TV audience favorites: June Lockhart as a teacher in "The Dove Affair;" Barbara Feldon (later to star in the NBC *U.N.C.L.E.* send-up, *Get Smart*) had her chance to live the life of a spy instead of a clerk in "The Never Never Affair." All the individual shows throughout the four-year run had the word "Affair" in the title of the one-hour segments.

Every episode of *U.N.C.L.E.* was crafted according to a formula. There would be an opening scene or two to serve as a teaser, often involving an ambush or attack by one of the nefarious agents of T.H.R.U.S.H. Then Illya and I would be shown strolling into a nondescript tailor shop on a side street near the United Nations building in New York. The mustachioed Italian tailor would tap twice on the handle of his pressing machine, opening up the back wall of the shop and revealing the hidden entrance

255

to U.N.C.L.E. headquarters.

Once Illya and I were inside the ultra-secret, high-tech lair (which in 1964 meant the presence of fake wall-size computers replete with spinning reels of magnetic tape and banks of meaningless, randomly flashing lights), a pretty girl at the front desk would offer us our triangular coded ID cards along with a flirtatious glance or two. Then Mr. Waverly, our avuncular, pipe-smoking boss, would give us our assignment, at which point the show really started.

The sequences that followed depicted Illya and me (usually operating separately until the last few scenes) engaged in derring-do and battling villains in exotic locales around the globe. During my *U.N.C.L.E.* years, people would often congratulate me on being able to travel around the world to film the show. They had no idea that all our international scenes were shot at the MGM studios within five minutes' walking distance of our dressing room. Lot 2 contained gigantic standing sets for every major world capital — London, Paris, Rome, Prague — while Lot 3 featured a jungle (where some of the Johnny Weissmuller *Tarzan* pictures had been shot), a lake (where the Mississippi River scenes for the musical *Showboat* had been filmed), and many other backdrops. We took full advantage of all of them, giving *U.N.C.L.E.* a cosmopolitan look that was very convincing and totally fake.

There were other common threads from show to show. There would usually be some kind of chase in the final scenes. David (I mean Illya) and I took turns driving — cars, sometimes motorcycles, even helicopters. At some point during the second act, the two of us would talk on our pen phones after uttering the magic instructions, "Open channel D." The props and special effects were incredibly simple, especially by today's standards. Bob Murdock, our prop master, prided himself on his ability to improvise a high-tech gadget that looked as if it cost thousands of dollars for just a few bucks. A cigar box covered with silver paper became "a three-meter range cyanide bomb." A rigged-up pipe with steam pumped through it turned an ordinary helicopter into a "rocket-firing helicopter."

Marketing considerations actually dictated some of our prop designs. Ideal Toys disliked the original look of the "*U.N.C.L.E.* gun," which was supposed to be a specially modified German Mauser pistol. They came up with their own design, which I understand made a mint at the toy stores during the

Christmas season.

When it debuted on a Tuesday night in the fall of 1964, *U.N.C.L.E.* was not an immediate hit. The first several episodes ranked near the bottom in the Nielsen ratings. (Despite what the pilot audiences had said, people were tuning in to Red Skelton and Ernest Borgnine instead.) In today's ultra-competitive media climate, the show would probably have been canceled. But we were given three months to find our audience.

In its original time slot opposite the powerhouse CBS offering *The Red Skelton Hour, U.N.C.L.E.* gathered an 8.3 Nielsen rating, which meant only 13 percent of the audience was tuning in. For the 1964–65 season, *Skelton* ranked sixth in the top ten shows watched by the American TV audience. Ironically, in the 1965–66 season, when *U.N.C.L.E.* had risen from the near dead, I was asked to guest twice on Red's show, including once with Joyce Jameson. By the end of 1964, we were ranked fiftieth overall. At that point in time, we were not on the 1965–66 NBC schedule. In December of 1964, the show was moved to eight o'clock on Monday nights. Even in the new slot, the rating was 14.1, which, in effect, meant it would be canceled.

But during October and November, college students began to discover the show. They got into the habit of watching it in dormitory lounges, bars, and frat houses around campus. Unfortunately, there are no Nielsen ratings boxes in these locations. But when the same students came home for the Christmas holiday break, they tuned their home TVs to *U.N.C.L.E.,* and suddenly the show's ranking shot up into the twenties. *Life* magazine's TV reviewer Scott Leavit credited this word-of-mouth promotion with saving the series from cancelation. These people in turn encouraged their friends to watch the show and the ratings began to climb.

The period from the airing of the last show of the first season through that season's summer reruns was the critical period for *U.N.C.L.E.* Those reruns produced a momentum that saw *U.N.C.L.E.* become for the week of October 18, 1965, the number one Nielsen-rated show in the country, edging out *Bonanza, The Dick Van Dyke Show, The Smothers Brothers Show,* and *Bewitched.* The show had climbed from fiftieth place to thirteenth place in the overall Nielsen with 24 percent of the audience, or twice the viewers it had at the beginning of the first season — a remarkable rise unparalleled in TV history at that time.

The surge was facilitated by a publicity tour for "Napoleon and Illya" orchestrated by my good friend, the late Chuck Painter, who took over as the show's publicist. Somewhere in the autumn, we three, Painter, David and I, set out from MGM every Friday and hit three Nielsen cities in two days, winding up in New York Sunday night and hopping the last flight back to L.A. and starting work at 7:45 A.M. Monday morning. When the tours began, the show was gathering a 17.4 rating. After these weekend tours in New Orleans, Dallas, St. Louis, Houston, San Francisco, Milwaukee, Chicago, Cleveland, etc. — twenty-four cities, and two thousand miles in all — the show's rating rose to 20, the magical threshold for survival.

Next, the national magazines began to run articles on the show. *Time, Newsweek, The Saturday Evening Post, TV Guide* — each ran an article on the fan reaction, calling the show's followers "The Mystic Cult of Millions."

Chuck Painter would move to Rome, became fluent in Italian, and do publicity for many features shot in Europe. He was later replaced by MGM publicist John Rothwell. By the time John came on board, the TV show and its two-hour feature spin-offs were shown all over Asia, Europe, the Philippines, Australia, etc. *One of Our Spies Is Missing,* a two-hour feature film cobbled together from TV's Parts 1 and 2 of "The Bridge of Lions Affair," set new house records at the Ritz Movie Theatre in Leicester Square, London.

Our secret weapon in the ratings war was David McCallum. Despite his tiny role in the original pilot (he was on screen for less than five minutes), America's ten- and twelve-year-old girls took notice. They began writing letters to MGM and NBC declaring their love for the Russian agent with the mop of blond hair. He was handsome, aloof, and a trifle mysterious — the epitome of cool. (It didn't hurt that David is also a fine actor with a remarkable degree of charm that viewers of every age and both sexes could appreciate.)

The producers of *U.N.C.L.E.* weren't stupid. They responded by expanding David's role, giving him greater prominence in the scripts, and ultimately making him my full-fledged costar.

With their love of trumped-up controversies, the tabloids of the day liked to depict me and David as locked in a bitter competition over fame and fans. Actually we got along famously. David was very sensitive about *not* being seen as displacing me or competing with me. So, for example, whenever we posed for publicity photos, David always let me stand on his right, traditionally considered the more prominent position, even after he'd achieved total parity with me in the eyes of the public. That's typical of David's thoughtful, unassuming character. We're good friends to this day.

Of course, Leo G. Carroll was the real class of *U.N.C.L.E.*. He was the sweetest, loveliest man I ever met. He told me that he was much older than the studio thought. And he was actually rather infirm, although a couple of times in the course of the series he did action scenes where he would use karate. Poor old Leo was hooked up to a catheter and had a plastic bag inside his trouser to catch his urine. One day we were out on Lot 2, and David heard Leo ask for directions to the nearest men's room. As Leo started walking, David said, "You don't have to walk, Leo. We'll get you a car." (There were little vans constantly whizzing around the studio lots.) Leo just kept on walking, calling back over his shoulder, "It doesn't matter, I'll be done by the time I get there." That was typical of Leo's wry, self-effacing sense of humor. His favorite spot when he wasn't working was the Hollywood library. He often said to me, with a sigh, "So many classics I have not yet read." Hitchcock considered Leo the finest film actor he'd ever worked with.

Through the fall of 1965 and after the winter holidays, personal appearances by Napoleon and Illya started to take on mob proportions. David was attacked by teenyboppers in Baton Rouge, Louisiana; Springfield, Illinois; Dallas, Texas; at Macy's in New York City; and in a host of other cities.

I first noticed that something was up when, in November 1965, I attended *The Royal Hunt of the Sun* at New York's ANTA Theatre. As I walked down the aisle with my ticket stub in my hand, I heard the sound of scattered clapping. When I got to my row, the clapping increased. I glanced around, and, to my astonishment, I realized that people were pointing at me as they applauded.

By the time I was seated, it seemed as if half the people in the orchestra seats were standing, clapping, and talking about Robert Vaughn, Napoleon Solo, and *U.N.C.L.E.*

It was then that I realized that our show was a genuine hit.

We began attracting first-class movie and TV performers to play guest-starring roles

— everyone from Joan Crawford, Rip Torn, and Vincent Price to Vera Miles, Broderick Crawford, and Sonny and Cher. We also drew fine actors whose greatest fame was still to come — Carroll O'Connor before *All in the Family,* Joan Collins before *Dynasty,* and William Shatner and Leonard Nimoy appearing together for the first time before *Star Trek.* A ten-year-old Kurt Russell appeared on the show, as well as two Miss Americas (Lee Ann Meriwether and Mary Ann Mobley) and, for good measure, the Bride of Frankenstein (Elsa Lanchester).

On the first season of the show, a pattern was established whereby we would have two leading ladies on the show each week — one for Illya, one for Napoleon. Since I was *The* Man from U.N.C.L.E., I felt it was incumbent upon me to be a gracious host to our leading ladies, so I arranged to have flowers sent to both dressing rooms. But none of the girls ever thanked me, so after about four shows I stopped bothering.

By the way, you might assume that having a parade of lovely starlets through our set might bring additional — ahem — "benefits" to a leading man. That didn't happen as often as one might think — or as often as jealous boyfriends believed.

For example, Judy Carne (later to achieve

great fame on *Laugh-In*) was a guest star on the third episode in our first season. I hadn't known her before, but she was very funny and cute, and I was always attracted to funny, cute girls.

One night after filming, Judy invited me to dinner, but feeling a little bushed, I begged off, saying, "No, I can't, I'm going home." But instead I went to the Aware Inn, an organic restaurant on Ventura Boulevard in the Valley where I liked to eat. They had reading lights at the tables so I could read magazines and newspapers while I ate dinner.

Well, while I was eating, I saw Judy come in. We both laughed, and I invited her to join me. I think she was separated at the time from her husband, Burt Reynolds, who, like Judy, had his greatest fame ahead of him.

Sure enough, Burt came in and spotted us together. He marched over and confronted me, accusing me, in effect, of having an affair with Judy.

I denied any such involvement. "As a matter of fact," I protested, "I didn't even want to have dinner with her." Judy laughed, and I laughed. But Burt did not.

I called over the owner of the restaurant. "Al, please bring another chair. Our friend

Burt is going to join us for dinner." But Burt took Judy and hustled her out the door.

The next day at work she apologized for the scene. Of course, no apologies were necessary — except perhaps one from Burt to Judy.

Another time, the lovely young actress Sharon Ferrell guest-starred on *U.N.C.L.E.* One day, I dropped her off at her home in Hollywood and she invited me in for a minute. When she excused herself to fix a couple of drinks, the front door flew open and there was Vince Edwards. "Sharon is my girlfriend!" he yelled, and marched into the room where Sharon had gone, slamming the door behind. As the two of them began yelling at each other, I decided that discretion was the better part of valor and quietly sneaked out.

For a decade, I'd been off the attendee lists for the young A-list Hollywood parties. Those earlier invites I'd had had been the result of my summer of '56 romance with Natalie Wood.

By 1966, my most steady girlfriend was Patricia Kennedy Lawford, by then the *former* Mrs. Peter Lawford. Pat was on all of the adult A-list invitations, and I was her date *cum* driver. Pat did not like to drive because she was afraid of besmirching the family's name with a DUI. (In 1966 the Kennedys still had a name capable of being besmirched by such an escapade.) So whenever we were in L.A. at the same time, I would pick Pat up at the Santa Monica home of Roger Edens, one of the great Hollywood composers and arrangers, and we were off to a party.

The same couples always seemed to be in attendance: Mr. and Mrs. Kirk Douglas, Mr. and Mrs. Fred Brisson (Rosalind Russell), Mr. and Mrs. Gregory Peck, Mr. and Mrs. Bob Brandt (Janet Leigh), and many more. Also in this crowd was Ruth Berle — Milton's wife — who was a staunch Democrat and Kennedy-family admirer. Milton called her "The Sergeant," and although Ruth had served in the Women's Army Corps during World War II, Milty's nickname for her was more of a comment on her personality than a tribute to her military career. She was one tough lady, and Pat loved her.

Fairly often, rather than driving back to Edens's house at the end of the evening, I'd drop Pat off at the Berles' home in Beverly Hills. On one occasion, after some post-party drinking at La Scala and some post-closing-time drinks as the guest of Manny, the restaurant's maître d', we went to the

Berle residence for a nightcap. After quite a few caps, Pat retired to the guest room, and Ruth urged me to stay: "Milton's out of town for a week — why don't you sleep in his room, and we'll have an early brunch when Pat awakens?"

I agreed, and stretched out on the king-size Berle bed. But after a few minutes, my eyes opened and on the booze-blurred ceiling I saw the hazy words: *U.N.C.L.E.* MAN FOUND IN UNCLE MILTIE'S BED WHILE COMIC IS AWAY.

I hopped up, paid my respects to the missus, and vamoosed. A wise judgment call by my subconscious alter ego.

One more word about Milton Berle. He and Mickey Rooney were alleged to have the two largest male members in Hollywood. But which one was the champ? According to legend, Mickey claimed the honor for years, repeatedly challenging Milton to a public face-off (although that's not quite the right word). Miltie always refused, until finally, one day, he agreed, with this proviso: "I'm only going to show enough to win." That was enough to end the competition forever.

Just as the rise of *U.N.C.L.E.* attracted guest stars to our show, so David and I, in our first flush of fame, were invited to make any number of guest appearances on other TV shows. I appeared on a Jimmy Durante special with a "Jimmy visits the arts" theme, where I recited Hamlet's "Oh, what a rogue" soliloquy and was billed above the brilliant dancer Rudolf Nureyev. I was on *Red Skelton* (twice), the *Today* show alongside Leo G. Carroll, and an ABC special with Phyllis Diller. David and I separately hosted the NBC music program *Hullabaloo,* on which I sang the Herman's Hermits hits "Mrs. Brown, You've Got a Lovely Daughter," "I Want a Girl (Just Like the Girl)," and "Second-Hand Rose," backed up by — wait for it — the Supremes. By any reasonable measure it was the low point of my career — and was it fun!

The *U.N.C.L.E.* days were, for me, the kind of experience most actors dream about but rarely experience.

At the height of the craze, David and I were receiving some seventy thousand fan letters every month — more than Clark Gable at the height of his fame. Two-part *U.N.C.L.E.* episodes released as theatrical movies in Europe, Asia, and Latin America did better at the box office than the James Bond pictures. Twenty-three original novels based on the *U.N.C.L.E.* characters were published (more than for any other TV series other than *Star Trek*) and sold by the boatload. When I visited the United Nations, African chieftains stopped me to ask for autographs. When David and I toured England, Scandinavia, the Philippines, Australia, Hong Kong, and Japan, we were treated more like rock stars than TV actors, complete with police-escorted motorcades from airports to downtown appearances. When I visited Finland on my way to Russia, children lined up for miles alongside the train tracks, waving and offering presents.

David and I — especially David — became favorites of the teenage fan magazines. Although we were both in our thirties, we were targets of the love fantasies of millions of readers of *Sixteen, Teen,* and *Tiger Beat,* and nearly every issue in 1965 and 1966 contained at least one article about the latest doings of "David" (no last name required).

By contrast, the adult magazines were more prone to retailing gossip about us, in particular speculating about my bachelor status and describing in detail what I was looking for in a wife. Many articles mentioned that I was actively seeking a "Jackie Kennedy" to solidify my plans to run for president. (Yes, of the United States of

America.)

Parodies and spoofs of *The Man from U.N.C.L.E.* proliferated. *Mad* magazine ran *The Man from A.U.N.T.I.E.*, and a Bob Hope TV special featured a similarly titled sketch. In the comics, Archie's friend Jughead appeared as *The Man from R.I.V.E.R.D.A.L.E.*, and an MGM Tom and Jerry cartoon was titled *The Mouse from H.U.N.G.E.R.* Spoofs of *U.N.C.L.E.* appeared on *The Addams Family, I Dream of Jeannie, My Favorite Martian, Get Smart, The Dick Van Dyke Show,* and *The Avengers.* I even got into the act, appearing in an uncredited cameo as Napoleon Solo in the movie *The Glass Bottom Boat,* with Doris Day. (Incidentally, I found Doris to be the sexiest star I ever worked with. Truly!)

As you can imagine, *U.N.C.L.E.* merchandise flooded the toy shops. Unfortunately, David and I didn't benefit from it. Our contracts supposedly gave us five percent of any merchandising revenues, but for some reason neither we nor our agents ever pursued the money. Only years later did we realize how much money we'd lost, especially when fans sent us all manner of weird *U.N.C.L.E.* souvenirs to autograph, things we'd never even seen before, from lunch boxes, games, baseballs, and aprons to two

271

life-size cutouts of me that some collector dug up God knows where.

As the show's popularity crested, millions of fans requested *U.N.C.L.E* identification cards. In Great Britain, MGM had to hire eight full-time employees to fill orders for the cards. When Vice President Hubert Humphrey and I cohosted the St. Paul Winter Carnival one year, one of the Secret Service agents protecting him sidled up to me and asked, sotto voce, if I could supply enough *U.N.C.L.E.* ID cards for the entire entourage. Many fans, assuming that the *U.N.* stood for United Nations, wrote to the international organization to ask for information about *U.N.C.L.E.* or to apply for jobs as secret agents.

A few of our fans wanted to offer us more intimate services. When riding in open cars, I often found myself bombarded with house and apartment keys labeled with the addresses of the adoring girls who lived behind those doors. At the end of our first season, I had to put up a very large (and expensive) electric fence around the grounds of Tolemac, my Mulholland Drive abode, to keep out the girls. But somehow they found new ways to get in, often surprising me with their shrieks and squeals as I breakfasted or showered. Finally I tried using recorded animal noises — fierce-sounding growls, barks, and howls — to fend off my visitors, but I never really figured out how to operate the sound system, sometimes setting it off in the middle of the night and annoying the neighbors. (My son, Cassidy, calls me technologically challenged.)

There's no doubt about it, being besieged by *U.N.C.L.E* fans was a terrible nuisance. And I loved every minute.

EIGHT:
SPEAKING OUT: WAR, PEACE, AND AN ACTOR'S VOICE

The time is out of joint; O cursed spite,
That ever I was born to set it right!

While relaxing in my MGM dressing room on a very warm summer afternoon in 1964, I came across an article in the *Los Angeles Times* stating that the United States Congress had passed the Tonkin Gulf Resolution.

It was an ominous piece of news, though few people recognized it at the time. In effect, this legislation gave Lyndon Johnson carte blanche to escalate a war that would cost the world's most powerful nation its aura of invincibility, without the legal or political complications of a declaration of war. It was shepherded through the Senate by Senator J. William Fulbright, Chairman of the Senate Foreign Relations Committee, who would later become a bitter critic of the Vietnam War — just one of the many ironies that would emerge in the tumultuous years of the late 1960s.

For a while, the resolution had few obvious results. Johnson ran for president against Republican Barry Goldwater on a peace platform (another irony), branding Goldwater a dangerous warmonger and promising "not to send American boys to do a job that Asian boys ought to be doing." But the Vietnam time bomb was ticking, and after Johnson won in a landslide and 1964 turned into 1965, the war began to heat up.

On February 11, 1965, the Johnson administration ordered air strikes against targets in North Vietnam in retaliation for guerrilla attacks directed by Hanoi against American military installations in South Vietnam. The first strike by Navy carrier planes at what was described as a Vietcong staging area in the southern part of North Vietnam was ordered up by LBJ after Communist guerrillas staged coordinated attacks against the U.S. installations at Pleiku in the central highlands of South Vietnam. Eight GI's were killed and 108 wounded. When the Vietcong (South Vietnam Communist guerrillas) then attacked a U.S. Army barracks in the coastal city of Quinhon, both Air Force and Navy planes, in the biggest air attack of the war, struck at coastal supply depots in the southern part of North Vietnam, for the first time expanding the war to the northern part of that divided country.

In that late winter of 1965, my mind was preoccupied with the slow crawl up the Nielsen ratings of *The Man from U.N.C.L.E.* But soon events on the world stage would find their way to the forefront of my attention. The process began in an unexpected way.

Working with me on the *U.N.C.L.E.* show was someone who would have been described by *Reader's Digest* as the most unforgettable character I've ever met. He had gone to Hamilton High School in Los Angeles with John Hackett, one of my closest friends to this day. He was also and remains a close friend of mine, and also a friend of my former acting student, and later megastar, Jack Nicholson. His name was Bill Tynan, and, among many other exploits and adventures, he once walked from Los Angeles to Mexico City. With his fiery red beard, wide-ranging knowledge of philosophy, religion, and American foreign policy, and a compelling Irish humor and wit, he rates as one of the great raconteurs I had the pleasure of having the odd jar with, ranking with such show businesses eminences as Richard Harris, Jason Robards, Rip Torn, and Ben Gazzara.

One evening on a late-night *U.N.C.L.E.* location on Lot 3 at MGM Culver City, Bill asked if I was paying attention to what was happening in Southeast Asia, or if I knew anything about the background of Vietnam vis-à-vis the French and Chinese. I said my knowledge was really limited to the French–Indo-Chinese War that had happened sometime in the mid-fifties in a place I believed was called Dien Bien Phu.

Bill then went on to explain to me the post-war history of Vietnam starting with Bao Dai, who ruled Vietnam as emperor in 1945, and then took me through Ho Chi Minh's time in Paris, and his return to lead his people in Vietnam in the expulsion of the French colonials in 1954, producing what were called the Geneva Accords. They provided for an all-Vietnamese election in 1956. The people of the country would have a chance at voting for self-government. Had the elections been held at the time of the fighting, they would have produced a victory for Ho, according to President Eisenhower's memoir, *Mandate for Change.*

According to Bill, the elections were never held due to the interference of John Foster

Dulles, secretary of state in both Eisenhower administrations. Bill concluded by saying, "We'll be in deep shit if we take on old Ho. He'll never be beaten if he and his Communist views and followers have to fight into the new millennium," then nearly thirty-five years away.

This was all virgin territory to me. My knowledge of twentieth-century geopolitics was limited to Western liberal democracy, Communism as practiced in the Soviet Union and later in China, national Socialism as formulated by Hitler in Nazi Germany, and some variant of Fascism in Spain and Italy — all with the exception of America and Britain were totalitarian regimes where power descended from above instead of from the people voicing their concerns from below. I said to Bill, "Tell me more."

And that's how it all began for me. A chance conversation with an old friend led to a quest that consumed most of my time and virtually all of my energy for nearly six years.

My natural curiosity about geopolitics sent me to the library to research the history of Vietnam and its relationship to its giant neighbor to the north, China. I also began to look more closely at how the war was being covered in the national press, in the New York and Washington papers, and in the liberal tabloids *The Nation* and *The New Republic.* I was also curious to find out what the staunchly conservative *National Review* had to say about the war. I discovered that, to Bill Buckley and his Republican brothers at that magazine, our burgeoning war in Vietnam was simply an extension of the Kennan containment policy that undergirded the Cold War since the mid-forties.

The reason articulated by Eisenhower for the Korean War, the so-called Domino Theory, was simply reactivated in Southeast Asia in the mid-sixties. That is, if one country fell to the commies, then one by one all those countries from the Philippines to Japan to Australia and ultimately to Hawaii and the West Coast of the U.S. would fall to the Red Oriental Menace. At this point in time, the Devil, who had formerly lived in the Kremlin alone, had split in two and was now also a permanent resident in Peking.

My research was not looking for an argument for the Domino Theory, but rather some historical evidence that would justify the policy beginning to be revealed to the public, now seeing American body bags on the nightly network news. My research mentors who opposed U.S. policy included, but were not limited to, French historians Franz Schurman, Jean Lacoutre, and most important, Bernard Fall, the Howard University Professor of International Relations and author of *Hell in a Very Small Place, Street Without Joy,* and *The Two Viet Nams.* These eminent historians were all very much of one mind on Vietnam. They all seemed to be saying, "Don't go there. But if you do, don't stay because tragedy looms for any country that tries to fight a counterinsurgency against Ho's guerrillas."

I found out that in 1919, Ho had endorsed Woodrow Wilson's ideal image of America, that it was the last best hope for mankind. He appealed to the Versailles Peace Conference on the basis of Wilson's principle of self-determination for all nations. In 1945, Ho used the United States Declaration of Independence for his own declaration of the end of the French colonialism. People often wonder, what if Kennedy had lived? What would he have done in Vietnam? But let's go back further to FDR, Harry S. Truman, and Ike, and their thinking on Ho. Would Franklin Roosevelt have responded favorably to Ho's request for a helping hand toward independence? Possibly, based on FDR's detestation of French colonialism.

After all, the French had not done for Vietnam what the U.S. had done for the Philippines; that is, prepare them for independence.

In 1945, Roosevelt died before the end of World War II, and Ho then wrote letters in English to engage Harry Truman in his quest for separation from the French leading to an independent Vietnam.

The OSS, forerunner of the CIA, and the State Department observers understood, as Washington did not, that the Viet Minh was a powerful nationalist movement with Ho Chi Minh as its hero.

For a brief period after 1945, there may have been a window of opportunity for Ho to become an Asian Tito — before Communism replaced Fascism as the International Political Devil. Truman, under pressure from domestic conservatives and European allies, yielded to the French interpretation of Ho's position as Red Colonialism, which must be stopped. The United States, in the fifties, truly believed, like General Electric, that what was moral and good in the eyes of America was also good for the balance of the planet. Few citizens thought otherwise. In other words, "We are the world."

The core of U.S. foreign policy then and

now is the conviction that our interests are quite consonant with those of the rest of humanity. Sometimes it's even true. But when the rest of humanity doesn't agree — as with the Vietnam War in the 1960s and '70s, and with the war in Iraq today — the results can be devastating for the United States and its people.

In 1952, after the Democrats had been in the White House for a score of years, Dwight David Eisenhower, Midwestern war hero, Republican straight shooter, was elected President of the United States. What if the new administration had chosen to let the Geneva Accords of 1954 run their stated course, holding all Vietnamese elections in 1956 with Ho winning the presidency of a united Vietnam? What if . . . ?

But that is not what happened. And four years later, JFK's new frontier got stuck with a smoldering, low-level insurgency in the south that had not yet become a civil war. Did President Kennedy put a premium on Southeast Asia as one of the world's trouble spots that needed his immediate attention? According to his alter ego, speechwriter, and biographer Ted Sorensen, no. Berlin was central, and the Soviet Union, nuclear testing, and the United Nations all took precedence over Vietnam.

As my research continued, I hoped to find an intelligent, thoughtful presentation of the arguments on behalf of the U.S. involvement. I contacted a friend in Washington, Carmela La Spada, an aide to Vice President Humphrey, and asked her to have the State Department send on to me documents justifying our presence in Vietnam. She said she would. In a few days, one ten-page document from State titled "Aggression from the North" arrived at Mulholland Drive. It was simply a rehashing of the Domino Theory and did not seem to reflect any strong reason for our Vietnam venture.

Surely, I thought, I'm missing something. But unfortunately I didn't find anything else in support of our ever-expanding war in Southeast Asia. Carmela later arranged a meet-and-greet tour for me at the famed Walter Reed Hospital in Washington. The day I spent with dozens of young men (average age nineteen) who were missing limbs and futures turned me intellectually and emotionally against the U.S. war in Vietnam.

I'd always been interested in politics. For example, I'd been an active supporter of the civil rights movement. One night in the mid-sixties, while visiting Stockholm as part of an *U.N.C.L.E.* publicity tour, I met Martin Luther King Jr. in his suite in the Grand Hotel. In fact, I cured him of hiccups using an old Minneapolis remedy: blow all your wind out, inhale as much as you can, and then swallow until you can't hold your breath any longer. Shortly after, Andy Young and Harry Belafonte, who had invited me to join their group after MLK had spoken that evening, explained to me how to use the "civil rights crouch" when people are out to hit you in the head. I don't know why they explained this to me, and I just as quickly forgot about it — until a later date when, as you'll see, it came in handy.

(My connection with Dr. King was revived under the auspices of the antiwar movement in the spring of 1967, when I had the honor of introducing Dr. King as the principal speaker at *The Nation*'s luncheon in Los Angeles. Against the wishes of many of his followers, he articulated again his clear opposition to the U.S. involvement in the Vietnam War.)

So getting involved in politics was not unprecedented for me. But taking a strong anti-establishment role — especially with my newfound celebrity status, thanks to *U.N.C.L.E.* — that was something new.

On January 29, 1966, in Indianapolis, I had my first opportunity to express publicly my disengagement with LBJ and his Democratic Party — the party I'd supported for as long as I'd been able to vote. The occasion was an address I'd been asked to make at the annual dinner in honor of Franklin D. Roosevelt and John F. Kennedy given by the Young Democrats of Marion County, Indiana. Traditionally, the principal speaker at such an event would deliver a stemwinder supporting the current leader of the national party — in this case, President Johnson. I'm sure that everyone in attendance assumed I would give such a speech, advocating Johnson's renomination and election in 1968. Instead, I came out foursquare against Johnson and his war.

In my speech, I said, among other things, "The war in Vietnam must end, because if it continues and expands, it will surely and eventually conclude with man's final solution to man: death of the human race." I went on to say, The hawks "point immediately to the misguided illegality of burning draft cards — or, in truly tragic cases — the burning of self, and fail to understand the reasons behind these protests . . . and shout these acts down as those of Communists and cowards. But they cannot shout down the thousands who burn nothing . . . but march in silent anguish to protest burning."

Reaction was stunned silence followed by a smattering of applause from the centrist regular Democrats who had gotten something so different from what they had bargained for.

A UPI story about my speech noted, "He believed the 'killing must stop' in favor of negotiations for free elections that the Vietnamese were promised at Geneva in 1954 but never experienced. He said we must gamble that our viewpoint will prevail in a free election, but if we lose, '. . . then we must learn to live with that [Communist] government . . .' as we have with others in various parts of the world." (I had the only copy of my remarks, so any quotations that appeared were mere paraphrases, not always accurate.)

The UPI story continued, "One veteran Democratic official said Vaughn's speech 'was just terrible. It sounded as if someone on the staff of the *Daily Worker* [the American Communist newspaper] wrote it. . . .' [But] a young party leader who declined to be identified thought 'it was a beautifully presented speech. Only deadheads resented it. Vaughn voiced the sentiments of a lot of people who are afraid to say what they think.' "

I received a mixed but largely negative reaction from the Indiana press, including both those who were there and those who were not there.

National and international reaction followed my return to MGM on Monday, January 31. A battery of lawyers from MGM, NBC, sponsors of *U.N.C.L.E.,* and others with a financial interest in my show-business career requested copies of my remarks; they were provided to those who requested them, made by me on an old-fashioned copying machine in my MGM office. Reuters was among the news organizations that requested a copy.

At that time, with the antiwar movement in its infancy, such a forthright peace message was rare and startling. My speech received more than its share of attention.

Senators Vance Hartke (Indiana), Wayne Morse (Oregon), and Ernest Gruening (Alaska) placed the speech in the *Congressional Record,* along with the chairman of the Foreign Relations Committee, J. William Fulbright. Morse and Gruening had been the only senators to vote against the Tonkin Gulf Resolution in 1964. My newly hired secretary, Patricia Manning (a Vivien Leigh lookalike), was besieged with requests for me to give speeches and participate in debates throughout the U.S. and Europe.

In February 1966, a month after my remarks in Indiana, Senator Morse was an overnight guest at my Mulholland Drive home. He explained to my Sunday-morning breakfast invitees that shortly before President Kennedy had left for Dallas on his fateful trip in November 1963, he had had a meeting with Morse regarding the future involvement of the U.S. in what Morse described as the civil war in Vietnam. Kennedy assured him that when he returned from Texas, the obligation we had to the South Vietnamese forces would be at the top of his foreign policy agenda. It was Morse's belief that Kennedy wanted out, if possible before the 1964 election.

There was one other bit of fallout from my Indianapolis speech, one with a curious connection back to my show-business roots. Sometime that spring, I got a message saying that Nancy Reagan would like to meet me for lunch. I hadn't seen her in more than twenty years, since the time we'd met during the tour of *Ramshackle Inn,* when she was an aspiring actress fresh from Smith College.

I wasn't sure why Nancy wanted to see me now, but I remembered that, just before my speech in Indianapolis, I'd appeared at a press conference. One of the questions was about the possibility that actor Ronald Reagan might run for governor of California against the incumbent, Pat Brown. Although the reporter's tone was sarcastic, I responded seriously, "Not only is Reagan going to run, but he has an excellent chance of winning." The room rocked with guffaws at my prediction.

Nancy and I enjoyed a nice lunch at the MGM commissary, and after some small talk, she came to the point. "From what I've been reading, I'm sure that you and Ron are poles apart politically, especially when it comes to Vietnam. But we both want you to know how much we appreciated your remarks in Indianapolis concerning his political future."

"How did you happen to hear about them?" I asked. They hadn't received very much play.

"Well, as I'm sure you know, Bill Buckley is Ron's political hero and mentor. Bill's brother-in-law, Brent Bozell, told us about what you said."

I remembered Bozell. He'd dubbed me "The Man from U.N.C.L.E. (Ho, That Is)," referring to my supposed sympathies for the North Vietnamese leader.

Nancy and I didn't cross paths again until

1983, when I attended the White House premiere of *Superman III.* She greeted me warmly and recalled our lunch at MGM in startling detail, while her husband was his usual vague and charming self. Nancy was her husband's wisest adviser and, I've always believed, his greatest asset.

In early March 1966, I received a phone call inviting me to meet with Sy Casady, president of the California Democratic Council (CDC), the Democratic Party's liberal wing, based mainly in Northern California. Casady had read my speech in the *Congressional Record* and asked me to give the keynote speech in Bakersfield, California, on March 15. A future senator from California, Alan Cranston, led a walkout prior to my speech protesting CDC policy of opposing U.S. involvement in Vietnam.

And then another key figure in the antiwar movement showed up at my doorstep. It was Allard Lowenstein.

An owlish intellectual and a gifted orator, Lowenstein was a Democratic activist whom I'd met for the first time in the spring of 1965, when I was doing *Hamlet* at the Pasadena Playhouse. Marcie Borie was then a fan magazine writer for *Photoplay* and *Modern Screen,* the two class operations in the motion picture press. She interviewed me a couple of times in connection with *U.N.C.L.E.* She called me and had tickets for *Hamlet* and wanted to get a couple of additional tickets. She wanted to bring along a man she'd known since college — someone she considered the most intelligent person and the best public speaker she'd ever heard. This was Al Lowenstein.

We all had a little supper after the show. There were three or four young guys with Al — he always had guys hanging around with him and driving him places (he didn't like to drive). After everyone said good-bye, I took Marcie aside and said, "I don't know which of the guys was the one you mentioned on the phone." She said, "It was the guy with the thick glasses. And the reason he was so quiet was that he'd never seen *Hamlet* before and he was so impressed that he was tongue-tied." In retrospect, this is pretty amazing because the Allard Lowenstein I knew was never tongue-tied about anything, whether speaking with Robert Kennedy or before the United Nations.

At the time, Lowenstein was a relatively obscure figure, but ultimately he would receive the credit he deserved for his remarkable political accomplishments. As author David Halberstam later characterized him, Allard Lowenstein, "the man who ran against Lyndon Johnson," would be the only real political hero of that terrible year, 1968.

A New York lawyer, the thirty-nine-year-old Lowenstein was a veteran of such liberal causes as the struggle against South African apartheid and the civil rights movement in the American South. He was a tireless organizer, a charismatic leader, and an eloquent speaker. Recent biographers have claimed that he was somehow affiliated with the CIA, which had in fact helped to fund the American student movement during the 1950s. But this had yet to surface in the mid-sixties.

By 1966, Lowenstein's focus had shifted to the Vietnam War, which he feared would destroy Johnson's social programs (the "Great Society") and alienate America's young people from the causes of liberalism and the Democratic Party. Working with Curtis Gans, a staffer for the liberal Americans for Democratic Action (ADA), Lowenstein drafted a paper calling for a gradual U.S. withdrawal and a negotiated peace settlement in Vietnam. The two spent the autumn of 1967 traveling to thirty-four states, speaking to student groups and political leaders about the need to "dump"

Johnson.

Lowenstein told me about his seemingly hopeless quest to unseat Lyndon Johnson in the den of my Mulholland home in the spring of 1966. He'd read my Indianapolis speech, and he wanted to know if I would be part of the "Dump Johnson" movement he was creating, serving as, in his words, "the high-profile Hollywood figure to get heard on all the talk shows."

I said with a chuckle, "I'd heard you were a political nymphomaniac, but this time you may have gone too far, considering who Lyndon Johnson is, how huge a margin he won by in 1964, and so on."

Lowenstein didn't catch, or chose to ignore, my attempt at humor. Instead, he said, "Well, I am kind of intense about politics. But this is the time to be intense, with what's happening in Southeast Asia." So I signed on, and from then on we were in constant contact. Al made it clear before he left my house that day that his first choice was Robert F. Kennedy. If Bobby refused Lowenstein's summons, he would approach other politicians. His preference would be for a Democrat, but he was willing to support an appropriate Republican if necessary.

In June, I was named National Chairman

of Dissenting Democrats. By year's end, the group had 160,000 members in more than twenty states and was tactically aligned with thousands of other Democrats throughout the country. (My oldest surviving high school friend, Bill Smith, put his teaching career on the line by heading up the Minnesota chapter of Dissenting Democrats before the antiwar position was acceptable in the political mainstream.) The press covered my activities with interest, repeatedly noting that I was the first prominent actor to publicly oppose the war in the Vietnam.

It was around this time that the FBI began to follow my activities. My 140-page file, which I obtained many years later through the use of the Freedom of Information Act, begins in May 1966, with a clipping from the Hollywood newspaper *Daily Variety* describing my interest in visiting Peking. It includes such items as this one:

A review of the Los Angeles files reveals an individual, who declined to furnish any name telephonically, advised the F.B.I. office at Los Angeles on July 6, 1966, that Robert Vaughn had recently appeared on the Merv Griffin TV show. Vaughn is the star from *The Man from U.N.C.L.E.* series and told about his recent trip to the Soviet Union, and called it "the most rewarding experience I have ever had." According to Vaughn, while he was in the U.S.S.R., a number of persons came up to him, embraced him, and said they hoped their children and our children would live in peace together. The person who furnished this information to the Los Angeles Division of the F.B.I. would not furnish any name and declined to elaborate.

Does it seem a little odd to you that the FBI would be taking calls from "informants" describing the contents of publicly broadcast television programs as if they were state secrets? It does to me.

A little over a year later, the Los Angeles chapter of the FBI was informed that the national office of the Bureau

has observed for some time that Vaughn, a well-known television actor and star of the television program *Man from U.N.C.L.E.,* has actively supported and participated as a speaker in various demonstrations and programs protesting U.S. involvement in Vietnam. In this regard, he has had the opportunity to associate and work with individuals who are a part of the

Communist movement and who are extensively engaged in protesting U.S. policy in Vietnam.

As a result of his activities and in view of his prominence as a nationally known television actor, you are instructed to promptly prepare and submit a report on Vaughn along with your recommendation concerning his inclusion in the Security or Reserve Index, if warranted. Your investigation should be limited to a review of your indices and contacts with logical confidential informants and established sources only in order to determine the extent of subject's involvement, if any, with the Communist movement. No additional active investigation is to be conducted in this matter without prior Bureau authority.

It's interesting to see what happens in this country in time of war. Notice that I was regarded as suspect, and as possibly in league with "the Communist movement," for no other reason than that I opposed the war in Vietnam — a position I shared with many U.S. Senators and countless fellow citizens, and which I was, of course, completely within my rights to take.

I received many death threats, such as a letter warning, "Come to Chicago and you'll leave in a cement overcoat." Thankfully, I was never personally attacked, indicted, persecuted, or, most important, blacklisted, which would have meant my being unable to work in the only profession I'd known since childhood.

My FBI file finally ends with this note, dated May 8, 1973:

> There is no indication to believe that Vaughn should be considered a security risk. His stated viewpoints and his current profession preclude him from any consideration for development as an informant. No additional investigation of Vaughn appears warranted and Los Angeles is placing this case in a closed status.

It took six years and who-knows-how-many thousands of taxpayer dollars for the FBI to reach this conclusion — six years during which I was speaking out on public issues in completely open forums where anyone could easily have seen exactly what I was doing and saying.

As the months rolled on and the war in Vietnam continued to worsen, the antiwar movement at home continued to grow. And as one of the more visible spokespeople for that movement, I continued to be in public demand. I appeared at many Democratic fund-raisers, and the University of Minnesota, where I had spent my freshman year in college, invited me to speak, along with UCLA, Harvard, USC, and other universities.

In January 1967, as I started on my second full year on the stump opposing publicly my government's foreign policy in Southeast Asia, I cited in my speech the following half-dozen arguments for staying in Vietnam, and tried to show why each one was wrong.

First, the legal argument: "The United States has a commitment to South Vietnam."

Secretary of State Dean Rusk had cited the SEATO Treaty, President Eisenhower's bilateral arrangements with the government of South Vietnam, and the Tonkin Gulf Resolution of 1964, among others.

In 1954, Secretary of State John Foster Dulles was invited to Manila, India, Pakistan, Ceylon, Burma, Thailand, Indonesia, and the Philippines. Vietnam was never a party to the SEATO Treaty. Britain and France also declined, refusing involvement on the grounds that there is no commitment possible under the articles of the SEATO

Treaty, and that there was no provision in that treaty for interfering in someone else's civil war.

Leading authorities on international law made the same point in a statement published by the *New York Times* of January 15, 1967, under the title, "U.S. Intervention in Vietnam Is Illegal."

The Tonkin Gulf Resolution was an act of respect to LBJ, never an authorization for a large-scale land war in Southeast Asia. President Eisenhower definitely stated that the aid he offered to President Diem on October 23, 1954, was only economic, and President Kennedy, three months before his death on September 2, 1963, said, "In the final analysis, it is their war. They're the ones who have to win it or lose it. We can give them equipment. We can send our men out there as advisors, but they have to win it, the people of Vietnam."

Argument number two, the political argument: "We must stop aggression."

The term *aggression* as usually defined in international agreements refers to one nation's unprovoked attack on another, or the imposition of one country's rule upon another by open force. In the case of Vietnam, we were not dealing with two nations at all, but one. The nation was temporarily separated into two zones, north and south, by the Geneva Accords of 1954, allowing time for regrouping to prepare for the nationwide free elections that would take place in 1956, which we, in complicity with our puppet President Diem in the south, prevented.

When we violated the Geneva agreements, sending in military assistance to back Diem, and then escalated that assistance, southern guerrillas representing 80 percent of the population formed up again to resist this latest oppression of their freedom and turned to their former leader, Ho Chi Minh, for help. When he sent that help to offset our illegal intrusion, we labeled that action "aggression."

Next, the religious argument: "We must stop godless Communism."

General William Westmoreland, Commander of the American Forces in Vietnam, alluded to the war as a latter-day Christian crusade. (Seven administrations later, George Bush would use the word *crusade* in the Iraq War, much to the delight of the Islamic terrorists.) Evangelist Billy Graham and Catholic Cardinal Spellman also joined the ranks of the "Hawks."

Senator Fulbright, describing the irony of the religious argument in 1964, said, "It has become one of the self-evident truths of the post-war era that just as the President resides in Washington and the Pope in Rome, the devil resides immutably in Moscow." Communism, whatever its spiritual limitations, was not the bastard child of Satan. It was an ideology, and an ideology cannot be killed with a gun.

Next, the strategic argument: "We must stop China."

The Rand Corporation, under contract to the United States Air Force, did an exhaustive research assignment to determine the extent of China's aggressive tendencies. To the probable irritation of the Air Force, they reported that China could not, the records showed, be accused of aggressive tendencies.

What were the critical issues that supposedly indicated that country's international aggressiveness? We usually cited the border disputes with India, Pakistan, and Burma. However, these disputes were the direct results of British colonialism, the result of Britain readjusting the territorial demarcation lines of the Chinese borders. (Our great friend in World War II, Chiang Kai-shek, openly supported mainland China on these issues.) China took back through negotiations or force what had been its for centuries, and having done so, sought no future gains and stood fast at those points.

And lastly, we cited the Communist Chinese influence in Vietnam. However, we should have recalled that Ho Chi Minh was waging his war of liberation long before China became a Communist country in 1949.

Next, the military argument: "Bombing the North will bring negotiations."

Bombing, as witnessed in Britain, in Germany, in Korea, has proven its ineffectiveness as an inducement to bringing an enemy to its knees. And we ended up dropping as much tonnage into Vietnam as we did into Europe at the peak of World War II.

In the South, it was estimated that we wounded a million Vietnamese children and killed a quarter of a million more. And despite this carnage, or maybe because of it, we only drove the enemy further and further away from the possibility of any discussion at the negotiating table. We had to recognize that the bombing did not reduce the enemy's will to fight, did not lower the morale in the North, did not reduce the flow of supplies to the South, and most certainly did not advance the cause of peace.

And last, the idealist argument: "We are fighting for freedom."

The question here is, whose freedom were we fighting for? Certainly not our own. The Vietcong constituted no threat to our territorial freedom. Neither did the Vietnamese. Who then? Not the 80 percent of the South Vietnamese people who had made it amply clear that they were not interested in the brand of freedom we offered them. We consistently failed to give them the one thing that they adamantly desired, restitution of the rights to their own land.

Whose freedom, then, were we fighting for? Air Marshal Ky (an admirer of Hitler) and his Saigon staff, with the exception of one man, were Northerners who fought with the French against their own people.

Senator Stephen Young of Ohio was of the opinion that "the only reason for our being in Vietnam today is our proud refusal to admit a mistake in our attempt to make Vietnam a pro-American and anti-Communist state."

More than anything else, we were fighting to avoid admitting failure. As Walter Lippman bluntly put it, "We are fighting to save face!"

These half-dozen reasons for our invading, fighting, and staying the course in Vietnam were fundamentally in error from the beginning because we did not understand that, for the North Vietnamese, *any* compromise was the equivalent of a defeat.

They had not fought for twenty years in order to reach a compromise. I didn't want to see the U.S. stuck in Southeast Asia for twenty years ourselves, fighting a pointless war against such a determined adversary. By 1967 neither did a large percentage of Americans. But the administration and its supporters weren't listening. So the debate raged on, eventually embroiling millions of ordinary citizens — including a few actors.

Perhaps the high point of my personal role in the antiwar movement came in 1967 when the archconservative William F. Buckley challenged me to debate him on Vietnam on *Firing Line.* It was his first year as host of the right-leaning opinion program, which would eventually become one of the longest-running programs in television history.

My friend John Hackett viewed the upcoming debate with Buckley as "the young challenger versus the old champ." I agreed with him and promptly made arrangements to go into near seclusion at St. Andrews Priory in Pear Blossom, California. I wanted to train for the event like Muhammad Ali preparing for a boxing match — or like an actor rehearsing the role of a lifetime.

I had stayed at the Priory before as the guest of Brother John Bosco. This time I asked Brother John if I could be allowed the indulgence of not speaking or being spoken to by the good monks. He agreed, and I arrived at the monastery with the collected works of Bill Buckley going back to his first published book dealing with his alma mater's relationship with the almighty, *God and Man at Yale.* I also reviewed my earlier examination of Vietnam history, adding additional information about the U.S. use of the Domino Theory vis-à-vis Vietnam and our government's other dubious reasons for interfering in this civil war.

The date for the *Firing Line* show was changed several times due to scheduling problems for Bill, until we finally settled on July 8, 1967, in Los Angeles. An earlier Constitution Hall date in Washington, D.C., was canceled at the last minute. Prior to that July date, I had agreed to speak at UCLA, USC, and Harvard, all in May 1967.

I remember Bill arriving in the studio at the last minute. He was running a little late, having just taken his son Christopher to

Disneyland. Spotting me, Buckley almost shouted in that strange mid-Atlantic accent, "How's peace?" More for my friends who were there to witness the "Great Debate" than for Bill, I semi-sang a retort, using the melody from *Carousel,* "It's busting out all over," bringing a crinkly smile to the word-smith's visage.

During that first year of *Firing Line,* Bill had his personal lawyer, C. Dickerman Williams, sitting between and upstage of Bill and his guest. His role was one of arbiter, moderator, and chairman, and he also uttered a final judgment as who had bested whom in the debate. I also noted that at Bill's left — upstage out of view of the audience — was a large button that allowed him, if he so chose, to alert Mr. Williams to step into the subject being discussed.

My researcher, Juanita Sayer, had come across a Buckley observation that I believe came from a *Harper's* piece where he said, "Some of the finest analyses of our Civil War were done by men who were not at Gettysburg." I had hoped that Bill would ask me if I'd ever been to Vietnam, allowing me to respond by quoting him. Unfortunately, it did happen, but not on camera.

In response to Bill's first question, "Is one of the reasons that a moral man can't 'rationalize Vietnam' is that the election schedule for 1956 there didn't take place?"

My three-hundred-plus-word answer seemed to have dazzled him with dates, as one viewer observed. Bill's response was that I was obviously a considerable student of the minutiae of that period.

We then continued to spar for a full hour, arguing over the historical causes of the Vietnam conflict, whether or not Americans' fear of world Communism was excessive, and whether or not U.S. interests were truly involved in this faraway war over a land with few vital resources and no obvious link to American security. Buckley drew parallels between Ho Chi Minh and Hitler, and between the Vietnam conflict and the prelude to World War II, parallels I fought against as vigorously as possible.

Along the way, Buckley quoted as many liberal Democrats as he could, hoping to embarrass me with evidence that people like John F. Kennedy, Arthur Schlesinger, and Theodore Sorensen had sometimes made statements contradicting my positions on everything from Vietnam to the Cuban missile crisis. That led to this exchange:

VAUGHN: I disagree with Mr. Schlesinger and Mr. Sorensen.

BUCKLEY: I think it's increasingly interesting how many people you do disagree
with.

VAUGHN: Yes.

BUCKLEY: And eventually maybe I can
find you disagreeing with Plato and
Aristotle, and then . . .

VAUGHN: Yes, I do. I've written a number
of papers on it, as a matter of fact.
(Laughter)

BUCKLEY: And I . . .

VAUGHN: And I'll be happy to send you
photocopies. (Laughter)

Reading the transcript all these years later
is an amazing experience. It's startling to
realize that, once upon a time, American
television viewers (at least some of them)
were willing to sit through an hour-long
debate on foreign policy that involved such
arcana as the exact significance of the 17th
Parallel, the history of the John Birch
Society, and the validity of the Geneva Accords.

C. Dickerman Williams summed up the
evening by saying:

Ladies and gentleman, tonight we've had
a conflict between a hawk and a dove.
Unfortunately, we must bring the conflict

to a close. Whose feathers were most ruffled, the hawk's or the dove's? I must leave that to you to decide. As chairman, I can't make a decision myself, I regret to say. Thank you, Mr. Vaughn. Thank you, Mr. Buckley.

Cort Casady, Sy Casady's son, and the student at Harvard who had invited me to speak there, was in the audience that evening. He remarked over drinks later, referring to a recent book written by J. William Fulbright on American foreign policy titled *The Arrogance of Power,* that said, "If for no other reason, Vaughn won the debate by the power of arrogance."

Buckley and I carried on a cordial correspondence for a number of years thereafter, and Bill appeared as a guest on my WABC radio show when I sat in for Bob Grant.

To complete my gradual entanglement in the antiwar movement, I was becoming friends, throughout 1966 and 1967, with the man who would become that movement's single most popular figure: Robert F. Kennedy.

I'd first met Bobby in the spring of 1960 in Los Angeles when he was his brother's national campaign director. He was thirty-four. I remember him as extremely reticent, both physically and vocally.

My friend and (at the time) my public relations man, Jerry Pam, who would eventually do publicity for Michael Caine, Roger Moore, Sean Connery, and others, was partnered with Bob Joseph, a consultant high up in Democratic politics in California. He was the man who introduced me to Bobby. We met, ironically, at the Ambassador Hotel on Wilshire Boulevard, where, eight years later, he would be assassinated.

We next met at USC in the fall of 1965, when I was concluding work on my Ph.D. The president of the university called and asked if I would host Bob and Ethel when they visited the campus for a speech to students and faculty.

While I was escorting Bobby to a student rally on campus, at one point the crowd seemed ready to crush the senator's car. Bobby turned to me and asked, "What would Napoleon Solo do in a case like this?"

After his remarks, RFK joined Ethel and me in the front row of the auditorium. She asked if I was going to be on the East Coast in the near future. I answered that when I finished this season of *U.N.C.L.E.,* I would be off to London and Venice to shoot a film with Elke Sommer and Boris Karloff titled *The Venetian Affair* — a *serious* spy movie. (If you are a man of a certain age, you surely remember the magnificent Elke Sommer, whom I found not only deeply attractive but also enormously bright. At the time, Elke was seeing my friend, writer Joe Hyams, who wrote *Bogie,* the definitive biography of his friend Humphrey Bogart. So Elke and I were a no-go in the romance department because of respect for my friend's feelings.)

In any case, Ethel Kennedy said, "Will you please save some time to be our guest at Hickory Hill?" That was their estate in McLean, Virginia, which had been owned briefly by JFK and Jackie. Of course I said yes.

I arrived on a Friday evening the following spring at National Airport (now Reagan) and was greeted by two station wagons filled with Kennedy children, friends, and assorted minders, sitters, etc. The children were beside themselves with excitement, particularly Joe Jr. and Kathleen, who were fifteen and seventeen respectively. The house was covered with *U.N.C.L.E.* posters inside and out, including pictures of me with my Walther P-38 at the ready.

The senator and his wife were in Mississippi making a speech and would not return until the next morning. For what remained of the day and throughout the evening I was put through the Kennedy baptism, playing numerous word games and having my mettle (or that of Napoleon Solo, since we were one and the same in the eyes of the Kennedy kids and their friends) tested in other ways.

I was given a bedroom in some kind of attic area that belonged to one of the younger Kennedy girls. Ethel had left a note saying she hoped I didn't get the bends from using the sink, which had been adapted for use by a small child.

This was the first of many visits to Hickory Hill, whose usual guests comprised a kind of Kennedy administration in exile, including Maxwell Taylor, John Glenn, Adam Walinsky, Peter Edelman, and Art Buchwald.

One of my trips to Hickory Hill happened to coincide with my first encounter with President Johnson himself.

Sometime during the months after my antiwar speech in Indianapolis, I was staying at the Madison Hotel in Washington, D.C., when I got a call from somebody representing Bess Abell, Lady Bird Johnson's social secretary. Bess was having a housewarming in Georgetown that evening and wanted to invite me.

I explained, "I'm going out to Hickory Hill to see Robert Kennedy tonight." In fact, I was planning to escort Pat Lawford that evening.

She laughed and said, "Why can't you stop by here before you go out to Hickory Hill?"

I said, "Well, I'll be in black tie."

She said, "That's all right, that won't be a problem." So I agreed to drop in.

However, when I got there, it was a Texas-style party. Everybody was in boots and Texas finery and I was the only one in black tie.

Nonetheless, I went in and was introduced around and chatted with a few people — various liberal Democrats and Lady Bird. Then I heard some mumbling behind me: "Mr. President, Mr. President." I turned around and there was LBJ, all six feet three of him in boots and a ten-gallon hat, looking closer to seven feet tall.

Someone said, "I want to introduce you to Robert Vaughn." I said, "Hello, Mr. President." He looked down at me, smiled coldly, and drawled, "Oh, yesss. You're the speech maker!" I smiled and nodded affirmatively and said nothing.

He then grabbed me and spun me around

so that I was next to him. He pulled me very close to him with an arm around my shoulders (as in all the pictures one sees of LBJ doing his thing to recalcitrant lawmakers). He put his face close to mine and said, "Well, good luck, son!" and then he flung me away into the crowd like a dishrag.

I laughed, and he didn't laugh at all. He walked away, and that was my big meeting with LBJ. A memorable one.

I met him once more — at Robert F. Kennedy's funeral.

The following morning, at "Hick Hill," I recounted my tale to Bobby, who roared with laughter, saying, "You got the LBJ lapel-to-lapel crunch and stare-down." It was one of the few light moments in my Vietnam hegira.

As you can probably tell, I deeply admired and liked Bobby Kennedy. But there's no denying that he was a complicated man who wasn't always easy to like.

This was widely understood even during his lifetime. In fact, there was a constant use of the terms "Good Bobby" and "Bad Bobby" by the press, referring to the two sides of his personality. I got to see both Bobbys firsthand.

One afternoon a friend of mine from

California asked me if I could take her daughter along when I went to the Kennedy place at Hickory Hill to play tennis. It was a little presumptuous of her, but I agreed. She was not the kind of slim young woman the Kennedys liked, but Kennedy sensed that she was uncomfortable and he couldn't do enough for her all afternoon. He was constantly coming over to her to ask if she was comfortable, was there anything she needed, did she want a drink, would she like to sit someplace else, etc. He couldn't have been nicer, although he'd never seen her before and would never see her again.

Later we played tennis — Kennedy and me against Maxwell Taylor and Ethel. We lost (I don't know why that stands out). Then we started playing some touch football. Art Buchwald and John Glenn were among the participants. Kennedy had a big old dog named Brumas who got out on the field somehow as Bobby went back to throw me a pass. He nipped Bobby, who responded by kicking that dog, showing immense anger — much greater than I've ever seen in a similar situation. An example of the Bad Bobby.

Many Democrats, including me, had pleaded with Kennedy to mount a challenge to Johnson. Some of his closest friends and advisers, including staffer Adam Walinsky and friend Richard Goodwin, had pleaded with him to run. But most of his brother's old counselors, including "the two Teds," brother Edward Kennedy and adviser Theodore Sorensen, had urged caution. So far, he'd declined, saying that although he opposed our nation's presence in Vietnam — and despised Johnson personally — he regarded the prospects for unseating Johnson as very remote: as likely as "a priest in Bogotá deposing the Pope," as he put it. In any case, he was unwilling to fracture the Democratic Party by opposing a sitting president. If he was to run for president, 1972 was more likely to be his year.

The logic of Kennedy's stance escaped me. Every week, the body count from Vietnam increased, and with each new casualty it became increasingly apparent that millions of Americans who'd voted for Johnson in 1964 largely on the strength of his promise not to involve our country further in the Vietnamese civil war would abandon the Democrats in November. Far from splitting the party, a Kennedy candidacy could save it.

I always felt that RFK wanted to oppose Johnson, and the war made that possible.

Otherwise there would be no possible ground for him to run against LBJ in 1968. The Kennedy heir apparent would have looked as if he were running simply because of the passion and anger that followed Dallas, evidenced by the thirty-five-minute cheering, crying, standing ovation that greeted RFK when he took the podium at the Democratic convention in 1964, just nine months after the President's murder.

In his bones, RFK may have sensed this. In late May 1967, he reportedly exclaimed to family friend Arthur Schlesinger, "How can we possibly survive five more years of Lyndon Johnson? Five more years of a crazy man?" But Hamlet-like, Bobby held back, still "thinking too precisely on the event," refusing to seize the opportunity to act in accordance with the wishes of his followers and the dictates of his own conscience.

To be fair, it's possible that personal fears influenced Kennedy's hesitation. First, there was the chance that one of his political adversaries — most likely FBI chief J. Edgar Hoover — would try to torpedo his candidacy by revealing embarrassing secrets like the old Castro assassination plot from his brother's administration. There was also, inevitably, the fear of assassination. Like his brother, Bobby attracted intense emotions, both positive and negative. In the super-heated atmosphere of 1968, it wasn't hard to imagine a crazed or ideologically driven gunman deciding to make his mark in history by murdering a second Kennedy brother.

So Senator Eugene McCarthy of Minnesota had stepped into the breach, prompted by the urgings of Allard Lowenstein.

In 1967, Lowenstein and ADA's Curtis Gans had begun seeking a candidate to lead an antiwar rebellion against Johnson within the Democratic Party. They approached several potential standard-bearers, including South Dakota senator George McGovern, Frank Church of Idaho, and General James Gavin, a military leader known for his opposition to the war. All declined.

Meanwhile, Lowenstein was meeting periodically with Robert Kennedy at his office in Washington and at the Kennedy family estate at Hickory Hill, Virginia. On September 26, he made a final plea to Kennedy at Hickory Hill, stating that Johnson could be forced out of the race.

Kennedy agreed with Lowenstein's assessment. He called Johnson "a coward" and predicted that the President might drop out on the eve of the Democratic convention.

But Bobby still refused to play the leading role in this drama. He said he'd be accused of "ambition and envy," and that Johnson (and perhaps others) would consider his candidacy part of a family vendetta.

Finally, in late October, McCarthy signed on to the crusade. In November, at a Chicago meeting of the Conference of Concerned Democrats (an antiwar group founded by Lowenstein, Gans, and Gerald Hill, chairman of the California Democratic Council), McCarthy announced his candidacy. I introduced Al at that meeting, who proceeded to give such a Hitler-like stemwinder speech introducing McCarthy that the fragile politician/poet seemed to me to be close to leaving the conference in anger and tears.

To most observers, it appeared a hopeless cause. Challenges to an incumbent president from within his own party were exceedingly rare, and in that era before the electoral reforms of the 1970s gave rank-and-file voters control over the nominating process, most of the power to choose a presidential candidate rested with state party organizations and bosses, who were staunchly committed to Johnson.

McCarthy's diffident personality didn't help matters. Scholarly, sensitive, a quoter of the classics and a writer of poetry, the fifty-two-year-old McCarthy lacked charisma and sometimes seemed listless. In the early weeks of 1968, his candidacy was driven not so much by his personal appeal as by the growing unease within Democratic circles — and the nation as a whole — over the war in Vietnam, and by the energy of Allard Lowenstein.

Meanwhile, Kennedy continued to agonize. In a startling exchange on the CBS news show *Face the Nation* on November 26, when the journalists on the panel continued to badger him about what he planned to do about his opposition to the war and to President Johnson, Kennedy replied, "I don't know what I can do . . . or what I should do that is any different other than try to get off the Earth in some way."

This was strange language for Sunday-morning political TV, especially from the brother of a slain president. (The famous soliloquy in which a psychologically tortured Hamlet ponders the morality of suicide — "To be or not to be" — inevitably came to mind.) Reporter Martin Agronsky hastily interjected, "Senator, nobody wants you to get off the Earth, obviously." But the note of despairing ambivalence was real, and reflected an anguish over the dilemma of Vietnam that was shared by much of the country.

The stage was set for 1968, one of the most painful and traumatic years in our nation's history — a time that neither I nor anyone who lived through it is likely to ever forget.

NINE:
THEY WANTED TO
SLAP MY FACE

O villain, villain, smiling, damned villain!
That one may smile, and smile, and be a
villain.

In the late fall of 1964, before the big hullabaloo over *U.N.C.L.E.* had begun, the
entire track team from the Soviet Union was
visiting California for an international meet,
and the honchos at MGM invited them to
lunch at the studios. This was a big deal at
the time, when Cold War tensions made
contacts between East and West relatively
sparse. The dining room was full, and
almost every important star on the lot was
present, but the Russian athletes seemed
singularly unimpressed, apparently recognizing no one. Suddenly one of the men
spotted me. Although his English was
limited, he moved quickly to my table,
extended his hand, and said, *"Magnificent
Seven, Magnificent Seven!"* I smiled and

shook hands with the young athlete, who I found out a few moments later through an interpreter was the world's high-jump champion and Olympic gold medalist Valery Brumel. *The Magnificent Seven,* I later learned, was one of the most popular American films ever to play in Moscow.

My new friend Valery, with much emotion, handed me a shiny gold medal, the Official Order of the First Class Athlete, a coveted award given by the Soviet government. Stunned and moved, I started to thank him, but Brumel made a sweeping gesture indicating that the medal was a gift of affection and esteem on behalf of the entire team.

When Brumel and the others started to leave, he turned to me and extended an invitation: "If you should ever be able to come to my country, I would like to show you Moscow as we like to have it seen, not only with the official Intourist guide — you know what I mean?"

I said, "I would love to come to your country very soon." I really meant it. Within one hour, I had arranged to add an extra day off to our Christmas taping hiatus, and with the help of the Russian interpreter, I put in motion a request for a special visa from the State Department. No doubt accelerated by Brumel's international celebrity, the visa arrived almost immediately, and within a day I was notified that I would be leaving Hollywood on Christmas Day, and arriving in Moscow on the 26th of December.

To repay Valery's kindness, I had a gold medallion with an image of JFK attached to a handsome key ring. I also took along a roll of newly minted JFK half dollars. Boris Sagal, a very successful MGM producer-writer-director, gave me an introduction to his brother, Dahleen Sagal, one of the Soviet Union's leading actors and a long-time member of the famed Moscow Art Theatre.

I also checked out what to wear in Moscow in the week between Christmas and the New Year. I was not surprised to read in a guidebook that the weather in Minneapolis any time of the year is exactly the same as in the Soviet capital.

I located my heavy black Chesterfield coat with its black velvet collar, which I'd bought for my trip to Germany to film *The Big Show.* One of the few pictures that I had of my father showed him holding me in his arms while I was less than six months old — he was wearing a coat almost exactly the same as the one I took on this trip. I also brought two new hats, one a black homburg that I fancied made me look like an international statesman, the other a warm fur hat that made me look like a Russian native. I also bought a set of thermal underwear designed for skiers.

At the time, tourists entering the Soviet Union had to pay for everything in advance by purchasing an Intourist coupon book, which covered lodging, meals, and the services of a private car and guide. I was not allowed to know which hotel I would be staying in until my arrival. Early Christmas morning, I boarded an American Airlines flight from LAX that would connect directly with an Air India flight to Moscow. But at the newly renamed Kennedy Airport in New York, I was advised that the Air India flight had been canceled. I had been reticketed on an Air France flight through Paris and then on to Moscow via Aeroflot, the Soviet government airline.

I arrived in Moscow at six o'clock in the evening of December 26. I waited a half hour at the airport and finally a man with a mustache and dark glasses came toward me saying in halting English, "Robert Vaughn? Follow me." He led me to a long black car and said, "I take you to the National Hotel." Just as I got in the backseat, another man, also wearing dark glasses and a tiny black mustache, joined us, opening the front door and sitting beside my driver. Neither man spoke on the hour-long drive into Moscow.

It seemed we were going in circles until we arrived at Gorky Street, where I was dropped off without a word other than, "National Hotel." I dragged my luggage inside (no anxious porters waiting for a tip) and in the lobby I saw in English: INTOUR-IST OFFICE. Behind the counter sat a short, fat lady who unsmilingly asked for my passport. After glancing at it briefly, she kept it.

I was taken directly to my room past similarly sized ladies who were in charge of the room keys.

I had paid top rubles for their grandest suite. I was left in a dark hall with my luggage and a gigantic room key from Czarist times. I found a light switch and proceeded to lug my suitcases into the semilit rooms. When my eyes grew accustomed to the meager lighting, I saw that there were two small rooms that looked like every rundown hotel I'd ever holed up in during my earliest days in Hollywood.

I then did a quick sweep of the room for the bugging devices I'd been told would be there. I found nothing and, since it was nearing midnight, I got ready to hit the Soviet sack. But just before I fell asleep, the phone rang. It was my Intourist guide and translator, Yuri Grishenko. We settled on a nine A.M. pickup time for my first full day in the USSR.

The following morning I got up early, truly excited about the start of my unique vacation. With a maximum physical effort, I managed to open the huge, heavy curtains, and there in the bright sunshine before me was Red Square, with the multicolored onion domes of St. Basil's in the background and a corner of Lenin's tomb directly below me. I was at last in Stanislavski's hometown.

I hurriedly made calls to arrange specific dates with people I'd promised to look up. Yuri arrived on time and in his car. His English was perfect, and his personality was warm and friendly. We hit it off immediately. (Later, in the early seventies, he became head of Intourist.)

Almost immediately we came upon a group of people in Gorky Park wearing bathing suits. They had cut holes in the ice pond and were swimming about. They seemed to recognize me and came toward me. I had explained to Yuri that I had just started filming a new television series in

America in which I played a secret agent not unlike James Bond. When my new friends heard this, each one greeted me with a shyly extended hand while smilingly calling me "Zero Zero Bondski man."

A huge fellow who seemed to be the leader of the group spoke some English. I told him jokingly that I was somewhat ashamed to be dressed as I was while they were in swimsuits. (I had donned my full winter regalia that morning, from the skiers' underwear through the velvet-collared Chesterfield and the fur hat.) I then remarked, "We have a group just like yours back in America. They're called the Polar Bear Club." The name brought great gusts of laughter as they promptly got the connection between the Arctic animal and Muscovites who enjoyed bathing in ice water.

When Yuri suggested we continue our drive, I took out my first JFK half dollar and gave it to the leader of the swimmers' club. When I saw his reaction, I was immediately sorry I hadn't brought hundreds of the coins with me. He turned the coin over in his hand, then emotionally embraced me.

"Aha . . . Kennedy . . . Kennedy," he sighed. "How we all suffered when we heard the news." He looked at me and added, "I hope only thing that will ever come between us is cold water, no Cold War."

I got back in the car, barely able to stop tearing up. The discomfort I'd felt on the no-frills Aeroflot flight and during my indifferent reception at the airport and the hotel all disappeared, vanquished by the eloquence of one plain Russian man expressing his friendship for me, an American guest in his country.

Throughout my stay, people were eager to greet me, recognizing me as an American by my clothes (I quickly shed the Russian fur hat). The words of the first middle-aged man who stopped me spoke for all: "I speak no good English . . . but I hope your child, my child grow up in peace."

During our first day together, I discovered that Yuri had been selected as my guide because of his interest in the theater. He helped me pick out as many plays and events as I could take in during my stay. Although Yuri was paid only to be my guide during the day, I invited him to the Bolshoi Ballet with me. He was thrilled, and I wound up inviting him to be my guest for all the subsequent evenings, whether at shows or in private homes where I was invited. Not only could he not have afforded all this but, more important, he got to meet famous artists and athletes he would otherwise never know. And, of course, I benefited from the presence of a skilled translator wherever I went.

Our second evening, we saw a performance of *Cyrano* by the Moscow Art Theatre's equivalent of our Actors Studio in New York. After the play, we were invited back to the apartment of Oleg Tabakov and his wife, members of the cast who had just celebrated their fifth wedding anniversary. They had some food left over and invited not only Yuri and me but also the star of the performance, Michael Kosakov, who played a brilliant *Cyrano* with a very small putty nose. We had a superb dinner cooked on a little grill on the outside balcony of their small apartment accompanied by some lovely Georgian wine. They were exceedingly kind, friendly people and kept giving me gifts from their home to take back as souvenirs of my trip. For almost five hours, till well after midnight, we talked theater, politics, with no taboos or restraint. They were particularly interested in Arthur Miller and his play *The Crucible,* which dealt with the Salem Witch Trials and their parallels to the McCarthy witch hunts in post–World War II America. We discussed the relative strengths and weaknesses of our respective countries, all in a spirit of frankness and friendship.

Midnight came and went. It was now snowing heavily, and Yuri had trouble finding our car. Michael Kosakov joined us out in the snowy street and suddenly started singing at the top of his powerful voice. Yuri immediately joined in. Since I couldn't understand a word of their Russian song, I started singing the first song that popped into my head, the Army Air Corp Hymn: "Off we go into the wild blue yonder, climbing high into the sky." I wonder what the Tabakovs' neighbors were thinking that night.

The following day, I visited the Moscow Art Theatre. I was in awe to enter this hallowed building, which I'd been studying and reading about since the mid-forties.

Dahleen Sagal had given me an open sesame to sit in on classes and watch a pantomime session. The clarity of the young actors' work required no translation. They were almost bewitching in their hypnotic movements.

The next day, Valery Brumel and I held a live press conference seen throughout the Soviet Union. I presented Brumel with the gold key ring and the JFK medallion. The live audience in the theater was ecstatic, asking me repeatedly what specific government medal it was. I didn't have the heart to tell them I had obtained the medal by walking into an American jewelry store and buying it over the counter.

The final highlight of my visit was a special screening at the Mosfilm Studio of their recent film of *Hamlet* starring, of all people, Russian's foremost comedian, Smolonovsky. I had no trouble following the play in Russian because of my years of studying the Bard's masterwork. Smolonovsky was brilliant and played the role entirely straight, except where humor was appropriate based on Shakespeare's text.

When I returned to the States just before the New Year, I was invited on the *Les Crane Television Show* for the ABC network, live from New York, to discuss my visit. The network got plenty of angry letters from viewers wanting to know why they would give airtime to this dumb actor who had obviously been brainwashed by the Commie devils. The response was a mild foretaste of what was to come when I began speaking out about the war in Vietnam.

Hollywood is a land of instant success,

instant stardom — where a person with the right face, the right talents, and a smidgen of luck can suddenly find himself riding a particular "property," a TV show or movie, to the very pinnacle of fame, adulation, and wealth. But what goes up in brilliance and light comes down with haste and in darkness because of that old harbinger of doom — greed.

And that's the story of the sudden demise of *The Man from U.N.C.L.E.*

We like to talk about movies and TV as "creative" industries, but in one way they can be anything but creative: The deepest instinct of a Hollywood mogul, it often seems, is to imitate anything that has worked for someone else. *U.N.C.L.E.* itself was an offspring of that instinct, representing TV's first attempt to cash in on the international spy craze triggered by the James Bond movies. When *U.N.C.L.E.* debuted, it was the only American spy series; within two years, it was one of a dozen. In this case, as in so many others, "creativity" meant riding the crest of a hot trend. We were fortunate enough to get in on the trend on the ground floor.

But by 1966, the spy trend was already showing signs of decline. The network honchos began looking around for the *next* trend. They believed they'd spotted one when a new series based on the adventures of a venerable comic book character became an unlikely hit.

The unexpected overnight success of *Batman,* an ABC midseason replacement in early 1966, launched an invasion of television by a new, ironic twist on pop culture. Under the guidance of producer William Dozier and writer Lorenzo Semple Jr., *Batman* used the essentially serious though somewhat corny superhero from the 1950s and '60s as the basis for a tongue-in-cheek satire. In the title role, Adam West was given over-the-top speeches about honor, courage, and patriotism to recite; his sidekick Robin (portrayed by Burt Ward) uttered such memorable (if nonsensical) exclamations as "Holy atomic pile, Batman!" Fistfights were punctuated with on-screen cartoon-style bubbles bearing legends like "Pow!" "Blam!" and "Splat!" And a pompous narrator (voiced by producer Dozier himself) closed each cliff-hanging episode by promising more thrills in the next show and urging fans to tune in: "Same Bat-time, same Bat-station!"

The whole thing was a determinedly goofy riff on traditional comic heroism — and in the antiheroic atmosphere of the mid-sixties, it became a giant hit.

Seizing on this rapid audience response, NBC wanted to capitalize on the pop movement, using *U.N.C.L.E.* as its chief weapon. So somewhere in the nether regions of NBC and in the fabled studios of MGM, the decision was made to transform *U.N.C.L.E.* into a kind of comedy, abandoning its previous success based on the Bondian format of lighthearted adventure. The new buzzword was *camp,* and suddenly the lemmings of Hollywood were marching in a new direction.

Sam Rolfe had been the line producer for the first year of *U.N.C.L.E.,* and the success of the show reflected his concept. He had supervised everything, and he also wrote many of the scripts for that first year. Then he walked away from the show, reportedly frustrated over his relative lack of recognition and modest compensation. A new producer named David Victor came on board, the first of several who would oversee the show in the next two-and-a-half years.

Of course, Victor wanted to leave his mark, and so the distinctive character of the show began to change. Unfortunately, it seemed that Victor really didn't understand the nature of *U.N.C.L.E.,* with its blend of a basically serious adventure tale with occasional dashes of wry humor. The story goes that Victor read a couple of magazine articles that referred to the show as a "spoof" of the spy genre, and he latched on to that idea, with *Batman*'s success as an additional spur. Victor decided to play up the humor, and the show was transformed into almost pure comedy.

The decline began in the second season (1965–66) with the new scripts. The understated humor was gradually transformed into farce, and the show ended up being positively campy, *Batman*-style. This might not have been so bad, were it not for the fact that most of the attempts at humor were more silly than funny. There were Popsicle hand grenades, golf cart cannons, exploding apples, Illya riding a bomb filled with skunk smell, and Napoleon dancing with a fellow in a gorilla suit.

Nonetheless, the momentum we'd built up during our first season kept us afloat. The second season of *U.N.C.L.E.* ended with us beating out such established shows as *The Lawrence Welk Show, Walt Disney's Wonderful World of Color, My Three Sons,* and *The Ed Sullivan Show.* The showbiz bible, *Variety,* called it a show that was "riding high and rightfully so," and predicted that if "pace and excitement are sustained, Metro will have a top 10'er."

The popularity of the show brought with it some serious acclaim. The Hollywood Foreign Press Association gave its Golden Globe to *U.N.C.L.E.* as the world's favorite TV show. I received the *Photoplay* Gold Medal award as the most popular actor in America. It was given to me by the previous year's winner, John Wayne.

Flush with the continued success of *U.N.C.L.E.,* NBC introduced a spin-off show in the fall of 1966. It was *The Girl from U.N.C.L.E.,* starring Stefanie Powers in the title role. (Stefanie had recently married and divorced my friend Gary Lockwood, the star of Norman Felton's *The Lieutenant* — the show that, as you'll recall, had been my springboard to *U.N.C.L.E.*) Stefanie was a lovely charmer and a talented actress, as millions of Americans came to see when she later starred with Bob Wagner on *Hart to Hart,* but *The Girl from U.N.C.L.E.* wasn't much of a vehicle. The show was canceled at the end of its first season, having ranked fifty-seventh among sixty prime-time network shows. It was a bad omen for the original show.

Throughout the third season of *U.N.C.L.E.,* the scripts got worse. It got to the point where David and I were actually shooting cupcakes out of guns into the sides of cars — that's how silly it got. Executive Producer Norman Felton and producers David Victor and Boris Ingster all agreed that if this pop/camp rendition of *U.N.C.L.E.* continued, the hit show was doomed to cancelation.

When people say that something "can't go on like this," it usually doesn't. The fourth season of *The Man from U.N.C.L.E.* was canceled after sixteen episodes had been filmed. "*The Seven Wonders of the World Affair*" (Parts 1 and 2) was aired on January 8 and 15, 1968. That spelled the end of the *U.N.C.L.E.* franchise — not counting a mediocre reunion show, "The Return of the Man from U.N.C.L.E.: The Fifteen Years Later Affair," which David and I made in 1983.

Ironically, when *U.N.C.L.E.* was canceled, it was replaced in its weekly slot on NBC by a show that was *all* campy pop culture, and it too became an instant hit. The show was an all-out, no-questions-asked, full-blown hour of goofy sketch and standup humor hosted by two well-known comedians, Dan Rowan and Dick Martin. Its name was *Laugh-In*. (And to compound the ironies, the very first episode of *Laugh-In* featured a cameo appearance by none other than Leo G. Carroll, gyrating on a dance floor with the likes of Goldie Hawn and Ruth Buzzi, and urgently speaking into a pen phone: "Open Channel D! Come in, Mr. Solo! I think I've found T.H.R.U.S.H. headquarters!")

Reflecting forty years later on how *U.N.C.L.E.* went from near-flop during its first season to international craze, and then, within eighteen months, to final cancelation, I would add these thoughts.

First, the survival of *U.N.C.L.E.* beyond its first few shows would probably never have happened in today's ultra-high-pressured, ratings-driven network environment. Back in the mid-sixties, a promising show like *U.N.C.L.E.* was given at least a little while to find its audience. Today, we probably would have been off the air by November, and we never would have had a chance to use the power of public relations and word-of-mouth to build our fan base. This change in our industry is not for the best. Who knows how many good shows have died prematurely thanks to short-term thinking at the networks?

Second, I wish that those of us who sensed what was going wrong during those second and third seasons of *U.N.C.L.E.* had used our clout to try to get the show back on track. Certainly David McCallum and I were aware that the tone and style of those farce-oriented scripts were a far cry from what had made *U.N.C.L.E.* popular. But we were young actors, thrilled to be enjoying our first major success, and we were probably a bit intimidated by the production honchos who were calling the shots. These were guys who'd been around the TV networks for years — surely they knew what they were doing? We kept our mouths shut and struggled to bring life to those dismal scripts, to no avail.

Today, of course, as two grizzled veterans of the show business wars, David and I know better than to assume that the guys in charge know what they're doing. I like to think we would speak up now before seeing a valuable franchise we'd help to create get mismanaged down the tubes. But that's hindsight, which is always twenty-twenty.

Of course, it would be silly to imply that my memories of *U.N.C.L.E.* are mainly sad ones. Quite the contrary: My time at the very top of Hollywood's celebrity culture may have been relatively brief, but it was enormously fun and rewarding. It also set me up for a less-spectacular but equally enjoyable four-decade run in a wide array of starring and character roles on TV, in movies, and on the stage. The iconic part of

Napoleon Solo has served as a powerful door-opener for me with countless producers, directors, and casting executives, as well as creating a loyal fan base that has followed me from one adventure to the next.

Best of all, I have wonderful memories of getting to know and work with two exquisite artists and gentlemen, Leo G. Carroll and David McCallum. Leo died after a battle with cancer in 1972, just four years after *U.N.C.L.E.* went off the air. David, happily, is still going strong, currently starring as Dr. Donald "Ducky" Mallard on the hit CBS crime series *NCIS*. I was tickled when a second-season episode of the series included this dialogue between the characters Jethro Gibbs and Kate Todd:

TODD: Gibbs, what did Ducky look like when he was younger?
GIBBS: Illya Kuryakin.

Hey, I wanted to shout at the actors on the screen — I knew him when!

For an actor, the end of a successful run on stage or screen brings mixed emotions. Of course, you hate losing the regular paychecks and the guarantee of interesting, rewarding work. But the disappearance of a demanding "day job" also opens up time and opportunities to explore other projects. My first big project after the death of *U.N.C.L.E.* was Steve McQueen's detective drama *Bullitt.*

Steve McQueen and I had remained friends after working together on *The Magnificent Seven.* His wife, Neile Adams McQueen, whom I'd met during the filming of that picture, also became a friend, and remained one after her 1972 divorce from Steve. Today, after almost half a century, Neile and I and my wife, Linda, are all quite close.

From time to time, I would get a call from Steve asking if he could drop by. We wouldn't do anything special — mostly just drive up and down the Sunset Strip. We'd usually stop by the famous Whisky á Go Go club, which was operated by a friend of his, Elmer Valentine, where we'd inhale a few brews and ogle the young chicks who ogled Steve and me back. We hardly ever spoke to any of them, although I'd occasionally pick one out for a subsequent rendezvous. As far as I know, Steve never did.

I never quite understood what attraction I had for Steve. I knew nothing about cars, bikes, racing, or any other kind of machinery — things that were always his chief passion.

(As his fans know, Steve was an avid collector and racer of sports cars and motorcycles, and he did many of his own motor stunts in the movies.) I also didn't share another of Steve's interests, which was experimenting with drugs. I'd had my single disastrous experience with pot in the fall of 1954, which Steve had heard about through Jim Coburn, and so we never smoked any joints together. Nor did Steve and I talk about the war, civil rights, or any other political topic; in fact, he never seemed to know or have any interest in what was happening in the world outside of Hollywood. So we didn't have anything in common, other than our shared profession.

Yet I enjoyed Steve's company immensely, and he evidently liked me, too — despite the fact that I kidded him frequently about his intense ambition and his ever-increasing paranoia.

And my friendship with Steve certainly led to some memorable experiences. One time while Steve and Neile were living on Solar Drive in Nichols Canyon, I got a call from Steve inviting me to join him at a car race at a place called Hansen Dam. I said, "Sure." The following day, Steve picked me up early, driving a red Type-D Jaguar convertible with the top down, a very exclusive, expensive car. His nerves were visibly on edge. When I asked why, he explained he'd wanted to participate in the race, but couldn't — the insurance company covering his current movie project had put its foot down. Steve was frustrated and annoyed.

When the race ended, Steve was even more highly charged. We jumped back in his Jag and took off at breakneck speed, hitting the closest freeway at full throttle. The next ten minutes were like a chase scene from the movies, except that the LAPD were nowhere in sight (where are they when you're praying for them?). I never had the courage to look at the speedometer, but let's just say that, although it had started to rain heavily, neither Steve nor I got wet.

When we pulled into the Solar Drive driveway, Neile was waiting. She took one look at my face and started laughing. She immediately poured me four fingers of Cutty Sark, which quickly returned my jangled nervous system almost to normal.

By 1968, Steve's career was in steady ascent. After *The Magnificent Seven,* he'd starred in *The Great Escape* (1963) and *The Sand Pebbles* (1966), for which he received his first (and only) Academy Award nomination. Buoyed by these critical and box-office successes, Steve signed a seven-picture deal for his own company, Solar Productions (named after Solar Drive), with Warner Bros. *Bullitt* was to be the first movie in the deal.

Early in the project, Steve sent me the script, hoping I'd accept one of the key roles in the picture. It was accompanied by a salary offer, for a fair amount that was basically in line with my expectations.

Based on a novel by Robert L. Fish, the script dealt with the machinations of organized crime and big-time politics in San Francisco. Unfortunately, when I read it, I found its mélange of mistaken identities, phony clues, double crosses, and betrayals to be so confusing that I became convinced several pages had gone missing during the photocopying process.

A few days later, Steve called me. "What do you think?" he asked.

"This is the first picture for your production deal?" I replied. "It doesn't make any sense. I can't follow the story line even after reading it twice."

"Hmm, that's a problem," Steve said. "What should I do?"

"Actually, I have a suggestion. I know someone who's a terrific script doctor — a British gal who has worked wonders with a lot of pictures. Why not give her a call?"

Steve followed my advice. He called the script doctor and paid her to analyze the script. She provided a long list of practical suggestions — scenes to delete and add, characters to simplify, crucial details to emphasize, motivations to explain, and so on.

The script was duly revised, and the new version was sent to me, along with a new salary offer somewhat higher than the first. However, when I read the script, I found that just about ten percent of the doctor's suggestions had been followed. The story was practically as confusing as ever. I called Steve and told him so.

Dismayed, Steve sent the script back to his writing team again and yet again. Each time, they made a number of changes, and Steve passed the revised script along to me, together with yet another salary offer, each one higher than the last.

Finally, I received another version of the script with a salary offer higher than any I'd ever received for a picture — my first six-figure movie payday, in fact. And although the script wasn't much different from the first version I'd read months before, when Steve called me this time, I told him, "You know, the picture is starting to look better and better to me!" We both laughed.

I figured I would let critics and audiences figure out the entanglements of the plot. I guess they did, since *Bullitt* was a box-office smash and is now considered one of the classic movie dramas of the 1960s, recently selected for preservation by the film archive of the Smithsonian Institution in Washington, D.C.

Bullitt was directed by British director Peter Yates and stars the incredibly lovely Jacqueline Bisset as McQueen's "love interest." If you watch the picture on DVD sometime, look closely at the cabbie in the taxi scene near the start of the movie; although he speaks only a few words, you'll recognize Robert Duvall in one of his first movie roles.

My role was that of Walter Chalmers, a slick and ambitious politician eager to use his public profile as a crusading anticrime legislator as a springboard to even greater fame and power. Think of an unscrupulous version of Robert F. Kennedy — smart, charismatic, and ruthless — and you'll have a pretty good idea of my character. It was a role that my *U.N.C.L.E.* fans might not have recognized, but one very similar to some of the parts I'd played when guest-starring on TV series in the late 1950s and early '60s.

Robert Relyea, assistant director on *The Magnificent Seven* and a producer on *Bullitt,* put it this way: "When Vaughn is doing that character he does better than anyone else, as soon as you see him you want to slap his face. And that was exactly the quality we wanted."

I found that working with the ever-touchy Steve McQueen — now not just the star but also the chief creative force behind the entire project — sometimes called for delicate diplomacy. The first day I came on the set, I asked one of the prop people for a Phi Beta Kappa key to wear on the vest of my three-piece suit. I figured it would be the perfect accessory for my character, who was both highly educated and vain. But when I put it on, Steve went over to director Yates and complained, "Why is Vaughn wearing that thing? People will think of *The Thomas Crown Affair.*"

That was Steve's most recent movie, in which he'd been miscast as a debonair millionaire art thief. It has since been remade in a 1999 production starring Pierce Brosnan, but it is remembered by ardent movie buffs for its sound track ("The Windmills of Your Mind" won the 1968 Oscar for best song), its erotically suggestive chess game between McQueen and Faye Dunaway (parodied decades later in the second *Austin Powers* film), and its prolonged kiss between McQueen and Dunaway — at fifty-five seconds, one of the longest in movie history. Anyway, Steve had worn a Phi Beta Kappa pin in that picture, a detail that not one fan in a million was likely to remember.

Peter told me that Steve was unhappy with my choice of accessory, and I said, "Why not have him come over to discuss it?"

So we talked it over, and when Steve mentioned his concern about the connection to *Thomas Crown,* I trotted out one of the oldest lines in the business: "If you really think the audience is going to make that association, the picture isn't written correctly." I didn't really know what that meant, but it served my purpose by putting the onus on the scriptwriter rather than on my choice of costume detail. Most important, McQueen bought it, and I was permitted to wear the key.

Steve and I also debated other details of my performance, right down to word choice. There's a scene in which Chalmers is condescendingly berating McQueen's character, Lieutenant Frank Bullitt, for failing to protect a chief witness in the spectacular organized crime hearings Chalmers is planning to stage in Congress. With a sneer,

Chalmers tells Bullitt, "Lieutenant, don't try to evade the responsibility. In your parlance, you blew it." That word *parlance* was a compromise that emerged after Steve decided that the word in the original script was "too tough" for movie audiences. I forget what the original word was, but I remember suggesting such alternatives as *patois* and *nomenclature* before I finally found a word McQueen was comfortable with: *parlance.*

Bullitt ended up being something of a landmark in movie history. Its insolent, hip young police officer, angry about interference from the politicized higher-ups in the department, became a model for many later characters, such as Eastwood's Dirty Harry.

The car chase through the streets of San Francisco is often cited as one of the great chases in movie history. In fact, in 2005 it was voted the best car chase in history in a poll of 5,500 British film fans. The scene, which runs nine minutes and forty-two seconds in the picture, took three weeks to film, with the cars reaching speeds of over 110 miles per hour in certain sequences. McQueen did some of his own driving, but stuntman Bud Elkins did many of the most risky maneuvers.

Bullitt was my most extended opportunity

to work with Steve McQueen. We later appeared together in *The Towering Inferno*, but our characters didn't interact much in that picture. However, we remained friends right up until his tragic death from lung cancer in 1980. (Steve blamed asbestos from a ship he'd worked on at age nineteen, ignoring the fact that he'd smoked two or three packs of cigarettes and a lot of marijuana every day for years.)

I even tried to help Steve in his final, desperate battle, after conventional medicine had proved useless. I had a friend who was the caterer for Renee, the hairdresser to the Queen of England, who had developed a machine that she was convinced had healing properties. It had electrodes that were attached to the patient's arms, producing a trancelike state that seemed to provide some relief from the worst symptoms. When McQueen was dying, I called Stan Kamen, who for a while was both Steve's agent and mine, and told him, "This woman I know has treated Laurence Olivier and members of the British royal family with some limited success with her machine. Would Steve be interested?" But it was too late — within days, Steve was gone.

A couple of final memories of McQueen:

In the early sixties, Steve, in one of our

drive-around outings, asked me, "Where do you get your hair cut?" I said, "Usually on movie sets." He said, "Man, I've found this guy named Sebring who just opened a shop on Fairfax Avenue. He does what he calls hairstyling for men. You should fall by and give him a shot." I did, and for the balance of that decade, Jay Sebring was my barber (though he never used that word). On many occasions he invited me to join him and his friends for a little partying. For no particular reason, I declined.

The last time I saw him, in the summer of '69, he again proffered an invitation. I again took a pass. The venue that time was Cielo Drive, where Charlie Manson's followers killed Jay, Roman Polanski's pregnant wife, Sharon Tate, and others. Following the massacres, Steve found out his name was on Manson's hit list. From that day forth, whenever possible, Steve carried a gun.

Although Steve was married three times, I think the key role in his life and career was played by his first wife, Neile. Without her help and her smarts, I think his rapid rise to success would have been much slower. She understood his appeal to women and could see that it was not reaching the screen in his first few pictures. (His first starring role was in the cheap 1958 horror flick *The Blob,* more or less Steve's equivalent of my *Teen-age Cave Man.*) By the time Frank Sinatra cast him in *Never So Few* (1959), his famous screen persona was beginning to appear, to finally be crystallized in 1960's *Magnificent Seven.* His three-year run as bounty hunter Josh Randall on CBS's hit television show *Wanted: Dead or Alive* contributed heavily to his growing worldwide fame. Neile did a lot to guide Steve toward these effective career choices.

In February 1963, Neile and Steve bought their "castle," as they called it, a spectacular stone house on Oakmont Drive in Brentwood. Standing on three acres and boasting eighteen rooms, it overlooked the Pacific and the city of Santa Monica.

In August 1964, they had their first big Hollywood-style party at the castle. I was invited along with a giant list of show-business celebrities: the Jim Garners, who were neighbors of the McQueens, Jimmy Coburn, George Hamilton, the Kirk Douglases, Sharon Tate, Carol Baker, Janet Leigh, Ben Gazzara and his wife Janice Rule, Gena Rowlands and her husband, John Cassavetes, Eva Marie Saint, Cloris Leachman and her husband, George Englund, and many, many others. Natalie Wood greeted me with the second biggest hug I've ever received. (The biggest? The one Dolly Parton gave me when I met her at 20th Century-Fox a decade later. When you've been hugged by Dolly Parton, you *know* you've been hugged.)

It was a spectacular party, as you can imagine, one that both proclaimed and solidified the arrival of Steve and Neile as two of the most important figures in Hollywood. Around midnight, I found myself on the patio looking toward the ocean and the flickering lights of Santa Monica. Steve joined me and we had a brief chat. Then there was a long pause, not unusual in a conversation with Steve.

Finally I said, "When you were back in New York in the fifties, living in a cold-water flat and courting Neile on your bike, did you ever think that you'd end up this way?"

There was another pause, and without looking at me, Steve replied, "What makes you think I'm going to *end up* this way now?"

I chuckled slightly, and after another long pause Steve walked slowly away. He was a very special friend, and I'll always miss his unique way of looking at life.

Meanwhile, as the tumultuous 1960s unfolded, my daily life, with its ups and downs and occasional odd episodes, continued.

It was Friday, October 13, 1967 (the date should have been a warning), when one of the more weird experiences of my life occurred — one that illustrates, among other things, the dark side of the celebrity life.

On that evening, I took my secretary, Sharon Miller, and two of her girlfriends, Diana Maitland and Mary-David Bramson, out to celebrate the end of the workweek at a Spanish restaurant called the Matador on Pico Boulevard in West Los Angeles. I had been there many times and always enjoyed their paella, which in Spain is considered the poor folks' dish. Usually it's made of saffron-seasoned rice together with whatever's available — sausages, chicken, shrimp, scallops, and what have you. It was just about a month before the announcement that *U.N.C.L.E.* would be canceled.

On one side of the table with our backs to the bar were Diana and me; I was occupying the seat nearest the wall, with Diana on my left. Mary-David was across from Diana, and Sharon was across from me.

A few minutes after we were seated and had not yet ordered, a man arrived at the table. We'll call him "John." He addressed me as Bob and asked me if I would come over and meet some of the people at another table. I said I'd be happy to meet them, but we had just arrived and I was quite tired, so if he wouldn't mind, I'd like to have the people come over to where I was. John said no: these people were from the Lakers Organization. He then handed me a business card, I assumed to prove his connection with the Lakers. (The Lakers basketball team was originally from Minneapolis, and I had seen many of their games when they were based there.)

I once again declined, saying I would be happy to meet them on the way out. John left, seeming to be unhappy with my suggestion.

A few minutes later, a blond man and a woman came to our table. The man asked me if I remembered the woman. I said I did not. She said she and her party were from the Kings and did I know the Kings? (They were an L.A. hockey team.) I said no, but I knew a few queens. The girls laughed and the blond man and the woman did not. I said hello to the woman, and she asked if I liked hockey. I said I did, which was not true. She then asked me to introduce her to the girls, which I did. The woman then said, "You don't know who the Kings are, do you?" And I said I did not. She said, "You know what you are? You are ignorant," and walked away with the guy.

At that point, Sharon and Diana left the table for the ladies' room. Mary-David and I were at the table talking about how bizarre fans are when drunk when another man appeared at the table, much drunker than the previous arrivals. He said something about the fact that JFK had given him a plaque for being the best athlete in Boston in some year that I don't now recall. He said he supposed I was not impressed by that fact. I said in a puzzled, friendly way, "No." The man said, "You could at least have looked at me." At that point in time, I was recovering from an ear problem caused by a gunshot going off next to my right ear during a shoot-out in one of the *U.N.C.L.E.* shows. As a result, I was bending my left ear toward his face with my face turned to the right and away from him. The man said, "We're having a hell of a conversation, aren't we?" I said quietly, "Yes." He said, "I bet you want me to get away from here, don't you?" I said quietly but firmly, "Yes." The man left.

About five minutes later, John came back to the table, just as our dinners were being served. I was at that time trying on Sharon's glasses. John reached across Diana on my left, grabbing my shoulder and saying something like "You're coming over to our fucking table." Diana told our intruder that he was hurting her, and John said something to me to the effect that, "It's you and me in the basement or it's you and me in the parking lot."

At that point, he dragged me out of the booth, knocking Diana to the floor, along with the table, the cutlery, the china, the food, the drinks, the candles, and everything else on the table. I had fallen to the floor facedown, and as I looked up, I saw shoes, high heels, dishes, fists, and other assorted stuff heading for my face. I suddenly remembered my lesson from Andrew Young back in Stockholm. I went into the Civil Rights Crouch, tucking my knees up to my face and covering my head with my hands.

Then there was a hell of a lot of yelling and cursing with the other members of the intruder's table arriving on the scene. A John Wayne–type barroom brawl ensued with, I later found out, no one connected with the restaurant trying to stop it.

Several people, I don't know who, got me upright and facedown on a table across the room. Sharon was then assaulted by the fist of one of the "ladies" with the group. At that point, I managed to disentangle myself from the drunken gang and instructed the girls that we were leaving, pronto. I could tell that my right eye was swollen, and I felt a scratch on the bridge of my nose. My shirtfront had also been ripped.

Sharon, feeling ill, went to the ladies' room and, at that point, one of the attacking women picked up a plate of food and attempted to throw it at me. Mary-David knocked it out of her hands. As we started to leave, another lady stopped us. She said she was embarrassed about the incident, that it was none of my responsibility, and she could be contacted as a witness.

I started to leave, asking Mary-David if she would get Sharon, who was still in the ladies' room. The parking lot attendant brought my car around, and after I got in, another woman attempted to fling her purse at me through the open window. And that was the end of our quiet, relaxing evening meal at the Matador, a restaurant that I frequented because it was not in the normal Hollywood mainstream. I never returned, needless to say.

The next day, I talked to Peter Allan Fields, one of the *U.N.C.L.E.* writers who was also an attorney, and gave him the business card I'd been given. He managed to contact "John" and got the names of the other people who were there and involved in the mayhem. John admitted to Peter that he was completely guilty, and further admitted that they were all drunk at the time and how sorry they all were.

Shortly after that, on February 14, 1968, I received a letter from my attorney, Guy Ward, formerly president of the California Bar Association, saying that he understood that John had entered a plea of *nolo contendere* and his sentence constituted a fine and a jail sentence, which was suspended. He ended his letter by saying I had until October 13, 1968, to file a civil complaint in the matter, which I most definitely intended to do.

However, two incidents of international consequence occurred after my receipt of Guy's letter that somehow overshadowed the Matador imbroglio.

While I was filming *The Bridge at Remagen* in Prague in August 1968, the Soviet Union invaded Czechoslovakia. After being under house arrest for a week, I was taken across the Czech-Austrian border, and finally released.

By the time I left Europe, in October 1968, Guy Ward had been hired as the chief defense attorney for the man accused of the murder of my friend Robert Kennedy —

Sirhan Sirhan.
I decided to drop the case.

TEN:
ANNUS HORRIBILIS

He was a man, take him for all in all,
I shall not look upon his like again.

The sudden disappearance of a very lucrative, steady job would usually be a painful shock to an actor. But, as *TV Guide* later commented, I "hardly noticed" the passing of *U.N.C.L.E.* No wonder: Most of my time that winter of 1967–68 was consumed with the effort to end the war in Southeast Asia. My head and heart had been ten thousand miles from MGM Culver City since January 1965, when the United States had expanded the war in Southeast Asia, bombing North Vietnam peasants and Agent Oranging their food supply. For me, nothing happening in Hollywood was as significant as the horror show we were staging in that benighted country so far away.

At the start of 1968 — a year many Americans would come to look back on as our nation's *annus horribilis* ("terrible year") — we antiwar Democrats had found a presidential candidate. He was Eugene McCarthy, a senator from Minnesota who was the first prominent politician with the courage to challenge the increasingly unpopular President Lyndon Johnson. But although many opponents of the war were rallying around McCarthy as he prepared to go toe-to-toe with Johnson in the New Hampshire primary in March, the Minnesotan was not their first choice. The man they considered the strongest alternative to Johnson was Robert F. Kennedy, brother of the slain president and the charismatic junior senator from New York.

Antiwar sentiment, however, was probably still in the minority when the year opened. That changed as the news on the ground changed.

On January 31, war news sent shock waves through American politics. In what came to be known as the Tet Offensive (after the Vietnamese lunar new year celebration), some seventy thousand North Vietnamese forces launched a broad attack that spread from the cities of the Mekong Delta to the highlands of the North, aimed at more than a hundred cities and other targets.

The scope of the offensive surprised and

dismayed Americans. So did its timing. As Gen. William Westmoreland, commander of U.S. troops in Vietnam, told an interviewer several years later, "I frankly did not think [the North Vietnamese] would assume the psychological disadvantage of hitting at Tet itself, so I thought it would be long before or after Tet." The fact that the United States was caught off guard reinforced the growing sense among Americans that their military and political leaders — up to and including President Johnson — didn't know what they were doing in Vietnam, and that the optimistic predictions they'd recited on television month after month meant little.

The North Vietnamese offensive began on the night of January 30 with attacks on seven towns along the coast and in the mountains, including Da Nang, the second-largest city in Vietnam. The next morning, Vietcong commandos attacked a series of targets in the capital city of Saigon. One group penetrated the outer wall of South Vietnamese navy headquarters before being repelled by gunfire. Another Vietcong band was destroyed in a cemetery before it could reach its objective, the main prison in Saigon. The headquarters of General Westmoreland at the Saigon Airport was attacked, while another group of fourteen commandos failed in a suicide mission to break into the presidential palace. A guerrilla band seized control of the studios of a Saigon radio station for six hours, but technicians thwarted their efforts to broadcast revolutionary messages.

In the boldest move of all, a group of nineteen commandos attacked the American Embassy in Saigon, blasting a hole through the high wall surrounding the compound. Ambassador Ellsworth Bunker had already been spirited from his nearby home as a security measure. The Vietcong held part of the embassy compound for six hours before they were killed or repulsed.

Within hours, a Communist division assaulted the American base at Bienhoa, and other Communist forces carried out well-planned attacks against thirteen provincial capitals. Two battalions invaded the beautiful northern city of Hue, previously a peaceful sanctuary in war-ravaged Vietnam. They targeted American advisers and the South Vietnamese who worked with them, killing almost three thousand soldiers, civil servants, and students. It took twenty-four days for the U.S. and South Vietnamese forces to retake Hue, including days of brutal hand-to-hand combat within the walled Citadel at the heart of the city. By the time the

South Vietnamese flag was raised over Hue, much of the city had been reduced to rubble.

Along with millions of other Americans, I watched with awe and horror as these events unfolded on the evening TV news. What did it all mean?

By phone I tracked down Allard Lowenstein. "Al," I asked him, "are you watching the news?"

"I sure am. And here's what it means: McCarthy is going to win the New Hampshire primary, and that'll force Bobby to step up to the plate."

Al was wrong about New Hampshire, but he was right about the psychological effect of Tet on the American public. Throughout February, media coverage of the offensive and the U.S. response was devastatingly negative. On ABC, Joseph C. Harsch criticized government officials for lack of candor, declaring that the U.S. needed a leader who would "admit frankly the fact that after two years of massive American military intervention in Vietnam, the enemy has been able to mount and to launch by far the biggest and boldest and most sophisticated offensive of the whole war."

The most serious media defection from the U.S. cause in Vietnam was that of Walter Cronkite, anchor of the *CBS Evening News* and the most widely respected TV journalist in the world. Stunned by the Tet attacks, Cronkite flew to Vietnam on February 11 and spent several days touring the country, including the ruined streets of Hue. On Tuesday, February 27, CBS aired Cronkite's special half-hour "Report on Vietnam," filled with clips of Vietnamese cities that resembled the bombed-out ruins of World War II. In his final summation, Cronkite repudiated the government's continued optimism about the conflict. Now, he said, it is "more certain than ever that the bloody experience of Vietnam is to end in a stalemate." Which raised the inevitable question: If victory in Vietnam was impossible, why were Americans still fighting — and dying — there?

Ironically, in strictly military terms, the Tet Offensive was a failure. Losses by the Communist forces were several times larger than those suffered by the Americans and South Vietnamese, and the territory captured by the Vietcong was rewon by the South within weeks. Most important, the pro-Communist uprising among the South Vietnamese people that the offensive had been intended to spark never materialized. But none of this really mattered. The shocking nature of the attacks, the apparent unwillingness of the U.S. leadership to level with the American people about the situation in Vietnam, and the growing sense that the war was a no-win situation all made Tet into a turning point in the evolution of attitudes toward the conflict.

The Tet Offensive and the shift in public sentiment galvanized the quixotic McCarthy campaign. In New Hampshire, the nation's first primary state, a brigade of youthful student volunteers (many of them having shaved and shorn their hair to be "Clean for Gene") suddenly materialized. Led by Sam Brown, a divinity student from Council Bluffs, Iowa, a peace advocate who served as student coordinator for the McCarthy campaign, the two to three thousand volunteers came from a hundred eastern colleges and fanned out across the state, ringing doorbells, making phone calls, and distributing literature. Many residents of the traditionally conservative state were charmed by their youthful idealism, which contrasted — favorably — with the drug-and-sex-soaked anarchism they perceived in their hippy counterparts.

As primary day, March 12, dawned, most observers predicted that McCarthy might win up to one quarter of the Democratic vote — a respectable showing but no disaster for the President. In the end, McCarthy collected 42 percent of the vote in New Hampshire, finishing within 230 votes of Johnson.

The meaning of McCarthy's near-victory in New Hampshire may not have been as clear-cut as it first appeared. Polls later showed that three-fifths of McCarthy voters in the generally hawkish state had deserted Johnson "because he was not hawkish *enough.*" Thus, rather than an endorsement of McCarthy's peace platform, the vote may have been simply a rejection of an increasingly unpopular president.

Nonetheless, the results from New Hampshire stunned the political world. They also prompted another round of agonizing reappraisal by Kennedy and his closest advisers. He actually proposed a political deal with Johnson. After meeting with his brother Ted, adviser Ted Sorensen, and Defense Secretary Clark Clifford, he asked Johnson, through Clifford, to appoint an independent commission to "reevaluate" the war in Vietnam. If Johnson would agree, Kennedy would stay out of the presidential race. But Johnson rejected the idea, viewing it as an abdication of presidential leadership that would only help the Communists.

Kennedy also offered an accommodation to McCarthy. The day after the New Hampshire primary, the two senators met at Ted Kennedy's Washington office, and two days later representatives of both campaigns met in Green Bay, Wisconsin. On both occasions, they discussed a possible joint effort to unseat Johnson. But McCarthy resented what he saw as Kennedy's opportunistic leap into the race after McCarthy had shown it was winnable. "It was a little lonely up there in New Hampshire," he acidly remarked. For his part, Kennedy was unwilling to comply with McCarthy's demand that he restrict his campaign to states McCarthy didn't plan to compete in. No deal was struck.

On Saturday, March 16, Kennedy announced his intention to seek the presidency in a press conference in the old Senate Caucus Room. It was the same venue where his brother had declared his candidacy eight years earlier. He said that the nation's "disastrous, divisive policies" could be reversed only by a change in the White House.

I watched RFK's announcement on television in the Sunset Boulevard living room of a lovely young Asian girl named Irene, who commented, "I'd vote for Bobby if I could. He's cute."

Irene wasn't the only one to think so. Like his brother in 1960, Robert F. Kennedy in 1968 quickly attracted a cadre of youthful female admirers who treated him more like a fifth member of the Beatles than a politician. When he arrived at a campaign stop, usually riding in a Lincoln convertible equipped with a flat-topped trunk for the candidate to stand on, his teenage fans in the crowd would begin jumping up and down and screaming, "Bobby!" Kennedy's attempts to shake the hands of those old enough actually to vote for him were often thwarted by his need to protect himself from the "jumpers."

Kennedy was well aware of the political power of charm and celebrity — so much so that he even briefly encouraged a certain TV actor to jump into the arena.

The last time I visited Hick Hill prior to Bob's announcement that he would seek the presidency, I was out back at the stables giving his horse, "Attorney General," a little brushing. Bobby arrived, and after some small talk, he said, "When are you going to join us?"

I replied, "What do you mean?"

Bobby said, "There's a Senate seat opening up soon in California. With your celebrity and speaking ability, you should go for it."

Flattered but a little nonplussed, I said, "Well, when you're sitting in the Oval Office, having stopped the war, we'll talk again."

He laughed, smiled, and said in his all-too-typical Hamlet fashion, "We'll see."

I never saw him privately again.

Events continued to unfold quickly that spring and summer. Fourteen Democratic primaries were scheduled for the March–July period, of which only four or five were viewed as competitive and crucial to the chances of McCarthy and Kennedy.

On the evening of March 31, President Johnson requested network time to address the nation on Vietnam. In his speech, he reviewed the troubled history of American involvement in the war, including the recent Tet Offensive. He recounted peace overtures his administration had made to the North Vietnamese, and announced a new unilateral de-escalation of hostilities that he hoped would be matched by equal restraint from the other side, and a possible initiation of peace negotiations.

In the closing moments of the speech, Johnson turned to the increasingly bitter atmosphere of domestic politics:

For thirty-seven years in the service of our nation, first as a Congressman, as a Senator and as Vice President, and now as your President, I have put the unity of the people first. I have put it ahead of any divisive partisanship. And in these times, as in times before, it is true that a house divided against itself by the spirit of faction, of party, of region, of religion, of race, is a house that cannot stand.

There is division in the American house now. There is divisiveness among us all tonight. And holding the trust that is mine, as President of all the people, I cannot disregard the peril of the progress of the American people and the hope and the prospect of peace for all peoples, so I would ask all Americans whatever their personal interest or concern to guard against divisiveness and all of its ugly consequences.

So far, this was standard political rhetoric from an embattled president appealing for public support for his increasingly unpopular policies. Coming from Johnson, the calls for "unity" sounded in many ears like pleas to stifle dissent. But then Johnson turned his rhetoric on himself and dropped the political bombshell of the year:

With American sons in the fields far away, with America's future under challenge right here at home, with our hopes and the world's hopes for peace in the balance every day, I do not believe that I should devote an hour or a day of my time to any personal partisan causes or to any duties other than the awesome duties of this office — the Presidency of your country.

Accordingly, I shall not seek, and I will not accept, the nomination of my party for another term as your President.

At the time of Johnson's speech, I was on a flight from Los Angeles to San Francisco, where I was filming *Bullitt* with Steve McQueen. When the pilot came on the public address system to tell us that Lyndon Johnson had just announced that he would not accept the Democratic nomination for president, the passengers erupted in cheers and applause. I was among the loudest.

In the Wisconsin primary on April 2, McCarthy won more than 56 percent of the vote over 35 percent for President Johnson, who had already withdrawn from the race.

Two days later, on April 4, on another of my commutes between Los Angeles and San Francisco, another announcement by a different pilot informed us that Dr. Martin Luther King Jr. had been shot and killed in Memphis. I was dumbfounded and sick when I heard the news.

Meanwhile, Vice President Hubert Humphrey had stepped forward to pick up the mantle of Johnson. A Minnesota liberal with a great track record as a champion of civil rights and other progressive causes, Humphrey was saddled with the Johnson legacy of Vietnam. Although his disaffection with the administration's war policy was widely rumored, his loyalty to Johnson would not permit him to publicly dissent.

On May 7, Kennedy won the Indiana primary with 42 percent of the vote. Roger Branigin, the Democratic governor of the state who was running as a favorite son candidate on behalf of the party establishment, received almost 31 percent, while McCarthy finished third with 27 percent. As party rules then stipulated, however, Kennedy's victory didn't guarantee him the state's backing at the nominating convention in August. The delegates would actually be selected by the party regulars at the state convention in June, and would be pledged to the primary winner only for one ballot; thereafter, they would almost certainly switch their loyalty to the candidate of the establishment, Hubert Humphrey.

A week later, Kennedy followed up Indiana with a 52 percent to 31 percent victory in Nebraska.

McCarthy won the May 28 Oregon primary race by a margin of 45 to 39 percent. Most of the remaining votes went to Johnson, whose name was still on the ballot. McCarthy benefited from the loyalty of antiwar activists who remembered the courage he'd shown in being the first to challenge Johnson. RFK's loss to McCarthy was the first electoral defeat suffered by any Kennedy in twenty-seven campaigns.

More significant for Kennedy — though little noticed at the time — was a particular campaign appearance in Oregon. At Portland's Temple Neveh Shalom, he made an impassioned speech in defense of the American commitment to Israel. "The United States must defend Israel against aggression from whatever source," he said. The next day, a newspaper in Pasadena, California, reported the speech alongside a photograph of Kennedy wearing a yarmulke. After seeing the paper, a Palestinian refugee named Sirhan Sirhan, living with his family in the Los Angeles area, wrote in his notebook: "Robert F. Kennedy must be assassinated before June 5, 1968." That would be the day after the California primary.

The completion of shooting for *Bullitt* in May enabled me to turn my full attention to work on my doctoral degree and my service for Dissenting Democrats. We'd continued to support McCarthy, but, like most other antiwar groups, we were torn between him and Kennedy.

I was one of the many Democrats struggling to decide what to do. Although I was on record as a McCarthy supporter, my heart was with Kennedy. I was certain he could win both the Democratic nomination and the general election. I was getting frequent calls from Tom Braden, a close friend of RFK, as well as from others in the Kennedy camp, asking me when I would be getting on board. At the same time, I was talking with Al Lowenstein constantly about my personal conflict; he was now running for Congress from the Fifth Congressional District on New York's Long Island and wanted me to campaign for him.

Of course, my acting career was not entirely on hold. My agent at the time, Max Arnow from Creative Management Agency (CMA), called to tell me that there was interest in me for a role as a Werhmacht major in *The Bridge at Remagen,* a World War II picture to be shot that summer in

Prague, Czechoslovakia. Producer David Wolper and Director John Guillerman wanted to meet with me to see whether I could speak German credibly. Having just spent a great deal of time preparing for a German exam as part of my Ph.D. candidacy, I arrived at the meeting feeling confident and bearing a copy of the German text I'd been studying from. Rather than using the film script, I read from the text. The filmmakers liked what they heard, and I was hired for the role.

The next day, I got a call from Jim Butler, an old college friend who was working as a Movie of the Week publicist at ABC-TV in New York.

"I saw you debate Bill Buckley on Vietnam last year," he told me. "What a job. You made the silver-tongued orator of the Right look slightly addled."

"Well, thanks," I remarked. "Does that have something to do with the reason you're calling?"

"Absolutely," he replied. "We've got Buckley scheduled to do live commentary from the broadcast booth at the party conventions this summer. Now we're looking for someone with an opposing point of view. Are you interested?"

"You bet your ass I'm interested. But I

just made a deal to shoot a picture in Europe during August." There was no way to resolve the timing conflict.

As it turned out, ABC paired Buckley with Gore Vidal, the distinguished novelist, playwright, essayist, and left-wing gadfly. Their on-air debates during the tumultuous conventions of 1968 produced one of the wildest moments in live television history. On Wednesday, August 28, an exchange between the two moderated by ABC newsman Howard K. Smith turned to the topic of war dissent. After someone referred to the treatment of American Fascist sympathizers during World War II, Vidal turned to Buckley and remarked, "As far as I'm concerned, the only pro- or crypto-Nazi I can think of is yourself."

Buckley was livid. He screamed, "Now listen, you queer. Stop calling me a crypto-Nazi or I'll sock you in your goddamned face and you'll stay plastered."

This was more than ABC had bargained for. The resulting litigation between the two gentlemen of letters went on for years.

Meanwhile, back in the spring, I whipped through my language exams and the written and oral doctoral exams and headed east. I gave several antiwar speeches at colleges and Democratic fund-raisers. It was apparent from the response that the stage was set for a thrilling final act in the end-the-war drama that Al Lowenstein had so skillfully scripted. In the primaries, Kennedy had demonstrated that the people were fed up with the war. Surely the Democratic convention couldn't turn its back on him. I hoped that Al himself would sit in Congress during the first administration of President Robert F. Kennedy. Perhaps I might even have some role to play in the new government. But above all I hoped that the wretched bloodletting of America in Vietnam would end.

I devoted the spring to working in support of Al's Congressional bid. I stayed at the homes of supporters in Long Beach, New York, rising early and spending long days in beauty parlors, bowling alleys, and supermarkets, shaking hands, kissing babies, and hugging female fans of *U.N.C.L.E.* It was no fun. But my respect for Al was such that I willingly did it all. I dreamed he'd be a powerful voice for good in the halls and cloakrooms of Congress.

June 4, 1968, was an unseasonably hot day on Long Island. The temperatures had fallen a bit by the evening when I returned to Al's house on Lindell Boulevard in Long Beach. The house was quiet; most of Al's student supporters were still out working the hustings. I untucked my shirt, grabbed a half-warm beer from the fridge, and settled down in front of the old black-and-white TV to catch the results from the crucial California primary.

This was the biggest battle of the primary season. California's 174 convention delegates were more than 13 percent of the number needed to win the nomination. So crucial was this state that Kennedy had even indicated that he would pull out of the race in favor of McCarthy if he lost California.

Bobby won a narrow victory — 46 percent to McCarthy's 42, with 12 percent for Thomas Lynch, attorney general of the state and a stand-in for Humphrey.

About three A.M. — midnight on the West Coast — Bobby appeared in front of the TV cameras to address his admirers and campaign workers at the Ambassador Hotel in Los Angeles. He looked haggard but happy. Ethel stood alongside, clad in a white-and-orange miniskirt and white stockings. Bobby joked about the Dodgers pitcher Don Drysdale, who had just pitched a record sixth consecutive shutout, saying he hoped "we have as good fortune in our campaign." After thanking the crowd and the many Kennedy supporters around the country who were watching, he said, "And now it's on to Chicago, and let's win there."

Al arrived home just in time to hear the news on TV that Kennedy had been shot.

Al began a succession of calls to Los Angeles to Dick Goodwin and other associates of Bobby. Between calls he reported to me on the unfolding drama as Kennedy was brought to Good Samaritan Hospital. For hours, hope and dread did battle. Just as in that half-hour period on November 22, 1962, between the announcement of the three shots fired at the Dallas motorcade and Walter Cronkite's confirmation that the President had died, we didn't want to believe the worst. But during one break between phone calls, Al and I walked over to the nearby beach. As the sun was rising, Al told me, "Goodwin says it's over. It's only a matter of time." Then he said, "I'm going to L.A. When I get back, I'm going to drop out of the race."

I was stunned. "You can't mean it, Al. It's because of you and all of us that Bobby ran for president. That's why he went to California. That's why he's going to die. Now you've got to win — for him."

Al was silent for a long moment. Fearing he hadn't understood me, I started to repeat my words. Al just raised his hands, removed his glasses, and mumbled, "I know, I know."

A few hours later, Al left for California. He would return two days later on the plane carrying the body of a second slain Kennedy.

Somehow — I don't know how — I got back to my apartment on Central Park West in Manhattan. I remember that I didn't shed a tear until early the next morning, some twenty-six hours after the shooting, when spokesman Frank Mankiewicz officially announced Bobby's death, adding, "He was forty-two years old." I fell apart and cried until I fell asleep.

It took months before I was able to function normally again. I sank into a depression that didn't lift until the following year, when I met my future wife.

On Thursday night, June 6, 1968, Bobby's coffin was brought to St. Patrick's Cathedral. That night, Barry Gray, the New York radio host who'd pioneered the talk show format, called and asked me to be on his program. When we finished the show around one A.M., Barry suggested we walk over to St. Pat's. The heat was unbearable, and when we arrived at East Fifty-first Street, a long line of people — perhaps a thousand or more — had already assembled to await the five-thirty A.M. opening of the great gothic cathedral to the public.

Those who were standing vigil next to the casket left. Then someone recognized me, and suddenly Barry Gray and I were asked to stand beside the light mahogany box that contained what was left of the man that I and many others had believed would be the next president of the United States.

On Saturday morning, I arrived at St. Pat's about a half hour before the scheduled eleven A.M. start of the funeral Mass. The first person I saw was Lyndon B. Johnson, striding unsmilingly through the crowd of people gathered outside the church.

I found myself seated near the middle of the great church, where I could see and hear all that was to happen.

An amazing assortment of notables crowded the cathedral. Statesmen such as Robert McNamara, W. Averell Harriman, and Douglas Dillon mingled with show people like Jason Robards, Shirley Mac-Laine, and Kirk Douglas, and writers like poet Robert Lowell, novelist Truman Capote, and journalists Jimmy Breslin and Stewart Alsop. Radical labor organizer César Chávez and a few fellow farm workers, unable to find seats, wound up standing in front of the congressional delegation, blocking their view — an "accidental" snub that the fiery Chávez and his supporters enjoyed.

My most vivid memories of that service are of two sounds. One was Edward Kennedy, eulogizing his second fallen brother with his powerful voice crumbling with emotion: Robert, he said, should be

remembered simply as a good and decent
  man,
who saw wrong and tried to right it,
saw suffering and tried to heal it,
saw war and tried to stop it.

The other was the surrealistically pure voice of Andy Williams, somewhere up high in the cathedral, singing "The Battle Hymn of the Republic" a capella.

When the Mass ended, a Checker cabbie on Fifth Avenue picked me up.

"I recognize you, buddy," said the driver. "I loved Bobby. Where can I take you? It's on me."

"Penn Station," I replied. I would be traveling on the RFK funeral train for Washington, D.C. "But take it slow. I need a little time to pull myself together."

At Penn Station I ran into Peter Edelman, one of Bob's aides from Minneapolis. We hugged silently. Words were impossible —

and unnecessary.

As soon as I boarded the train, I headed for the bar car. The next eight hours were like the Irish wakes I'd attended so often as a child. They'd always involved an open coffin in the living room of somebody's home. (In this case, the last car of the train played the role of the living room.) The coffin was always the centerpiece of a drunken blowout filled with jokes, toasts, and stories about the departed.

I'd often been part of the gatherings at Hickory Hill, Ethel Kennedy's home in McLean, Virginia. They'd included many of John F. Kennedy's closest friends and advisers as well as newer faces that had become part of Bobby's entourage after Dallas. Ethel referred to this gang as the "Government in Exile." Now they were all there on Bobby's funeral train.

I ran into Al. "You know," I told him, "if there's a conspiracy to kill off the remaining liberals, all they have to do is dynamite this train."

Once again he covered his eyes. "I know, I know."

We pulled out of Penn Station. No one could have anticipated what we glimpsed through the windows of the train as we journeyed south from New York. It was a

386

world that those of us who habitually traveled by plane rarely saw. As columnist Russell Baker later said, "These people were out doing their Saturday things. But they ended up at the railroad track, and the reaction was kind of varied, as you would expect; a lot of solemn people and a few carrying flowers and signs and whatnot. But it really impressed me to see America with its hair down on a Saturday afternoon. It was like seeing one's whole country."

I'd put it a little differently. Looking through the windows of that car, I saw the downtrodden of America — overwhelmingly black — watching the passage of a train that they believed carried a man who might have been a hero for them. For some reason, not discernible from his political record, black Americans in 1968 saw RFK as a friend and a possible savior. They held heartbreaking makeshift signs: REST IN PEACE, ROBERT, I'LL PRAY FOR YOU. WHO WILL BE THE NEXT ONE? WE HAVE LOST OUR LAST HOPE. GOOD-BYE, BOBBY. WE STILL LOVE YOU.

Then there were the people standing alone and saluting. Some were police officers or firefighters in uniform. Others were women in hair curlers holding children in one arm while saluting awkwardly with the other.

While the train was passing through New Jersey, Bob's oldest son, Joe, just fifteen at the time, visited the car. I was seated next to Lucy Jarvis, a producer for NBC. She said, "My God, maybe all the Kennedys are going to do a trip through the train." She was right. Moments later, Jackie appeared, looking as stunned as she had during her husband's four days in November five years earlier. Her smile was fixed, her eyes glassy and remote. She was quickly gone; I wouldn't see her again until 1980, when we met at a memorial service at the old East Side Synagogue after the assassination of Al Lowenstein.

After Jackie's departure, there was a moment of awful silence in the previously boisterous bar car. It was broken by the unmistakable voice of Ethel Kennedy: "Guys, this is the only car that isn't on the tilt." (She was referring to the fact that the train ride had been exceptionally bumpy.) She proceeded through the car, shaking hands and exchanging personal words with everyone. She smiled, laughed, and cracked jokes, even as she looked monumentally wounded.

The train ride was a gloomy affair. Brake troubles and crowds along the tracks prolonged the trip from the normal four-and-a-half hours to over eight. At Elizabeth, New Jersey, the crowd of mourners overflowed onto the northbound track. At 1:24 P.M., the Admiral roared past the funeral train, hitting a group of mourners. Two were killed, six others injured. I heard nothing about the accident till much later.

We passed through Baltimore. Darkness fell. The food and booze ran out. The air-conditioning stopped working. The train grew quieter, damper, gloomier. We all sensed that we were witnessing not merely the end of a political campaign or even the life of one worthy man, but the end of an era. Public life, we knew, would never again be as exciting or uplifting. Nothing I've seen in the forty years since then has changed my mind.

The train arrived at Washington's Union Station around nine o'clock. I was invited to share a limo ride with someone in the funeral cortege. As I took my seat, the door was slammed on my right hand.

It was quite dark when the procession rolled out from the station toward Arlington. We passed the shantytown called Resurrection City, where thousands of blacks had gathered to protest the persistence of poverty in America. They recognized the procession with clenched fist salutes, lit candles, and torches fashioned from rolled-up newspapers. A chorus sang "The Battle Hymn of the Republic" one more time. Crossing the bridge into Arlington, I noticed a hill high up in the cemetery that seemed to be ablaze: more candles and newspaper torches.

The procession rolled to a stop. We exited the cars. Someone handed me a candle (I have the burned-out stump of wax to this day). In the candlelit darkness, the pallbearers carried Bob's coffin toward the burial plot, looking terribly desolate, young, and fragile — like friends burying not a great statesman but a buddy from the office.

The brief ceremony was quickly over. The big shots departed, led by President and Lady Bird Johnson. I hung around, nursing my bruised hand and carrying my candle forlornly. The coffin hadn't yet been interred. Gradually the crowds that had been held back for security reasons climbed the hill and made their way toward the grave site. Sobbing, they knelt by the coffin, touching it and praying. Suddenly we all felt much older. I closed my eyes and thought of the line from *Hamlet:* "Flights of angels sing thee to thy rest . . ."

I'd made no plans for an overnight stay in Washington, expecting the service to conclude by seven P.M. Now, however, it was almost midnight. I had nowhere to go till Sunday night, when I was ticketed to fly to London and then to Prague, where filming of *The Bridge at Remagen* would shortly begin. I found myself wandering around Georgetown in a kind of daze. I ran into Al again and we embraced. Al suggested a nearby hotel where I could get a room for the night. I thanked him, then said, "You know, I'll be in Czechoslovakia all summer. Come and see me. I think some kind of freedom is happening there. Anyway, it's better than being here."

"Thanks for the invitation," Al replied. "But we still have to win in Chicago. The Democrats have to nominate someone who will stop the war."

"And who is that going to be?"

"What about Hubert?"

I was incredulous. Whatever his instincts, Hubert Humphrey had staunchly supported Johnson and his war. "Hubert is Lyndon's man."

"Maybe not," Al replied. "I'm hoping we can get to him. Talk him into resigning as vice president. Make a clean break. Then run as an independent Democrat on an antiwar platform."

It sounded implausible, but I knew better

than to doubt Al. "Well, I never thought you'd get Johnson to quit. Maybe you can pull it off a second time."

Al gazed at me sadly. "Maybe," he said quietly. "Maybe. But I don't think so." He gave a long sigh. "I don't know anything anymore. The world is upside-down." That's how we parted.

Subsequently Al and Eugene McCarthy organized a group called the Coalition for an Open Convention to give antiwar Democrats a focus for their ongoing efforts. On August 12, McCarthy urged his supporters not to show up to demonstrate in Chicago during the convention. His goal was to avoid clashes with police. Some followed his advice, others did not.

The debacle in the streets of Chicago during the August convention has become legendary. Estimates as to the number of demonstrators in the city vary, but most accounts suggest only about five thousand protestors turned up. Disguised police officers acting as agents provocateurs mingled with the crowds, helping to stir up trouble. (Ten years later, CBS News investigators claimed that as many as one-sixth of the demonstrators were undercover agents.) After several days of minor clashes, the conflict came to a head on Wednesday evening. The police launched a full-out assault on protestors, whose taunts and minor attacks they'd tolerated with growing frustration and anger. Demonstrators, reporters, camera operators, and innocent bystanders alike were clubbed, kicked, beaten, and arrested. Later, the Walker Commission, examining the events, would call the violence "a police riot."

Meanwhile, on the floor of the convention at the International Amphitheatre, the Humphrey steamroller piloted by the party regulars pushed on. Some insurgents rallied around George McGovern; others talked of drafting Ted Kennedy. Both efforts quickly faded.

When images of the mayhem outside reached the floor of the convention, an uproar ensued. While making a nominating speech for McGovern, Connecticut Senator Abraham Ribicoff departed from his text to denounce the police: "With George McGovern we wouldn't have Gestapo tactics on the streets of Chicago." TV cameras quickly shifted to Chicago's Mayor Richard Daley, sitting near the stage among the Illinois delegation. Apoplectic, he was screaming at the podium. His words weren't picked up by the network microphones, but lip-readers recorded them as, "Fuck you, you Jew son of a bitch, you lousy motherfucker, go home."

Humphrey had continued to search for a way to extricate himself from Johnson's legacy. The Vice President's staff actually prepared an antiwar statement calling for an immediate cease-fire. But when Humphrey showed it to Johnson, the President lashed out and promised to use all his power to "destroy" Humphrey if he dared to release it. Humphrey did not.

The devastating images of the convention were broadcast to the world: violence on the streets of Chicago; confusion, division, and anger among Democrats; and at the center of it all, an ineffectual Hubert Humphrey, desperately trying to evoke the spirits of unity, peace, and forgiveness in the face of the storm.

Many have said that the chaotic convention cost Humphrey the election. If this is taken to mean that a Humphrey victory was rendered impossible even before the start of the fall campaign, it's certainly incorrect. In the final days before the election, every poll showed Republican candidate Richard Nixon's once-wide lead over Humphrey rapidly shrinking. On November 5, Nixon was elected with just 43.42 percent of the vote, defeating Humphrey by a popular-vote margin of just over half a million out of 63 million votes cast. (Most of the remaining votes went to the right-wing independent candidate George C. Wallace of Alabama.) If the campaign had lasted, say, five more days, it's very likely Humphrey would have won.

In fact, Humphrey might well have won had he simply had the nerve to speak out against the war. There are any number of scenarios imaginable, including one in which Humphrey would have resigned the vice presidency in order to free himself to chart a new political course. But Humphrey refused to do this. Under the circumstances, he had the worst of both worlds: saddled with Johnson's hated war, he was also treated with barely disguised contempt by the President, who refused even to keep Humphrey informed about the latest developments in Vietnam and at the Paris peace talks. In a race as close as the 1968 election, this anchor was more than enough to drag the Democrats to defeat.

In October 1968, I was sitting at a desk in London's Savoy Hotel, gazing at an absentee ballot for the U.S. presidential election. Humphrey's failure to take the public stand against the war that represented how he truly felt would undoubtedly cost him millions of votes. It nearly cost him mine; I even briefly contemplated voting for his Republican opponent as a vague act of protest against Humphrey's weakness. "I can't do that," I finally concluded. I placed my X in the box next to Humphrey's name, knowing it would make no difference.

In the years to come, Richard Nixon would preside over student riots, increasing racial polarization, the Watergate scandal, and almost six more years of death in Vietnam. In retrospect it was all practically inevitable. The best of their generation — John, Martin, and Bobby — had all been snuffed out. We won't see their likes again.

ELEVEN:
PRAGUE SUMMER

But in the gross and scope of my opinion,
This bodes some strange eruption to our
state.

Desolation is the word that best describes
how I felt upon my arrival in Prague in the
late afternoon of Monday, June 10, 1968. It
was less than a week after the horror of that
Tuesday midnight at the Ambassador Hotel
in Los Angeles, when the brightest American hope of that dismal year had been
gunned down in his moment of triumph.

I hadn't slept on the overnight British
Airways flight to London, nor during the
layover at Heathrow prior to the short flight
to Prague. I had barely eaten since running
into Al Lowenstein in Georgetown on
Saturday night.

My secretary, Sharon Miller, had gone
ahead to Prague, and she met me at the
airport, which was really just a group of

World War II vintage Quonset huts strung together in helter-skelter fashion.

"Julian would like you to join him for dinner," Sharon said. This was Julian Ludwig, the line producer for David Wolper on *The Bridge at Remagen.* "He'll be at the Paris with some others from the cast. They say it's the only decent restaurant in Prague."

"Must I?" I groaned. I was exhausted and haggard, my nerves frayed — in no condition for my first meeting with my new colleagues. But Sharon said, "They all know what you've been through. Go ahead, Robert — it might do you good."

"Then call Julian and say I'll be happy to join him."

To my surprise, the evening worked out very well. Julian and I were joined by George Segal, Bradford Dillman, and Ben Gazzara. I knew George mainly from his guesting on talk shows, where he was witty, charming, and played a musical instrument that looked like an Elizabethan banjo. He'd also starred with Liz Taylor and Richard Burton in the Mike Nichols film of *Who's Afraid of Virginia Woolf?,* for which he received much critical acclaim.

Brad had been the last guest star on the final two-part *U.N.C.L.E.* show, "The Prince of Darkness Affair." A graduate of Hotchkiss, the posh New England prep school, he'd gone on to Yale, where he'd supposedly turned down William F. Buckley's invitation to join the hush-hush Skull and Bones Society (of which both Presidents Bush are members). I'd marveled at his stunning — and chilling — performance opposite my buddy Dean Stockwell in the terrifying movie *Compulsion,* the story of the infamous Loeb and Leopold murders.

And then there was Ben Gazzara, whom my dear friend Jason Robards always referred to with great affection as "Benny the boozer." In 1969, while filming and editing John Cassavetes's *Husbands,* Ben would be my house guest on Mulholland Drive. We'd first met in June 1956, when he was starring on Broadway in *A Hatful of Rain* with Shelley Winters. Later (in 1961), Shelley and Dominick Dunne would be two of my neighbors and friends for a summer in Malibu. We saw many a sunset together — none of them while strictly sober. Shelley, alas, has since passed away, while Nick has gone on the wagon and become a very successful chronicler of crime among the ultra-wealthy.

At the time of our first meeting, Ben was going with Elaine Stritch, no shrinking violet with the bottle herself, and I spotted the two of them in a booth at Jim Downey's bar on New York's Eighth Avenue, a popular actors' hangout. As soon as I saw Ben, I recalled what my friends Paul Lambert and Will Sage had told me. They'd seen Ben as Jocko de Paris in the New York production of *End as a Man,* and they'd urged me to introduce myself to him as their friends. "And be sure to tell him that you played Jocko, too," Paul had added.

It turned out that this was not a great icebreaker. When I introduced myself as they suggested, Ben responded with complete silence.

Thinking he might not have heard me, I tried again: "Mr. Gazzara, I'm Robert Vaughn. We have a couple of mutual friends, Paul Lambert and Will Sage. I just got through playing the role of Jocko de Paris in *End as a Man,* and Paul and Will tell me you were just wonderful in the play." Gazzara stared into space as if I were invisible and inaudible.

Well, I can take a hint. But as I started to leave, Elaine upbraided Gazzara using her full stage voice: "Oh, for Christ's sake, Benny, say hello to the kid!" (Ben was all of two years older than me.)

Gazzara mumbled some halfhearted greeting, and I made good my escape. We next met when we worked together on *Playhouse 90,* acting in a teleplay called *The Trouble-makers* directed by John Frankenheimer. Gazzara was practically as uncommunicative then as he had been that night in New York.

But by the time we had dinner that first night in Prague, we were friends, and we remained so, at least for the filming of *The Bridge at Remagen.* My mother had a saying about show-business relationships: "He loved her, but the season closed." The four of us — George, Ben, Brad, and I — grew terribly close during the months of August to November 1968. We four shared many more dinners in Vienna, Hamburg, Rome, and New York; we laughed and drank and cried and drank and told stories and drank — and then we topped the evening off with a drink or two. (Actually, George Segal was the exception; he drank very little, saying, "It interferes with my suffering.") If anyone would have said at the time, "You four won't see one another again once Election Day has come and gone," we would have scoffed at the prediction. But that proved to be the case.

That summer, Prague was, of all the world's great cities, arguably *the* place to be. Change was in the air. The stirrings had begun earlier that year, encouraged by Party Secretary Alexander Dubček, at forty-six one of the youngest men ever to lead a Communist country. From the beginning he'd displayed a very different style to that of his predecessor, Antonin Novotný, a distant, repressive man whose only leadership technique was arresting people and who was sometimes described as conducting "a personality cult without the personality." By 1967 he'd led the country to the brink of economic collapse.

Then, in January 1968, at a crucial vote in the Czech Praesidium — then equally divided between the Old Guard and reformist followers of Dubček — Novotný turned to a wavering supporter named Hendrych and threatened to blackmail his daughter if he didn't vote the right way. Hendrych tapped a rare vein of decency: He stood up to Novotný, switched his vote to Dubček, and broke the deadlock. The Prague Spring had begun, and leadership of the country fell into the hands of Dubček and Ludvik Svoboda, a seventy-two-year-old veteran of two world wars and himself a victim of Stalin's purges. Fittingly, the word *svoboda* is Czech for "freedom."

The shift in government struck a responsive chord among the Czech people. On

April 14, Václav Havel — the actor/writer who would lead the Velvet Revolution of 1988–91, serve four-and-a-half years in prison, and ultimately serve as president of the Czech Republic — published a groundbreaking article in *Literárni Noviny,* then Czechoslovakia's most influential weekly. Titled "On the Theme of an Opposition," it was Havel's contribution to the burgeoning debate on the political future of his country and the first time that the demand for "a new democratic opposition party" had been voiced publicly. Only the unprecedented relaxation of censorship by the Communist regime had made such a publication possible.

The new Dubček regime responded. That same month, Dubček published his Action Programme. It called for freedom of the press and the church, the right to assembly, rehabilitation for the victims of Stalin's purges, and multiparty elections with secret ballots. The economy was to be reorganized to include more trade with the West, and the right to emigrate and travel abroad would be guaranteed. Key government posts would be open to non-Communist-party members, and political detentions would be done away with. Writers who'd criticized the regime were released from prison. For the first time, policemen had to wear numbered badges for identification, and workers were allowed to go on strike. Dubček's program must have terrified the Kremlin.

By the time we started filming in the second week of June, it was a joyous time to be in Prague. Western newspapers and magazines like the *International Herald Tribune, Time,* and *Newsweek* had sprouted on the kiosks in Wenceslas Square. Western music was playing everywhere. On TV, newsmen, philosophers, and academics debated how to consolidate and advance the liberal reforms taking shape without antagonizing the hard-liners who'd long held sway in the country. The restaurants were packed with young people excitedly talking, laughing, and swapping clippings from newly available, once-banned documents and speeches. The smiles they wore and their exuberant anything-is-now-possible mood exemplified the "socialism with a human face" then making headlines the world over.

It seemed like a nationwide coming-out party for millions of happy Czechs. But there was also ominous talk about the troop exercises being conducted by the Warsaw Pact countries in the Soviet-controlled nations bordering Czechoslovakia. No one really dared to believe that the Kremlin would stand by idly while one of the nations in its orbit tried to break away.

In that time of excitement tinged with anxiety, even our movie got caught up in the political intrigue. One Czech newspaper still parroting the party line wrote that we were actually agents of the CIA, in Czechoslovakia to support the prodemocracy insurgents. One Comrade Sadovsky, Soviet adviser to the Ministry of Culture, declared that, using the pretext of filming a "story of the Second World War," we were smuggling guns, tanks, and other military equipment to prepare "a Vietnam-style American invasion of Czechoslovakia." Another national newspaper ran the screaming headline AMERICAN TANKS AND TROOPS HAVE ENTERED PRAGUE.

Rumors flew that our quarter-century-old tanks, vehicles, and weapons were to be impounded. We were informed that pending an investigation of the "real" reason for our importation of military equipment into Czechoslovakia, we would not be allowed to continue filming. But for whatever reason, these threats were never acted upon. Of course, the Soviets weren't only threatening us, they were shaking a fist at the whole country, especially its new leaders.

Meanwhile, we pushed ahead with our filming. I made my first appearance at the Remagen Bridge location. As I exited the vintage car that would be my on-screen vehicle, I noticed some of the middle-aged locals, who'd been watching with great excitement and laughter, suddenly go silent. In a moment, I realized why. I was dressed in the uniform of a major in the German Wehrmacht. The Czechs were horrified: To them, I was a Nazi, a reminder of the German occupation of their homeland in World War II.

I immediately told my secretary, Sharon, to have the distressed observers come into the makeup trailer. I enlisted the help of our excellent translator, the buxom Pepsi Watson. Czech through and through (despite her last name), she spoke perfect English with no apparent accent. I'd been attracted to Pepsi from the time we first met, though I sensed that she was a very high-strung, perhaps excessively emotional person. (I like high-strung women, but not *too* high — as Ring Lardner supposedly warned, "Never sleep with anybody who has worse problems than you do.") So I kept our relationship professional. Now, with Pepsi's help, I told the Czechs the story of our film: Set during the last days of World War II, it recounted the Allies' desperate search for a bridgehead across the Rhine in order to launch a major assault, only to discover that the retreating German army had destroyed all bridges except one — the bridge at Remagen.

Hearing the story and putting my German uniform in a historic context seemed to defuse the anxiety felt by the local people. As the days and weeks went by, we became very friendly with the Czechs. We got to know many of them by name and learned about their hopes for freedom and justice, particularly for their young children.

As that summer's political drama unfolded, skeptical members of the world press corps were stationed at the Alcron Hotel off Wenceslas Square, waiting for the Red hammer to fall.

Benny, George, Brad, and I spent a portion of nearly every night in the same hotel, often joined by Ben's then wife, Janice Rule. It was a faded museum whose green marble pillars, potted palms, and jazz orchestra bespoke an elegance right out of late silent and early talkie European movies. Each evening, the musicians honored us with renditions of World War II songs, romantic and martial, and we took turns twirling

Janice around the dark rooftop dance floor. Janice was a very gifted dancer, and she made even me look slightly more than adequate. Sometime during the summer, we had started playfully referring to Brad as "our tower killer" — partially because of his performance in *Compulsion,* partially because his smile looked, well, kind of scary. When Brad took his turn dancing with Janice, Ben would pound on the table, Upman cigar firmly clenched in his mouth and yell, "Watch the tower killer grinding it into J.R!"

We usually wound up at the Alcron bar for a nightcap and a report from the newsmen on the stories they'd filed that day. Charles Collingwood, one of the original "Murrow Boys" from the glory days of CBS News, presided over the press corps' nightly gatherings, accompanied by his Hollywood actress wife, Louise Allbritton. Always meticulously dressed in a Savile Row suit, Collingwood was the most eloquent of the scribes even after a few Rémy Martins, and I was frankly more starstruck in his presence than in that of any of the actors I'd met.

Throughout the summer, celebrities would wing in to Prague for a meal and a look at the historic events unfolding in that tiny country. Governor Edmund G. "Pat" Brown, who'd been my luncheon guest in 1966 at MGM, flew in for a quick tour and a chat. (He'd been followed in the Sacramento State House by Ronald Reagan and then by his own son, Jerry Brown — sometimes known as Governor Moonbeam; a whirlwind succession of Center, Right, and Left that makes political sense only in California.) Shirley Temple, then the American Ambassador to Ghana — her days on "The Good Ship Lollipop" far behind her — came for lunch one warm afternoon at the International Hotel, where most of the crew and actors lived during the shoot.

Another time, I was in my room, trying to decipher the evening news on one of the few TVs in the hotel, an old black-and-white model that the manager had given me on condition I keep it secret. A loud knock came at my door. "Who is it?" I called, thinking it might be Brad Dillman, one of the few people who knew about my TV.

A voice answered, "Winston Churchill."

A bit nonplussed, I called out, "Come on in, Winnie." It was, of course, not the great wartime leader of Britain but his grandson, Winston Churchill III, visiting Prague on assignment from BBC News. We had a hell of a good evening, chatting and drinking brandy (he would have done his grandfather proud in the booze department that evening). I never saw him again.

To celebrate American Independence Day, the cast of the movie was invited to the American Embassy for the Fourth of July, along with Charles Collingwood, his wife, and some of his colleagues. I tried to use the opportunity to learn what was really happening inside the Dubček administration and the significance of the Warsaw Pact troop exercises, but even after I told the ambassador's wife I was in my Ph.D. countdown at the USC, she revealed nothing. Later that day, over drinks with Collingwood, I found he'd been stonewalled, too.

Little by little, the foreign press began to drift away from Prague, having concluded that nothing dramatic would be happening in the short term. But rumors and stories continued to circulate around the Czech capital. In mid-August, according to one widely circulated account, a Czech train carrying Dubček from Prague arrived at a border town called Čierna Nad Tisou at the same time as a Russian train from Kiev carrying the Soviet premier, Leonid Brezhnev himself. The two trains were parked head-to-head for three days as ultra-secret negotiations supposedly took place between the two leaders. One reporter spoke to a railway worker who said he'd seen a man walking along the line at three in the morning. It turned out to be Dubček. "I can't sleep," he told the worker, "I'm thinking about the price I'm going to have to pay the Russians." But whatever was going on behind the scenes, nothing was revealed publicly.

Just a couple of days later, we got word that Dubček would be making an important statement. Filming came to a halt on the set as cast and crew gathered around a radio to listen as Pepsi Watson translated. "I am being asked whether our sovereignty is threatened," Dubček said. "I tell you sincerely that it is not. We kept the promises we made to you. We continue without turning away from the path on which the Communist party and the whole Czechoslovak nation set out to walk this January 1968. There is no other possibility for our people."

Now another rumor began to circulate — that all of the Prague street signs would soon be taken down in order to make Russian maps of the city useless. This one was true.

On the evening of August 20, our gang of four — Benny, George, Brad, and I — had finished our evening brandies around one

A.M. Brad and I had returned to our digs at the new Park Hotel next to the Exhibitions Palace, a vast wrought-iron love child of the British Brighton Pavilion and the Eiffel Tower located more or less in central Prague. I finished off a final cognac at the bar and retired with the early summer dawn — it got light between three and three-thirty — already faintly tingeing the skies.

I'd scarcely dozed off when I was wakened by a hammering on the connecting door between my suite and Brad's. I unlatched the door and there was Brad, yelling "Look out the window — the cocksuckers did it." There in the square in front of the Exhibitions Palace was a circle of tanks bearing the Soviet red star emblem. Standing atop the tanks was a collection of very nervous and confused-looking young men — Soviet soldiers who, I later learned, had been brought in from places like Mongolia and told that, when they reached Prague, they would be joyfully greeted as liberators. (As Dick Cheney discovered in Iraq thirty-five years later, such predictions rarely come to pass.)

There was nothing for Brad and me to do but wait for instructions. Around eight A.M., word came that Brad and I, and my secretary, Sharon, should grab our passports and a few essentials and meet the car and driver waiting for us downstairs. (I didn't realize that this would be the last time I would see the Park Hotel.) As we headed for the International Hotel, our driver translated what was being said on the car radio. President Svoboda had reportedly been in his pajamas as the tanks rolled into the Hradčany Palace courtyard. His reaction to the Soviet demand that he lend his support to a new puppet government was one word: *Ven!* — Out! A moment later, we heard that a Czech protestor had been killed.

Later, we heard that when Dubček had first been told that foreign troops had violated his country's borders, he was unwilling to believe that the men with whom he'd been negotiating only a couple of weeks before could possibly be attacking his country now. Only when Soviet armored cars drove into the square below his window and machine-gunned a Czech civilian right in front of his eyes did he realize the score.

Our translator, Pepsi, provided further details. KGB men had forced their way into Dubček's study and ripped the telephones out of the wall. His personal bodyguard — a childhood friend — had tried to protect Dubček and was shot by the officer in charge. Dubček and the other Czech leaders were tied with ropes around their necks, bodies bent backward, feet and hands lashed, so that they were unable to struggle without strangling themselves. We later heard from another reliable source that they were taken across the border, all the way to Ukraine, lying on the floor of an armored car.

Despite our horror over what was happening, at first it seemed exciting to be part of an extraordinary historical incident. It was as if we were performing in another scene of the movie, one that somehow had been omitted from the scripts we'd received. But soon we began to realize that all of us, cast and crew and director, were pawns in an international chess game, and the initial thrill was soon replaced by a genuine fear for our well-being — and perhaps even our lives. We were told to stay at the International Hotel for the time being. What would the government do with us? We'd have to wait and see.

Built in the 1950s, the International Hotel was from the architectural school of Stalin. Nicknamed the Little Empire State, it was a very large building with a tall central tower and spire topped with a red star. Now that most of the Americans in town, including our movie team, had been collected there, the orchestra stationed on the top floor devoted themselves to playing World War II songs for us to dance to.

At first there was plenty of food and wine to cushion our imprisonment. We kept hearing that the next day we'd get out, then the day after that and the day after that. A week passed, and the wine began to run out, and then the food. Word came from our producer, David Wolper, that a curfew had been imposed, and that the Russians were under orders to shoot on sight anyone who violated it. Our humor turned macabre; we began joking, half in earnest, about writing last letters to loved ones.

Around this time, I realized that I had left all of my doctoral dissertation materials back at the Park Hotel. I'd spent years accumulating this information, interviewing blacklisted actors and writers, many of them colleagues and friends of mine, and recording their memories and reflections on tape. All of these notes and recordings were now out of my reach — a terribly frustrating situation.

Pepsi had been out of sight for some time. Now our translator suddenly appeared and announced that she had been distributing underground newspapers outside the embassy. Evidently she did not know that two young boys had been machine-gunned for driving around Prague and handing out copies of the *Freedom Press*. But I admired the fact that she'd been willing to take such chances for a cause she believed in — she was a true revolutionary in the best sense of the word.

As our confinement continued, so did the rumors. People were saying that Dubček and the other Czech leaders had been executed in Moscow. But the Czech resistance was fighting back, using sabotage and surreptitious radio and TV broadcasts. Daily at noon we were serenaded by sirens and car horns signaling a general strike.

Then, a week after the invasion, Svoboda and Dubček returned from Moscow. When Dubček spoke to the nation via TV and radio, he appeared pale and haggard, with a bandaged head, obviously a man who had been tortured and broken. In halting tones and with many unaccountable verbal and linguistic errors, he appealed to the people to be calm and not to provoke further violence. He tried to assure them that the Russian troops would withdraw as soon as the situation in Czechoslovakia had been "normalized." As the speech went on, he seemed almost to faint in front of the microphone. Finally, when he began to speak about what had gone on in Moscow, he broke down completely and sobbed.

Dubček's public breakdown was a devastating moment for our Czech friends.

Pepsi was with us when Dubček's speech ended. Suddenly she ran off, clearly with some mission in mind. For a moment, I considered running after her, but not knowing where she intended to go, I stayed put, waiting for the next shock.

I didn't have to wait long. Word got back almost immediately that she had run up to the roof terrace of the hotel, where she'd torn the Russian flag and flagstaff from its support and launched it, javelinlike, at the tanks below. I never heard of her again.

In a moment, all those tanks had turned their guns toward the facade of the hotel, and we Americans were ordered to sit on the stairs inside the front of the hotel facing those guns. We followed orders, though they seemed to make no sense at that time — and still don't today.

Soon word arrived that cars and buses were on their way to take us to the Austrian border. Ben and Janice were to be taken over the border in their own car. Traveling with them would be a young woman who had been Ben's personal waitress at the International Hotel and who had served as the nanny for Ben's daughter Liz when she visited. (In Ben's memoir, *In the Moment,* he calls her Apolina, and I will do likewise.) Like almost everyone else in Prague, Apolina wanted to leave once the Russians came, and the Gazzaras were ready to help. Brad, Sharon, George Segal, and I would travel in my car with my driver. All of the others were assigned spots in specific cars or buses.

The actual departure was chaotic and hasty. We took our passports, whatever we were wearing, and the few things we could stick into a small overnight bag. All of my dissertation materials remained at the Park Hotel. But at last we were escaping house arrest at the International, and that fact eclipsed any other worries.

It was a long, nerve-racking trip, not least because we had to slow down repeatedly for roadblocks manned by young, scared-looking Russians with machine guns. But the arrangements were almost flawless. Gas had been provided by the American Embassy, and David Wolper had somehow obtained the proper papers needed to get us over the border — all of us except one.

It was evening by the time we reached the checkpoint just inside the Austrian border at Gmünd. The guards scrutinized the vehicles in front of ours, one by one, and let them through . . . and then it was time for Ben and Janice's car, and mine.

The oldest-looking border guard told us all to get out of the two cars with passports at the ready. Within seconds, the guards found Apolina — the one person among us whose papers were not in order. They dragged her toward a little guardhouse. We were held at bay by very frightened but menacing young soldiers with large weapons shaking in their sweaty hands. The scene was completely dark, silent, and frightening, lit only by the moon and several searchlights (like the ones you might see at a Hollywood premiere) casting erratic shadows over the border crossing.

With Apolina in custody, the rest of us were taken across the border to a kind of café, a border way station of the kind found in a noir film about Cold War espionage. There we would wait for her, and meanwhile take part in one of the more macabre press availabilities I've ever experienced — we were plied with food and beer while several journalists interviewed us about our experiences in Prague.

Three hours went by. It was now after midnight, the reporters had gone, and there was still no sign of Apolina. We were arguing with great fervor and increasing intensity about what we should do: Leave Apolina there, or somehow get back across the border into Czechoslovakia and try to rescue her? Was that even possible? Wouldn't it only get the rest of us into trouble? And how could we be sure Apolina was even within reach? By now, she might have been taken back to Prague.

Suddenly, as we argued, a shadowy figure emerged from the darkness at the checkpoint, yelling and waving her arms. It was Apolina. Somehow this young, terribly frightened girl had distracted her captors and escaped. Soon we were weeping with joy and excitement.

Eventually, Ben managed to get her back to the States.

Relieved and exhausted, we were now billeted in a run-down border motel about as restful-looking as the one run by Anthony Perkins in Hitchcock's *Psycho.* I'd finally managed to begin a fitful night's sleep just before dawn when the phone rang. I snarled into the line only to be greeted by a typically hyper American disc jockey's voice saying, "Hey, music lovers! A special treat! We're about to speak with Robert Vaughn, who you know as super-agent Napoleon Solo from *The Man from U.N.C.L.E.* He's just outwitted the Russkies, escaped from Communist repression, and has crossed the Czech-Austrian border to safety in the small town of Gmünd. Tell us, Robert, how it feels to be free!"

I screamed every profanity I could think of, smashed the rickety old phone down on its cradle, and fell fast asleep. I never learned the identity of the insensitive jerk on the other end of the line.

We hadn't managed to complete the filming of *The Bridge at Remagen* before world events had interrupted us. We resumed the picture that fall, first in Hamburg, Germany, and then in Rome, where Wolper had, at great expense, rebuilt half of the Remagen Bridge at Castel Gandolfo, the Pope's summer residence just outside the city.

In Hamburg, we four were put up at the very grand Atlantic Hotel. We spent our time there shooting interior scenes that were to have been done at Barrandov Studios in Prague.

Our first week there, some of the younger American actors in the cast were discussing a bar named Sherry's near our hotel. They claimed it was populated with gorgeous young German girls, beautifully dressed and speaking perfect English, and each resembling (at least at a glance) an American movie star. They even identified themselves as "Linda Darnell," "Marilyn Monroe," "Elizabeth Taylor," and so on, just in case the impression wasn't quite exact. According to our young colleagues, the price for a "date" with one of the "stars" was $37.50. But there was supposedly some unwritten deal with the Atlantic Hotel that you had to first wine and dine her in the hotel's very posh restaurant.

Our curiosity piqued, the four of us went over to check out Sherry's, and sure enough, the whole story turned out to be correct. I found three "Marilyn Monroes" almost immediately and had to quickly choose one without offending the other two. And how was she? Well, if Joe DiMaggio wouldn't tell, why should I?

One night shortly before we left for Rome, Brad, George, and I were in George's suite, which was connected by a very large gothic door to Ben's digs, when we heard a great deal of laughing next door. Fortunately for the curious, all of the suite doors at the Atlantic Hotel had enormous keys, with equally enormous keyholes. George took a quick peek and announced, "Benny is with 'Arlene Dahl' tonight." (Arlene was a very red-haired American movie actress whom you might remember from 1950s pictures like *Woman's World* and *Slightly Scarlet*. She'd married, then divorced, the Latin lover and matinee idol Fernando Lamas who lives on in Billy Crystal's spoof: "You look mahvelous!")

Somehow we managed to arrange ourselves so that all three of us could peer through the keyhole at once. Sure enough, there was Benny, clad in a huge white terry-cloth bathrobe and smoking an enormous Romeo and Julieta cigar. He was reclining on the giant gothic-carved bed reading a copy of the *International Herald Tribune* with the headline JACKIE TO WED ARI. The *ersatz* Arlene Dahl was sitting at the foot of the bed, also in a robe, holding a very large brandy snifter in her well-manicured, lovely white hand.

As we watched, Ben, lowering the paper and smiling, said to the German hooker, "Drink deep, my angel, my sweet Nazi." Ben had a habit of calling everyone "angel," male or female, but "my sweet Nazi" was too much. George, Brad, and I broke up in giggles. And that is my last memory of four rapidly aging actors having a grand old time in Europe on David Wolper's dime.

Months later, after we'd all returned to the States, my dissertation materials were retrieved from the Park Hotel and returned to me by the State Department on Christmas Eve. No reason was given why it took so long.

For Prague and Czechoslovakia, things got worse before they got better. Alexander Dubček was found to have radioactive strontium in his blood, suggesting he'd been poisoned in Moscow. He was shortly removed from office and expelled from the party, spending the next eighteen years as a clerk in a lumberyard for the Slovak Forestry Commission. Happily, Dubček lived to see the Velvet Revolution of 1989 and reemerged as a symbol of democratic freedom in what has become today's Czech Republic.

As for Pepsi Watson, I never found out what happened to her — my personal heroine from the short-lived Prague Spring.

TWELVE:
STILL UNSOLVED?

Foul deeds will rise,
Though all the earth o'erwhelm them, to
men's eyes.

On January 20, 1969, Richard Nixon, the dark prince of American politics, at long last achieved his goal — the presidency of the United States. It might never have happened if the shots fired at Robert F. Kennedy the previous June had missed their mark. And subsequent history would surely have been profoundly changed. The American involvement in Vietnam would almost certainly have ended several years earlier than it did . . . and the Watergate would have remained forever just another hotel in Washington, D.C.

Like the murder of his brother almost five years earlier, the assassination of Robert Kennedy was a tragic watershed for America. But unlike the earlier killing, at least the RFK assassination was a noncontroversial, open-and-shut case with a single, obvious suspect.

Or was it?

Millions of Americans today can recall how RFK's assassin, Sirhan Bashara Sirhan was seen on TV firing a .22 Iver Johnson pistol at the senator. But those memories are illusory. Contrary to most public opinion, *no one* saw the assassination on TV because there was *no* live coverage of the murder. There's not a single film still or photograph of Sirhan committing the crime.

This is not to say that there is no evidence linking Sirhan to the crime. He was seen by many people in the pantry of the Ambassador Hotel firing his weapon and quickly being subdued by a group of onlookers who included former pro football player Roosevelt Grier, Olympic star Rafer Johnson, and author George Plimpton.

Sirhan was arrested, charged with the killing of RFK, convicted of the crime, and sentenced to die in the electric chair. However, the State of California abolished capital punishment in 1972, and today, forty years later, Sirhan is serving a life sentence for his crime.

Practically all Americans assume that Sirhan's responsibility for the death of RFK and his role as the lone assassin have been established beyond all reasonable doubt. I shared that assumption until 1972, when my continued involvement in political debate brought the real questions about the RFK killing to my attention.

I was asked by Bob Walsh, manager of Los Angeles radio station KABC, to host a four-hour talk show on Sunday afternoons. I wasn't a novice host: I'd previously filled in at KABC for Marv Grey, who had been the producer for the legendary Joe Pyne, an archconservative in a talk-radio world then dominated by liberals. Pyne's favorite expression when he disagreed with a caller was, "Why don't you go gargle with razor blades?" — quite a contrast with KABC's highest-rated host, the very eloquent, British-educated liberal Michael Jackson, whose intonations and manners resembled those of Prince Charles. (Around the station, people talked about the time Jackson interviewed Senator Ted Kennedy from D.C. about the war then raging in Vietnam. Kennedy concluded the interview by saying to Jackson, "Also, I just wanted to tell you how much I enjoy your music.")

I was happy to take on the KABC assignment. It required making some special arrangements, since I'd been signed by the

British commercial Channel ITV to star in a television series titled *The Protectors,* to be shot in Europe and England. I found I could broadcast from Britain once a week, thereby keeping my Sunday slot alive even while I was overseas.

I launched the new show just in time to interview almost all of the many Democratic candidates vying to oust Richard Nixon in the upcoming 1972 election. And amid all the usual calls about matters political, I received my share of dingbat conspiracy theorists, eager to explain in great detail that JFK did not die in Dallas, but was alive in a vegetative state in a rest home off the coast of Zanzibar; that Martin Luther King Jr. did not die in Memphis, but was directing Communist coups in South America; and that similar implausible alternatives to conventional history ought to be considered, going back to Lincoln's assassination in 1865.

But one of my conspiracy-monger callers was different. He was a former ABC journalist named Jonn Christian, who believed that Sirhan Sirhan had not acted alone; that there was more than one gun firing at Bob Kennedy in June 1968; and that Sirhan was, in Jonn's words, a "Manchurian candidate." The reference, of course, was to the 1961 film directed by my friend John Frankenheimer in which a brainwashed Korean War veteran is turned into a robotic killer programmed to assassinate a presidential candidate as part of a plot to seize control of the government. (Ironically, it was John Frankenheimer who had driven RFK from Malibu to the Ambassador Hotel on the June evening when he met his death.)

After taking several calls from Christian, I asked Bob Walsh, the station manager, about the advisability of inviting him into the studio to elaborate on his theory. Walsh replied, "Well, I figured you'd be filling the middle ground on the political spectrum, not the wacky fringe. But your ratings look good. Follow your own judgment." But he added, "You might think about having a bodyguard in the studio when you interview him."

Also scheduled that Sunday was an interview with my old friend Jack Nicholson, whose career post–*Easy Rider* was just taking off. Jack declined my offer to have him guard my body, and I went on the air with Jonn without benefit of protection.

Jonn Christian resembled a rough-hewn Santa Claus: He wore a full white beard with a few strands of red and boasted a girth almost equal to that of the canonical St.

Nick. He spoke rapidly with great confidence and an obvious mastery of hundreds of relevant facts — a far cry from the usual ditzy conspiracy-peddler.

Christian agreed that Sirhan had indeed fired a gun in the pantry of the Ambassador Hotel on the evening of June 4, 1968. But he claimed that Sirhan had no recollection of the events of that night because he was, in Jonn's phrase, "the robot of another." Furthermore, there must have been a second gunman in the pantry, because Sirhan's .22-caliber Iver Johnson weapon only held eight rounds, while a minimum of nine bullets had actually been fired — and possibly as many as twelve.

My years as Napoleon Solo hadn't equipped me to judge the accuracy of Christian's assertions. After we went off the air, I asked Jonn if he could show me further evidence for his theory. He arranged a meeting with Bill Harper, a retired ballistics expert who lived in Glendale, not far from my Mulholland digs. I brought along Linda, then my fiancée and one of the brightest persons I've ever met (as well as a longtime detective-book aficionada).

Linda and I spent two hours with Harper and Christian, and although we quickly got lost in the weeds of advanced ballistics science, we understood two key points on which Harper and Christian agreed: first, that RFK had been shot from behind; and second, that the bullets had been fired at point-blank range, defined as within several inches. Furthermore, they agreed that the autopsy report, grand jury records, and trial data would confirm these facts — both of which *flatly contradicted* the official theory of the killing.

What should I do with this potentially explosive information? I thought about my friend, Al Lowenstein, the creator of the "Dump Johnson" movement and one who shared my deep admiration for Robert F. Kennedy. I picked up the phone.

"Al," I said, "can you stop by my place the next time you're in L.A.? I've got something important to run by you."

"What about, Bob?"

I gave Al the thirty-second version, and he replied, "Count me out. I want no part of any conspiracy theories. And especially not when it comes to Bobby. I feel bad enough about him as it is. You know, if I hadn't convinced him to run he might still be alive today."

"I feel the same way, Al," I told him honestly. "And you know I don't usually pay any attention to the conspiracy mongers. But this fellow Jonn Christian is different. Just sit down with him for a half hour and let him tell his tale."

Al agreed, and in early 1973, we sat down for a chat in three wooden captain's chairs on my front lawn facing the lights of the Valley below. Christian outlined his theory succinctly, and he captured Al's interest. Al agreed to examine the autopsy, grand jury, and trial records and to meet Bill Harper.

For the next three years, Al and my friend Vince Bugliosi, famous as the prosecutor of Charles Manson and his gang in the horrific "Helter-Skelter" killings of 1969, worked on efforts to reopen the RFK case. They researched the evidence, aided by the efforts of other individuals who were experts in specific fields of forensic science. As their work continued, Al became more and more convinced that Christian's conspiracy theory was essentially correct. In 1976, in an essay titled "Who Killed Robert Kennedy?" published in a collection of pieces entitled *Government by Gunplay,* Al wrote: "I do not know if there was a conspiracy to murder President Kennedy, Senator Kennedy, Martin Luther King Jr., or Governor Wallace; I do know that it is *possible* that there was a conspiracy to murder one or more of them. If there were such conspiracies, I do not know if there were connections between them; I do know it is *possible* there were connections of some kind between some of them."

What facts made Al Lowenstein, Vince Bugliosi, and many other rational and intelligent people believe that Sirhan Sirhan did not act alone in the murder of Robert F. Kennedy? Here's a summary of those facts as I understand them.

First of all, Sirhan Sirhan was apparently not positioned so as to fire the bullets that killed Kennedy. The autopsy clearly shows that Kennedy was shot from behind, from below, from the right, and from point-blank range, with a gun positioned no farther than three inches from his head. Yet all the eyewitnesses said they saw Sirhan in front of Kennedy and between one and a half and five feet away from him — completely different from the location he would have had to be in to fire the fatal shots. This contradiction was withheld from the defense counsel until after the defense, in its opening statement to the jury, had already conceded Sirhan's guilt — a violation of all norms of proper jurisprudence.

Evidence based on bullets recovered at the scene also contradicts the theory that Sirhan killed RFK. Thanks to the Freedom of Information Act, Bernard Fensterwald, a Washington attorney, was able to obtain an FBI report on the shooting in 1976. This report indicated that at least twelve bullets were fired in the hotel kitchen that evening. Two were recovered from the body of RFK, and five from the bodies of wounded bystanders. Two more passed through Kennedy's body, one through his chest and one through his left shoulder pad. Three more bullets were found lodged in ceiling panels, and additional bullets made holes in the frames of doorways. Yet the Sirhan theory relies on the notion that Sirhan's gun, which held a maximum of eight bullets, was the only one fired.

It literally doesn't add up. What's more, criminologist William Harper swore in an affidavit that the bullets that killed Kennedy could *not* have been fired by Sirhan's .22 Iver Johnson pistol, because the ballistics characteristics of the bullets didn't match those of the gun.

Finally, there are reasons to believe that the L.A. police either obstructed or neglected specific aspects of the Kennedy murder case, thereby helping to ensure that the truth might never be known. For example, although an armed security guard stated that he was standing to the rear of

Kennedy at the time of the shooting — in the location from which the fatal shots must have come — and even admitted dropping down and pulling his gun when the shooting began, the guard's weapon was never checked to see whether he might have shot any of the bullets that killed Kennedy, whether deliberately or accidentally. And the one person who photographed the assassination had his camera seized by the Los Angeles Police Department. His photographs were never recovered.

There's more evidence that could be cited, but I think this is plenty to give you some idea of just how shoddy the case against Sirhan Sirhan really is.

As I write these pages (in January 2008), some brand-new evidence has just come to light. Dr. Robert Joling, past president of the American Academy of Forensic Scientists, and Philip Van Praag, sound expert, have concluded, based on exhaustive analysis of audiotapes from that fateful night, that at least twelve shots were fired using at least two different guns. They tell me they plan to put their data online for other researchers to examine shortly.

And what about the mental state of Sirhan himself? Is it really possible that Sirhan could have been a "Manchurian candidate" programmed to take the fall for RFK's murder? This may sound implausible. But Dr. Herbert Spiegel, a New York psychiatrist who teaches at Columbia University and is considered a major expert on hypnosis, supports this theory. He believes that Sirhan was probably acting in response to hypnotic directives when he fired at Kennedy. He appeared badly disoriented after his arrest, and when he was given a psychiatric examination before his trial, he was found to be highly susceptible to hypnotic suggestion, even climbing the bars of his cell like a monkey upon command. In all probability, Spiegel suggests, Sirhan remains today in a state of hypnotically induced amnesia forty years after the assassination.

Beginning in 1973, when I introduced Al Lowenstein to Jonn Christian, Al spent the last seven years of his life seeking answers to questions others were unwilling to ask. And when Al himself was assassinated in the spring of 1980 by his former protégé Dennis Sweeney, he was on the verge of getting a commitment from President Jimmy Carter to reopen the investigation of RFK's death if Carter were reelected that November. Instead, Al was killed, Carter lost to Reagan, and the official veil of silence over the RFK murder has remained intact.

But the questions continue to attract interest from a few intrepid private researchers. Was there a second — or even a third — gunman? If so, who was it? Could the security guard behind RFK who admitted pulling his gun and dropping into the firing angle suggested by the autopsy report have had something to do with the killing? And, most important, assuming that more than one shooter was involved — as the ballistics evidence overwhelmingly implies — who was the mastermind behind the plot? Even those most eager to blame the crime on Sirhan Sirhan don't pretend that he had the cleverness, the resources, or the organizational ability to pull together an assassination conspiracy, still less to keep it secret decades after the fact.

Most recently, my friend the respected investigative journalist and foreign correspondent Peter Evans has suggested in his book *Nemesis* that none other than Greek shipping magnate Aristotle Onassis was responsible in part for the murder of Robert F. Kennedy.

In that book, Evans devotes more than three hundred pages to describing what he learned about the RFK assassination plot in over twenty years of research. Rather than repeat the whole story, I recommend *Nem-*

esis to any interested reader. It's a fascinating piece of work and deserving of much greater attention than it received upon its publication in 2004. But I will describe a little of Evans's theory, since it's a necessary prelude to a rather fascinating interview I conducted late in 2007 that rounds out my own involvement in this tragic mystery.

According to Evans, the paths of Aristotle Onassis and Robert F. Kennedy first crossed in 1953, when RFK became assistant counsel to Roy Cohn, the chief investigator working for Senator Joseph McCarthy's notorious anti-Communist crusade. One of Bobby's assignments was to study what McCarthy, with his sense of drama, called the "blood trade" between certain American allies and Red China, whose soldiers were fighting U.S. troops in Korea.

RFK found that more than three hundred New York Greek shipping families were regularly trading with China. And although none of Onassis's vessels was involved, Ari was afraid that anyone prying into his business would discover that he was secretly negotiating with Saudi Arabia to supply a fleet of tankers to transport oil under the Saudi flag. Onassis's fears were realized in October 1953, when sealed indictments were handed down to seize any ships owned by Onassis that came into an American port. Ari blamed Bobby for his predicament, the huge financial loss it entailed, and the (at least temporary) derailing of his dream of becoming the richest man in the world.

Despite — or perhaps because of — his resentment of RFK, Onassis gradually became socially and romantically entangled with the Kennedy family. He met then-Senator John F. Kennedy and his wife, Jacqueline, in the summer of 1956 when he invited the two of them aboard his yacht, the *Christina*. And shortly after JFK's ascension to the presidency, Ari began an affair with Lee Bouvier Radziwill, Jackie's sister, who was then married to a faux Polish prince named Stanislaw ("Stas") Albrecht Radziwill. (This was at the same time as another Ari affair, with the great opera singer Maria Callas.)

But Ari wasn't satisfied with the president's sister-in-law. He wanted Jackie herself. He took advantage of the First Lady's vulnerability in August 1963, shortly after the devastating death of her two-day-old son, Patrick. Onassis urged Lee to invite Jackie aboard the *Christina* for as long as she wanted while she recuperated from the grief of her loss.

From a political standpoint, it was almost inconceivable: to have the first lady cruising the Greek Islands with her sister and her sister's lover — a man who had been sued by the U.S. government for fraud and was openly conducting an affair with the world's most famous opera star — was not the kind of photo op the Kennedy family needed with the 1964 re-election campaign just months away. But Jackie accepted the invitation.

More than thirty years later, in 1995, Evelyn Lincoln, JFK's secretary and perhaps his most trusted courtier, spoke to Peter Evans about the significance of that cruise. JFK, she said, had warned Jackie, "It would be a terrible mistake to accept Onassis's hospitality because he would eventually want something in return." "Had Dallas not happened," Lincoln told Evans, "the cruise would have been seen as a catastrophic wrong turning. . . . It would have exposed everything. The Kennedys' marriage had reached such a nadir . . . that if the President had survived and won the election in November, there would probably have been the first divorce in the White House."

For Robert F. Kennedy, his brother's closest political adviser and something of a family "enforcer," the way Onassis thrust himself into the Kennedys' personal drama at this sensitive time heightened the tension and hostility between himself and Ari.

The feuding between Onassis and the Kennedy family continued through several more episodes, including an effort by Onassis to publicize the apparent involvement of the Kennedy brothers in the still-mysterious death of Marilyn Monroe. But, according to Evans, the notion of killing a Kennedy did not take shape in the mind of Onassis until after a meeting early in 1968 between him and Mahmoud Hamshari, a follower of Yasser Arafat and a fanatical anti-American and anti-Israeli activist.

Enraged over the U.S. support for Israel during the Six Day War of 1967, Hamshari suggested that killing "a high-profile American on American soil" would make the U.S. government "think twice about backing the Jews." And when Hamshari had an opportunity, through a business connection, to meet Onassis, he used it to shake down the Greek magnate for the money needed to carry out the plot.

In *Nemesis,* Evans provides extensive detail about the dealings between Onassis and Hamshari. He describes the apparent involvement in the conspiracy of a Dr. William J. Bryan, a well-known expert in hypnosis based in Los Angeles (and the technical adviser, creepily enough, on John Frankenheimer's *Manchurian Candidate*). He quotes a defense witness from the trial of Sirhan describing the accused killer as being "out of control of his consciousness and his own actions, [and] subject to bizarre disassociated trances in some of which he programmed himself to be the instrument of assassination." And he describes pages from Sirhan Sirhan's notebook, once in the possession of Christina Onassis, that seem to implicate Onassis not just in the killing of RFK but also in two other business-related murders.

And then there is Hélène Gaillet, one of the players in Evans's story, whom I myself have had the opportunity to interview.

On a very dark, misty late-fall afternoon in 2007, I met with Hélène Gaillet de Neergard at the spacious apartment on New York's Upper West Side that she shares with her husband, William. Statuesque and elegant, Hélène served me tea and delicious cakes while she told me her long, amazing story.

She was one of five daughters of a northern French bourgeois family who were frantic to marry off their girls. Valedictorian of her high school class, Hélène received scholarship offers from several fine universities, but since the family was moving to New York, her father advised that the only choice she had was Barnard. Hélène enrolled at that college, where she studied history, practiced her knowledge of four languages, became an expert fencer, cut classes, and hung out in the Village listening to jazz.

At nineteen, she quit school and worked as a sales rep for her father's company for a year. Later, she met and married a Hungarian count, Charles de Barcza. She bore him two daughters, but the marriage was loveless and ended in separation. However, because de Barcza died before they were divorced, technically Hélène remained a countess. She moved to a rental apartment on New York's East Side, became a U.N. interpreter, and then turned to freelancing in advertising and publicity.

In 1968, she met Felix Rohatyn, the Wall Street investment banker of the firm of Lazard Frères who would make his name as the man who saved New York City from bankruptcy during the 1970s — "the most fascinating man I ever met," Hélène says. Later Rohatyn and Hélène took a penthouse suite at the Alrae Hotel on East Sixty-fourth Street — the same hotel I lived in, on and off, after returning to New York from

Czechoslovakia in 1968. It is now one of New York's most sought after hotels, renamed the Plaza Athénée after its sister hotel in Paris.

Eventually, Hélène realized a long-held dream by becoming a professional photographer. She worked as a stringer for *The New York Times, New York* magazine, and *The Village Voice,* photographed many society parties, gallery openings, and other events, and worked for the Metropolitan Museum of Art, the New York Public Library, and other major institutions.

Thanks to Rohatyn, Hélène also made the acquaintance of Jacqueline Kennedy. After the President's assassination, André Meyer, Felix Rohatyn's associate at Lazard Frères, served as a watchdog for his estate and the wealth inherited by his widow. Felix and Hélène often visited Meyer and his wife at the Carlyle Hotel, and they dined there with Jackie Kennedy several times. And although Hélène was never allowed to photograph the ex–First Lady, she did sit in with André Meyer when he was arranging Jackie's prenuptial agreement prior to her marriage to Onassis.

Hélène met Ari for the first time at the Coach House — one of my favorite New York restaurants — when she dined there with Felix in the early seventies. As the dinner came to a close, he raised the palms of her hands to his lips and told her, "The next time you are in Paris and need a place to stay, you must call me."

And this chance meeting led to the curious circumstances that give Hélène a place in the story of Robert F. Kennedy's assassination.

In 1973, Hélène was on assignment to travel to Kinshasa, Zaire, to cover the George Foreman–Muhammad Ali fight. But when the fight was postponed for a month due to a cut eye suffered by Foreman, she was stuck in Paris with time on her hands. Not sure whether to return to New York or stay in Paris, Hélène suddenly remembered Ari's invitation.

She got Ari's number through Rohatyn. Fifteen minutes later, Ari was inviting her to come to the island of Skorpios as his guest.

Peter Evans actually heard the story of Hélène's visit to Skorpios not once but twice. He interviewed her in 1983 when writing his biography of Onassis, *Ari.* But on a tip from a mutual acquaintance, he visited her again in 2003. When they met this second time, Hélène confessed she'd not been entirely forthcoming during their first interview. She told Evans, "When I knew you were coming to see me again, I thought: 'Oh my God, am I ever going to tell this story or not?' Because I am a proper person: I don't talk about things I've done. Then I thought, 'Well, you know what? I think this is the right time for me to tell this story. This is the right time.'

"I believe that what really happened should be put down by an historian," she added, "so that a hundred years from now people will know the truth about at least one part of our history."

She then told Evans the same version of the story that she told me as I was writing this chapter.

Onassis's sister, Artemis, and his daughter, Christina, were also at Ari's estate in Skorpios. Christina had become intensely concerned about her father's health and welfare. She made Hélène promise not to take any pictures of him on the island. Onassis was dealing with some difficult business issues, Christina explained, and she worried that unflattering pictures of her father would make him more vulnerable to the schemes of his enemies.

During her stay on Skorpios, Hélène said, she stayed aboard Onassis's yacht, while Ari remained at his estate on shore. Onassis had lunch with her aboard the *Christina;* other days she didn't see him at all. One day, they went skinny dipping, and Ari came on to her. Hélène reciprocated enthusiastically. It was the first and last time that happened between them.

One evening a few days later, Hélène dined with Ari at his beach house. They talked about many things, including religion. Hélène had been raised a Catholic, and she found inspiration and solace in her faith. Ari questioned her closely about the subject, saying that he was fascinated by the ideas of confession and absolution.

In the course of the conversation, she asked Ari whether he agreed with Hemingway's famous remark about the difference between rich people and the rest of us — "They have more money." With a laugh, Ari replied, "The rich get laid more, I know that . . . even that little runt Bobby Kennedy got laid more."

More disturbingly, however, Onassis then went on to speak freely about his hatred for Bobby. Kennedy had been killed five years earlier, yet, according to Hélène, Ari's hatred for him was still vivid and intense.

In the wee hours of that night, Ari walked Hélène to the beach. A launch would soon be taking her back to the *Christina.* But the mood of intimacy they'd shared that evening seemed to make Ari reluctant to say good night. They stood together, gazing out to sea, for a long time. After a while, Hélène realized that Ari was talking to himself, in low, murmuring tones, almost like someone deep in private prayer. Finally, as she strained to hear what Ari was saying, he turned to her, and, quite clearly and simply, said, "You know, Hélène, I put up the money for Bobby Kennedy's murder."

It was six P.M. when I left Hélène's Upper West Side residence. We had spent almost two hours together. She is a woman of great sensitivity, awareness, and self-confidence, and has an encyclopedic memory for dates, places, events, and the extraordinary people with whom her three score and ten years have brought her in contact.

I was most impressed with her ability to place herself in the time and emotions of some of the world's most powerful and famous people and her conversations with them. I have been similarly blessed.

Back in the 1960s and '70s, I interviewed dozens of people for my book *Only Victims,* dealing with the Hollywood blacklist. I learned to recognize when their answers to my questions were devious, veiled, or dissembled. Not once did I feel that Hélène was anything but honest. I'm convinced that her story is a faithful rendition of what happened to her, recounted now out of a sincere desire to clear the record about how the life of Robert F. Kennedy was cut short.

That last morning on Skorpios, Hélène quietly entered Ari's dressing room and, using lipstick, wrote a message on his mirror conveying her appreciation and affection. She closed with Onassis's favorite expression: "Fate happens!"

Many years later, Hélène again wrote a message in lipstick, this time on her own dressing room mirror. She wrote an ironic version of the fairy tale rhyme from *Snow White*. Hélène's version concludes with these lines:

Mirror mirror on the wall,
One day I will see it all,
But by then it'll be too late,
For I will have met my fate.

Hélène has not yet met her fate. But her secret is a secret no more.

Does her story settle forever the question of who killed Robert F. Kennedy, and why? Not in a legal sense, and perhaps not even in a moral sense. But along with the other evidence uncovered by so many friends and admirers of RFK, it makes abundantly clear that one of the greatest crimes of the twentieth century remains emphatically unresolved by the official verdict, even to this day.

Thirteen:
"If You'll Put Your Head Between Marisa's Legs . . ."

'Tis in my memory lock'd,
And you yourself shall keep the key of it.

There's something inherently picaresque about the life of an actor. He flits from role to role, from theater to theater, often from city to city, donning in each place a different set of costumes, attitudes, and expressions — almost, in fact, a different self. If he appears in movies, he may travel the world for location shots in dozens of exotic places, none of which he ever calls home. All are merely vivid backdrops for the world of make-believe that he and his fellow actors create on screen. It's a life of disconnected and discontinuous episodes, each with its own unique and never-to-be-recreated energy. And after a lifetime in service to Thespis, it leaves behind — in addition to the usual memories of marriage, family, and enduring friendships — thousands of fragmentary recollections: that time on Broadway . . . that night in London . . . that crazy scene on the set in Istanbul or Los Angeles or Edinburgh or Milan — or was it Paris?

Maybe you can see where this is going. Having recounted as best I can the most important and meaningful stories of my life — on stage and screen, yes, but also in the political and social arenas — I find myself holding a bag of colorful leftovers, shreds of memories that don't connect very well with any of the larger narratives of my life but that I'm loath to leave out. Call them my "nightcap stories," if you like — the kind of anecdotes I usually share late in the evening when I'm with a few friends and we're all reluctant to call it a night. And so we take another brandy and swap a story or two . . . and then maybe a couple more.

So in this chapter, I ask you to forget about finding any narrative arc or unifying theme — except, maybe, the fun I've had wandering the world as a purveyor of make-believe.

Let's start with some stories related to my first and most enduring love — the live theater.

In September 1954, at the Summerhouse

Theater in Albuquerque, New Mexico, producer Karl Westerman decided to do a post-season production of *I Am a Camera.* This was the Christopher Isherwood play of between-the-wars Berlin that would become the enormous film and Broadway musical success *Cabaret,* winning Liza Minnelli an Oscar for her portrayal of Sally Bowles. I was tapped to play the role of Chris, while a lovely young actress I'll call Betty was chosen to play Sally.

To my surprise, however, I found myself on opening night playing *both* roles. Here's how it happened. In the first act, Betty knew the lines for her character — kind of. In the second act, she knew her lines the way actors know them the first day the director says, "Let's try today's rehearsal off book," meaning without holding a script. And in the third act, Betty knew nada, zip, zero, nothing. The play ran a full half hour longer than its normal running time because whenever Betty couldn't remember her line, she would turn to me and say with great enthusiasm, "What do you think, Chris?" And I would say her lines, somehow melding them into my words.

It's a good thing I'd done the play before — otherwise it would have been an even greater disaster than it was.

Another time that same season, I was directing and playing the title role of *Mr. Roberts,* a play I'd already done in college. The second act began with a one-line speech for which we hired a local actor who also was responsible for running the very complicated lighting cues using an old-fashioned hand-operated light board. During the first of our two final dress rehearsals, when the bright white lights (operated by the stage manager) flooded the stage, our actor/lighting man looked at me with terror in his eyes. He yelled, "It's the limelight! I'm outta here," and he ran off the stage, never to be seen again.

We stopped the rehearsal and grabbed the first civilian available, a chubby little twelve-year-old girl, to step into the light booth to learn the fifty-some cues. We opened that night, and that frightened little thing never missed a single cue. We made her an honorary member of the ship's crew with a sailor hat that was just a bit too large for her preteen head.

Dress rehearsals have a way of generating confusion. When I directed *Light Up the Sky,* we were using the real set for the first time. Our leading lady in this production was named Louise, and for four weeks of rehearsal she had successfully pantomimed the opening of an imaginary door on our empty rehearsal stage. Evidently, the gesture had become second nature, because in the dress rehearsal she walked right through the *real* front door, then stopped long enough to mime opening a door that wasn't there.

Fortunately, she was able to master using the actual set door that evening for our opening performance.

Back at the University of Minnesota, on closing night of a production I was in of Melville's nautical drama *Billy Budd,* the actor playing the title role, standing at the top of a rope ladder, delivered the last line of the play — a stirring tribute to the man who has condemned him to death, "God bless Captain Vere!" On this occasion, however, as a dramatic ruffle of drums began, Billy Budd lost his balance and fell fifteen feet, right into the ruffling drums in the orchestra pit. It was quite a thrilling sight and might even have made for an effective conclusion to the play if only we'd planned it that way. (Fortunately, the hapless actor suffered the loss of neither life nor limb.)

You never know what will happen in live theater — and that's true not only in local or regional theater but even on Broadway itself.

Back in 1965, I went to see the wonderful

Christopher Plummer as the conquistador Pizarro in *The Royal Hunt of the Sun* by Peter Shaffer in New York. I was there on an *U.N.C.L.E.* publicity tour, and I was sitting in nice tenth-row seats with a couple of friends from Los Angeles. About two minutes after the curtain went up, we heard mumbling near the front of the theater. As the murmuring from the house intermingled with the onstage action, the effect was surrealistic:

OLD MARTIN
(a grizzled Spanish hidalgo of the mid-sixteenth century)

I used to lie up in the hayloft for hours reading my Bible — Don Cristobal on the rules of Chivalry. And then *he* came and made them real. And the only wish of my life is that I had never seen him.

PIZARRO enters
(Christopher Plummer in full military regalia, a tough, wasted commander)

I was suckled by a sow. My house is the oldest in Spain — the pig-sty.

VOICE FROM AUDIENCE

Mumble, mumble, mumble . . .

OLD MARTIN

He'd made two expeditions to the New World already. Now at over sixty years old he was back in Spain, making one last try . . .

VOICE FROM AUDIENCE
(louder than before)

Mumble, mumble, mumble . . .

The mumbling got louder and more obtrusive. Then, later in the first act, Pizarro had a heart attack on stage. (All part of the script, of course.) He collapsed onto the floor and lay there writhing in pain.

As Plummer groaned and squirmed on the stage, the mumbling audience member yelled, "Eisenhower had a worse heart attack than that!" And then we saw him and his female companion being ushered out of the theater.

During the intermission, I rushed out to the lobby to get a drink and found myself being served by a cockney bartender. He said, "I heard they threw one of your mates out." It turned out that the overinvolved audience member had been the actor Gary Merrill. Gary had been in *All About Eve* and later married the star of that movie, Bette Davis. The two had divorced in 1960 after ten years of marriage. Gary would later be involved with another great screen star, Rita Hayworth.

The evening's fun wasn't over. After the show, we went downtown to Sardi's. This evening happened to be the opening night of a long-forgotten (and evidently highly forgettable) musical called *Skyscraper* starring Julie Harris, Charles Nelson Reilly, and Peter Marshall, and the cast had gathered here for the customary reading of the reviews as they appeared, taking the main floor rather than the usual second floor. We looked over and there sitting in the corner was Gary Merrill and his date. He had stuffed handkerchiefs in his ears (they were hanging down) and he was barking like a dog. Then he got down on his knees and started nipping at the heels of people sitting at tables. Of course, he and his date were kicked out again.

(A week later, I invited Gary to breakfast with Senator Wayne Morse. He was perfectly sound and sober, and asked the senator many excellent questions regarding Vietnam.)

The evening wore on. We went to the now-famous restaurant Joe Allen's, then a new watering hole. Plummer himself came in, and we ended up talking at the bar till around two A.M. I was staying at the Plaza Hotel (paid for by MGM and NBC, of course), and when it got late, I said, "Come back to my suite, and we'll have a drink on Leo the Lion." Of course, we'd already had a lot by then. In the crowded hotel lobby there was a very tall, very well-dressed black hooker. The group of us invited her up to the suite. She evidently didn't recognize us. We ordered drinks, and Chris and I got into a deep conversation about Hamlet, a role which Plummer had played. Our guest ordered some fine wine and had a meal before leaving. But while she ate, Plummer and I were out on the balcony overlooking Central Park, reciting the soliloquies from *Hamlet*, speaking alternate lines.

A perfect ending to one of the more bizarre evenings of live theater that I can recall.

One time in the early sixties, I was killing some time in London during the Christmas holidays. I had been invited to a black-tie event in Belgrave Square just off Chester Street, where I would spend the first half of my stay in England with my future wife, Linda, while filming the first twenty-six episodes of my ITV series *The Protectors* in 1971–72.

I had recently purchased an English bobby's black rain cape lined in red, especially made for civilian use.

Also at the party was Zsa Zsa Gabor, whom I had met in the fifties when she was a continuing guest on an L.A. TV show titled *Peter Potter's Jukebox Jury.* At that time, she was in her thirties and had been Miss Hungary in 1936, before World War II.

I refreshed her memory about our early meeting and complimented her on her performance in John Huston's picture starring José Ferrer as Toulouse-Lautrec, *Moulin Rouge* (1952).

I was certain I would be leaving with Miss Gabor, returning to my lovely suite at the Dorchester Hotel. However, an actor whom I much admired for his brilliant performance in *The Sporting Life* (1963), a British film about rugby, arrived also wearing the same cape I had purchased. We got to chatting and laughing and laughing and chatting about acting, specifically *Hamlet,* and by the time we were ready to leave, I had traded Zsa Zsa Gabor for Richard Harris.

Under the British laws of that time, all pubs were closed at ten P.M. sharp. Richard said we should go to the house of his current girlfriend, who was a print reporter for a London syndicate, and pick up a stash of hooch he had squirreled away at her place. While I waited downstairs in the salon, a pitched battle occurred on the second floor involving much yelling and the sound of glass breaking. After about fifteen minutes, I was considering leaving when Richard suddenly appeared with a bottle of one of my favorite brandies, a multistarred Greek Metaxa.

We then hailed a cab and proceeded to drive aimlessly around Hyde Park and its environs, while passing the grape back and forth. Light was coming up and we were still thirsty, but the pubs did not open until ten A.M.. Suddenly, Richard said, "I've got some mates who will give us a nightcap" (more accurately, a dawn cap), and off our driver went to Covent Garden, where the lads were unloading and negotiating that day's produce for sale. They all knew Richard, and the Rémy Martin brandy was broken out to salute our arrival. We then went for breakfast in some dreadful little kitchen that made wonderful bangers and eggs scrambled with lox and onions.

I did not see him until many years later crossing the main road to Elstree Studios. He had a very long white beard and was wearing a long brown gown, carrying a staff and a pint of ale, looking like an Old Testament prophet. I caught his eye, but we didn't connect.

Shortly after the beginning of the new millennium, my driver for the BBC show *Hustle,* Ben, had also been Richard's driver on one of the British fantasy films of the period. Ben said that during the last years of his life, Richard lived at the Savoy Hotel, and it had been Ben's responsibility to get him to the studio on time and to watch out that he didn't take off and not return during the lunch break.

One day after combing Richard's normal pub haunts, he found him sitting on a chair between four lanes of traffic, concentrating very heavily on the passing vehicles. When Ben found him, he told Richard he was late getting back to the set and asked why he was sitting in such a dangerous place. Richard replied simply and with great energy, "I'm watching the world go by and when my house comes around, I'm going in." It made sense to me.

Unfortunately, Richard Harris left us too soon, like so many of the great British rogues whose talents were commensurate with their capacity for the drink. I'm sorry we didn't have the opportunity to spend another crawl together.

Another, even briefer encounter with a well-known denizen of Hollywood occurred during this same period. I consider it memorable not mainly for what happened but for *where* it happened.

In 1962, I was sitting in Schwab's Drug Store, mulling *Daily Variety,* when I spotted an article announcing the opening of the first topless restaurant and bar on the Sunset Strip. I noted the date and the address, and when the great day arrived, I made sure to get there early. (There had been quite a bit of subsequent publicity about this epochal event, and I was concerned that the crowds might make it difficult for me to get in the door.) The opening was scheduled for 11:30 A.M., so I arrived at ten o'clock and parked my new Lincoln Continental right outside.

I walked inside. The place was very dark, especially by contrast to the bright Southern California sun outside, but as my eyes adjusted I could see nothing but empty tables and chairs. Taking a seat at the bar near the entrance, I wondered whether I had the wrong date. But in a few moments I realized that I wasn't quite alone. At the opposite end of the bar was a fellow actor, someone I'd encountered once or twice in social situations and who now sat there smiling at me: Warren Beatty.

He would soon become an international movie star, an acclaimed director, and a political activist, but at the time he was best known as Shirley MacLaine's little brother. And now I also knew that he was the only other guy in L.A. who would get up early to check out a new topless bar.

I love the stage. But my career has been enormously enriched by the opportunity to act in movies — and not only financially. I've had some wonderfully entertaining experiences on and off soundstages around the world, and seen dozens of countries that I would never have had the opportunity to visit had I not been sent there to do location shots for motion pictures. And movie acting has also introduced me to many of the world's best actors — as well as some of the most eccentric ones.

In late November 1968, before returning to the States after my summer-long adventure in Prague, I was sent a script titled *The*

Mind of Mr. Soames. The picture was to star Terence Stamp, who had scored big in the title role of the film version of *Billy Budd* (the same play I had done at the University of Minnesota). I read it and liked it, particularly the role of the very liberal psychiatrist who offers counsel on the best way to raise the weird character of Soames. (Why do I say "weird"? The first time you see Terry's character, he's wearing sleepers and spending his nights in a specially designed crib — at age thirty.)

The cast had a brief read-through of the script before starting filming. Terry wasn't there, which didn't bother me because, in the role of a great overgrown baby, he seldom spoke. However, a few days into filming, Terry had still not spoken, either on or off the set. I realized that he was applying some kind of British "method" to the role, and remaining mute was his way of staying in character.

Anyway, I heard from someone that Terry would be going to India when we finished the picture, in search of a spiritual guru. This was, of course, at the same time that the Beatles and many others were traveling to India on a quest for enlightenment. What was unique about Terry, however, was that he planned to bring no luggage with him on his journey — he would take only what he was wearing. I rather admired this quixotic gesture on Terry's part, although I later learned he had squirreled away a packet of British pounds somewhere in his clothes — just in case.

Terry and I have since run into each other, and he has always been warm and gracious to me — as well as quite a fascinating character.

Before I finished *Soames,* I was approached by someone from *Playboy* magazine asking if I would like to appear in a filmed version of *Julius Caesar.* A rather good version had been done in the early fifties, directed by Joseph Mankiewicz and starring Marlon Brando, James Mason, John Gielgud, Deborah Kerr, Louis Calhern, and Edmond O'Brien. Mankiewicz was no shrinking violet — he tinkered with the script and actually had the chutzpah to include a title in the picture that read, "Shakespeare's *Julius Caesar* with additional dialogue by Joseph L. Mankiewicz."

I asked the *Playboy* fellow whose idea this was. Apparently Charlton Heston, while a student at Northwestern, had done a black-and-white 16-millimeter film of *Julius Caesar* in which he played Marc Antony, and he had always wanted to do a big-screen color version. Somehow he'd finagled Play-boy Enterprises to come up with the gelt, and they were going to shoot in Spain and England in the spring of 1969. I asked who else was involved, and they listed a stellar collection of names: John Gielgud, Diana Rigg, Richard Chamberlain, Richard Johnson. Jason Robards was set to play Brutus, the role James Mason had played in the Mankiewicz film.

I had never met Jason, but I'd heard some great stories about his jarring and carousing, and the prospect of getting to know him made the project especially attractive to me. I said okay, and I volunteered to play Casca, the role played by Edmond O'Brien in the fifties version. Casca had not yet been cast, and I was on board.

I'd worn a beard in the *Soames* picture, and I decided to keep it for *Caesar.* We had our first reading and blocking rehearsal in a typical low-end London building in Earl's Court that looked more like a squatter's residence than a legit theater rehearsal space. During the table read-through, I noticed two things. One was that Jason, whom I had just met for the first time that morning, was either seriously jet-lagged (he had just flown in from Hawaii), terribly hungover, or somewhat out of his element in tangling with Shakespeare's words. What's worse, our putative star, "Chuckles" Heston (as Jason called him — though never to his face) didn't seem any more at ease with his interpretation of Antony than Robards did with Brutus. The air seemed heavy with potential catastrophe.

At the end of the day, Jason and I had a few drinks together. He confessed that he'd never read or seen *Julius Caesar* before, and he decided that he'd like me to help him with learning the role. I suggested we work with a tape recorder, which, to my surprise, he agreed to. The only one we could find was a large, very heavy reel-to-reel Wollensak machine (remember, this was back in the sixties; the Wollensak was an old clunker even for that time). We began working together on scene after scene, trying desperately to get the very American Jason Robards comfortable with the very Elizabethan diction and cadences of Shakespearean verse.

Despite our efforts, Jason sensed doom for the project. "Heston and I are gonna bring this thing down in flames!" But of course he was under contract. So Jason gathered together all the money he could get his hands on, even mortgaging his house in Norwalk, Connecticut. He went to the producers with his nest egg and tried to buy his way out of the picture. But they said no, so Jason had no choice but to try to make the movie work — at least his part of it. We proceeded to shoot the gobbler.

During my stay in London, I was living on a houseboat, the *Mayflower II,* which was anchored at the bottom of Church Street, just off the Hogarth Roundabout in Chiswick. (A friend of mind, Mary Oreck, had heard I was going to London and gave me the name of Phil Brown, a blacklisted actor who owned the *Mayflower II* and would be spending the summer on the Adriatic coast. I loved staying on Phil's boat.) One night, Jason and his future wife, Lois O'Connor, unexpectedly dropped by, our fellow actor Rip Torn in tow. The two gents were more than six sheets to the wind. Some time later, well after dark, we noticed that Rip was missing. This was odd, since the only way to exit the vessel would have required the departed to pass us. This had not happened, but we were so well stoked with John Barleycorn that we didn't bother to investigate Rip's whereabouts. We found out later that he had fallen overboard and had had a titanic struggle getting to the shore.

I didn't see Rip again for several years,

and when I did, he had no memory of the evening.

The first scene we shot for the movie depicted Caesar, played by the great John Gielgud (Johnny G to his friends), being feted by the populace of Rome upon his successful return from the Gallic Wars. Because of scheduling problems, the scene was shot without the street crowds, who were filmed at a different time. Unfortunately, no one told Sir John that in the crowd would be *Playboy*'s contribution to the Bard's work — a group of bare-breasted beauties, looking for all the world like time-traveling refugees from a Hugh Hefner house party. When these shots were intercut with the images of Gielgud smiling and waving to the crowd, they give Caesar's grins a wolfish, leering quality that I'm sure Shakespeare never intended.

A duplicate of the Roman Coliseum had been built at MGM Studios in London, but the structure had been scaled down a bit for financial reasons. In his role as Mark Antony, Heston, who was a very large, powerfully built man, had enhanced his already broad physique by some sort of golden wings that broadened his shoulders by at least a half a foot on each side. When Jason noticed this, he said slyly to me,

"Maybe Chuckles will be too wide to get through the tunnel, and then we can all flee this fucking fiasco." Alas, Heston was too resourceful to let that happen; he simply turned sideways and navigated the narrow passageways of the mini-Coliseum with surprising grace.

Somehow we all got through the filming, although the scent of failure hung over the entire project. Months later, I saw the finished film in a small movie theater in Studio City, California. The tiny crowd, after getting a good chuckle during the opening scene with Gielgud and the bunnies, slowly drifted from the theater. By the time of Caesar's death, the place was empty except for me and my popcorn. It goes to show, yet again, that no script is idiot-proof — not even one by old Bill Shakespeare.

Heston, Robards, and I may have shown bad judgment in getting involved in that ill-fated production of *Julius Caesar.* But at least we weren't literally nuts, which is more than I can say about some of my erstwhile costars.

In 1975, I received a call from my agent Joe Funicello (the brother of Annette, everybody's favorite Mouseketeer). It seems that the Rome office of ICM, the big global talent agency, wanted me for one of the principal roles in a film to be titled *The Babysitter*. It would be directed by the celebrated French director René Clément and star Maria Schneider, Marlon Brando's leading lady from the controversial 1972 film *Last Tango in Paris*. Exalted movie critic Pauline Kael had called that picture "the most powerfully erotic film ever made, and may turn out to be the most liberating . . . Bertolucci and Brando have altered the face of an art form." Nowadays most people who buy or rent the DVD of *Last Tango* do so merely to see what all the fuss was about — and to check out the imaginative purposes to which Marlon and Maria put a stick of butter in one of the movie's more famous scenes. (While publicizing the picture, Schneider told the press that she and Brando had one thing in common — "Our bisexuality." Ah, those swinging seventies! Years later, she told Roger Ebert she had said these things merely as "a joke." I have no personal testimony about her sexual proclivities one way or the other.)

I signed on for *The Babysitter* and flew to Rome to begin work. Our early scenes were filmed on the streets at night with Clément directing from the warmth of his car, his wife at his side, while we actors labored in the chill Roman air. I met Maria only briefly. She was quite youthful-looking, pretty and polite, and very feminine in a schoolgirlish, Lolita sort of way. I thought I noticed a bit of flirtation, but I was wrong. Shortly thereafter, Maria disappeared, and shooting stopped. After several days, we found out what had happened. Under Italian law, a person can be self-committed to a mental institution if she can prove that someone she's emotionally involved with is already institutionalized. This is what Mademoiselle Schneider had done, evidently out of love for someone in an Italian booby hatch.

Once the producers managed to track her down, she announced that she would return to work on the picture only if I took over as director — that's how daft she was. I declined the honor.

Maria did ultimately return to finish the film, and Monsieur Clément paid no attention to me for the balance of the filming. (I suppose that if I were directing a star fresh from a mental institution, I too would want to give her all of my attention, and then some.) The picture was released in France under the title of *Jeune fille libre le soir,* and to this day I've never seen it. However, a videotape copy was sent to me by an Italian fan, which I look forward to viewing . . .

someday.

I don't mean to imply that my acting career has brought me into contact with a large number of mental incompetents. Actually, I've had the pleasure of working with some of the smartest and most talented people in Hollywood. Among this number I count my friend Blake Edwards, whom I first worked with way back in 1960.

At that time, Blake was best known for his fine touch with sophisticated detective shows: He'd created *Peter Gunn* and *Mr. Lucky,* two of the most fondly remembered dramas of the late fifties and early sixties. He called on me to play the role of detective A. Dunster Lowell, scion of a distinguished Boston family turned private eye, in a TV pilot titled *The Boston Terrier.*

Our first meeting to discuss the project, however, did not go well. Blake and the television show's writer, Tom Waldman, asked to have lunch with me at Romanoff's, the famed restaurant that was Bogey's number one luncheon stop in the Hills of Beverly.

For some reason, at the time of the meeting with Blake and Tom, I was very pale of face — which bothered me quite a bit. Normally I stayed quite tan throughout the year in Southern California, a quality I cultivated because I did not like wearing makeup while working. (I wore none at all during *U.N.C.L.E.*)

I had heard of a new product called Man Tan that supposedly made you look like a resident of Barbados after a single application. So I tried it the night before our luncheon meeting. I awakened the following morning, looked in the mirror, and saw the countenance of a man in the final stages of cirrhosis of the liver.

What could I do? I proceeded to Beverly Hills and joined Blake and Tom. They were both teetotalers, but I ordered several vodka gimlets. Combined with my appearance, my drinking frightened them into thinking I might be an insurance risk. Nonetheless, they valiantly went forward with me and the pilot, and there was no problem — at least, not from an insurance point of view. *The Boston Terrier* never got picked up.

Now I always travel with my Ben Nye makeup #3, a suntan look recommended to me by Cary Grant. It doesn't guarantee a trouble-free makeup session, but it helps.

I can't help adding another, somewhat unrelated, anecdote from my *Boston Terrier* days.

The evening before we were to start filming, I was sitting at the bar in the very swank Ritz-Carlton Hotel in Boston. I began chatting with a lovely, beautifully dressed young lady who called herself Lisa.

Gradually, I became aware that the charming Lisa was a working girl who viewed me as a potential "date." Not wanting to waste her time, I hastened to tell her that I wasn't interested in that sort of arrangement.

Lisa smiled. "Don't worry," she said. "I'll be happy to spend the evening with you gratis. After all, it's George Washington's birthday."

I didn't see the connection, and said so. "Well, he would never tell a lie, would he?" The logic still escaped me, but I liked Lisa's sense of humor. We enjoyed dinner together, and on the way to my hotel suite, I asked her whether Lisa was short for Elizabeth.

"No," she said, "Lysistrata. You know, the woman who denied her favors to the men in order to end a war." I wasn't sure what she was driving at, but I decided that Lisa was the best-read hooker I'd ever encountered.

In my suite, I excused myself, went into the bathroom, and proceeded to secrete my money clip in the neck of the toilet bowl, just beneath the upper rim. (Not that I didn't trust Lisa . . . but I didn't.) When I emerged, Lisa said, "Now it's my turn," and she went into the bathroom, still carrying her winter coat.

I went to the bar to mix a couple of drinks. When I returned to the living room, Lisa was nowhere to be seen. I rushed to the bathroom. It was empty — and so was my money clip, which was sitting on the marble-topped sink where she'd left it. The only other sign of her presence was a crooked smile scrawled in red lipstick on the mirror.

Happy Washington's Birthday.

Years later, I got to work with Blake on his feature film titled *S.O.B.,* standing for Standard Operational Bullshit. It was a showbiz story built around a script that Blake had written while producing several films with his wife, Julie Andrews, at Paramount. At the time, the studio was run by Robert Evans (the man who was caught in bed at the age of fourteen with my friend Patty Wheeler). These Andrews/Edwards films tanked at the box office, and, in a fit of pique, Evans said to Blake, "You'll never work in this town again!" — a great line that has since become one of those classic showbiz formulations (like "Show me the money!") that everybody recognizes.

Anyway, in *S.O.B.,* Blake cast me in the role of his studio tormentor, a thinly veiled version of Evans. However, the most memorable aspect of the experience was the way my first day of shooting started, which can only be described as unique.

I'd been told in advance that I would be required to be in drag for one scene. That was okay by me — a man who does make-believe for a living can't be too proud. My first day on the set, I met my girlfriend in the film, played by the famous and elegant model Marisa Berenson, granddaughter of fashion designer Elsa Schiaparelli. Then I was taken off to be properly costumed.

Not having scrutinized the day's script too carefully, I was a bit surprised to see what my outfit looked like: not just drag but a filmy red negligee, mesh stockings, and four-inch heels. In my full regalia, I was led onto the bedroom set by an assistant director. The crew had already prelighted the scene, Marisa was in bed, and Blake announced, "Ready to shoot. Now, Robert, if you'll put your head between Marisa's legs, we can start."

If you're wondering what kind of action could possibly follow a setup like that, it's not what you're probably thinking. The scene opens on a shot of a telephone ringing at bedside. Marisa reaches over, answers the phone, says, "It's for you," and hands it down to me, at the other end of the bed. Hey, it may sound easy being an actor, but just try it sometime.

If you've never seen *S.O.B.,* it's a brilliant put-down of Hollywood, starring Julie Andrews, William Holden, Robert Preston, Larry Hagman, Shelley Winters, Loretta Swit, and Richard Mulligan. It's still loved by everyone who has ever had a beef with the movie industry. Best of all, I got a chance to say many times during the film, "You'll never work in this town again" — to carhops, taxi drivers, waitresses, and so on. A fantasy dream of power that ranks with The Donald's "You're fired!"

S.O.B. offers an interesting example of life imitating art. The film recounts the tale of an internationally famous movie star, known for her roles as a sweet, virginal ingenue, who is forced by a tyrannical studio head (me) to bare her breasts in order to spice up a musical number. The only way the director and producer can achieve this is to get their shy leading lady drunk over lunch.

When the day came to shoot this scene, Blake closed the set to all except the key people needed to film the sequence — not including me. But the story that later circulated was that Julie Andrews couldn't bring herself to remove her top until after a long, liquid lunch. True or not? Despite my sleuthing, I've never been able to find out — nor did Julie divulge the truth in her wonderful memoir, *Home.*

High in my pantheon of unforgettable characters I've worked with is English actor Oliver Reed, probably best remembered for such films as *Women in Love, The Devils,* and *The Three Musketeers.*

I met Ollie during the eighties, when for the first time, I had the opportunity to work in Africa. My late friend Bill Holden, one of the sweetest gents I've ever acted with (*S.O.B* and *The Towering Inferno*), had advised me over several long liquid lunches during the *Tower* shoot, "Bob, if you ever get a chance to work in Africa, say yes." Bill was one of the founding members of the Mt. Kenya Safari Club and spent most of his downtime on the Dark Continent.

In the mid-eighties, I got my chance. It came via a call from Joe Funicello saying that producer Harry Alan Towers — the HAT, as Joe liked to refer to him — wanted me to do *Skeleton Coast,* a picture to be filmed in Namibia and South Africa with Ernest Borgnine, Oliver Reed, and Herbert Lom.

Harry Towers had allegedly somehow

been involved in the famous Profumo scandal of the sixties that rocked the British government (or so said Joe Funicello). I also heard that Harry was often referred to as the Fourth Man in *The Third Man* British political spy story. I could never quite nail these references down when talking to the HAT; whenever I brought up either subject, he always gave me his best noncommittal smile.

Anyway, I arrived in Johannesburg (Joburg to the locals) on Holy Saturday, 1983. Before I'd left home, the HAT had called me and said, "Ollie and his date would like you to join them and me for Easter Sunday lunch. You'll like it — we'll go to a very posh Joburg restaurant."

I wanted to beg off. "Won't I be terribly jet-lagged?"

The HAT scoffed. "It's a twelve-hour flight from London, but you only shift one time zone. You'll be fine." So I agreed to the luncheon date.

The restaurant was indeed a beautiful one, and it was filled with families celebrating Easter in their very nicest holiday attire. It was apparent from the get-go that Ollie and his date had gotten a considerable running start on the rest of us in the drinks department. After a brief exchange of pleasantries,

481

Ollie called the waiter and pointed to the empty bottle of wine in the ice bucket. A fresh bottle arrived almost instantly, and Ollie proposed a toast to our upcoming film adventure. After more toasts to the heavens, several dead actors, and some deceased animal pets of the Reeds, Oliver suddenly stood up, climbed onto his chair, and asked me, "Would you like to see my living, beautiful bird?"

Not wanting to diminish his energy for the festivities, I replied, "Absolutely." At which Oliver proceeded to unzip his fly and produce his penis, on which was tattooed some kind of winged creature. (I never did find out exactly what kind of bird it was, since I was afraid to ask or look too closely.)

The diners at the nearby tables said and did absolutely nothing. I think they were so shocked by what Ollie had done that they simply refused to believe it. They went on with their Easter lunches and pretended it had never happened. And so did Ollie's date, the HAT, and I, though the rest of our lunch was admittedly a rather nervous affair.

Harry later told me that Ollie's tattoo was actually quite famous, and that I should be honored that he'd showed me such fondness only a few minutes after we'd met.

At the time, my reaction was to wonder, "What have I gotten myself into?" But Ollie was a joy to work with. Although half in the bag during the workday, he was never late, never missed a line or a cue, and was the quintessence of professionalism on the set.

Better still, in the grand tradition of the British actor/drinker, he regaled the cast during our downtimes with wonderfully funny show-business stories. One concerned Richard Burton.

Richard Burton, Ralph Richardson, and John Gielgud were doing one of Shakespeare's histories — what Burton referred to as the "King plays" — and after a matinee, Richardson and Burton went out and got pretty well sloshed before the evening's performance. Gielgud, who was onstage for the opening scene, had heard about his carousing mates and prepared himself. When Burton came onstage, Gielgud said, "Well, it appears that the Duke of Norfolk has had the odd flagon of Rhenish."

Burton replied, "If you think I'm pissed, wait until you see the Duke of York."

Most movie shoots conclude with a cast party, but when we filmed *Skeleton Coast* we had a party almost every night. During the *final* cast party, Ollie was eloquent and stone sober, drinking one bottle of diet

Coke after another.

At one point that evening, he asked me where I stayed when working in London. I answered, "The Cadogan Hotel on Sloane Street in Knightsbridge." It was famous for having been owned by the celebrated English actress Lily Langtry, who gave the writer Oscar Wilde free lodging there — and for being the place where Wilde and Lord Alfred Douglas did the nasty, leading to Wilde's trial and imprisonment for homosexuality. Decades later, the neighborhood became known as the haunt of wealthy young girls who were called "the Sloane Rangers," the most famous of whom grew up to be Princess Diana.

When Ollie heard that I stayed at the Cadogan, he told me that whenever he was near Sloane Street around midnight, he would ask his driver to stop in front of the historical plaque honoring Sir Herbert Beerbohm Tree, the great actor/manager. He would then briefly exit the vehicle, "drain his snake," and hoist a jar to Sir Herbert. I later found out that Ollie and Tree were related through the acting dynasty that included the famous British film director Carol Reed.

Ollie exited this "vale of tears" (his words) in May 1999. He was sitting at a bar in

Malta when his mighty and seemingly unbreakable heart seized up and silenced him forever. The bar, I've heard, is now named Ollie's Last Pub after this charismatic, charming character. The next time I'm in Malta, I plan to pass by and hoist a wee drop to this rascal of rascals.

In the early seventies, after my three years in London doing *The Protectors* and before my marriage to Linda in June 1974, I signed on to do a film in Venezuela to be titled *Next Week Rio.* It was to be a coproduction among companies from Venezuela, Germany, Spain, and America, and would star me and two as-yet-unnamed actors from Germany and Spain. My salary for the film was paid in advance and held in escrow for me at ICM in Beverly Hills.

One of the several producers called to tell us that we would be billeted at the Hotel Avila in Caracas, which was supposedly owned by the Rockefeller family and was the best the city had to offer. "Would you like the Catherine Deneuve suite or the Yves Montand suite?" he asked.

More or less arbitrarily, we selected the Deneuve suite, and the three of us arrived in Caracas — Linda, me, and our little white poodle, Pip — and were properly

485

picked up by a chauffered car. The suite was okay, and the food was palatable, if not exactly four-star. But these were the last normal things that happened on this film shoot.

The director was a sweet British gentleman named Gordon Hessler. We had no cast get-together for introductions or a read-through of the script. Instead, we were simply given a work call for the following Monday, and we were allowed to relax for the weekend.

On Monday morning, I reported as directed and gave the *Rio* makeup man, who spoke no English, a try at giving me a suntan look. He failed, producing instead a Halloween orange glow. I handed him my Ben Nye #3 and asked him to try again, applying the makeup sparingly. He washed my face with something that felt like carbolic acid and slathered me generously with makeup — another disaster. So I washed my face again, using some Irish Spring soap I always travel with, and the third go-round was reasonably successful.

At this point I called Linda. "Don't finish unpacking our things until I give you a call," I told her.

"Why not?"

"I sense doom. And where showbiz is

concerned, I'm usually right."

We completed the first day's work as planned, the only delays being caused by bad weather. The following morning, I had my first scene with dialogue. After we were finished blocking for the camera, we were ready to commence filming when I looked around and saw neither microphones nor soundman.

I asked Gordon, our director, "What's up?"

"Well, in this country, they do the sound later."

"Don't they record a guide track while filming?" I asked.

"They don't bother with that."

Rather nonplussed, I replied, "Well, Gordon, I'll be in my Catherine Deneuve suite. Let me know when the normal Hollywood sound equipment arrives. If it isn't here within forty-eight hours, I'll be on my way back to Beverly Hills."

Linda and I had a lovely candlelight dinner poolside at the Avila, interrupted only by a phone call reporting that the sound equipment would be arriving tomorrow. Intimidation, I've found, always breeds a quick response — one way or the other.

The rest of the week went by without any major catastrophe, but I still sensed an unquiet atmosphere permeating the Venezuelan crew.

On Friday, rumors were flying around the set. The crew, we were told, had expected to be paid that morning, and this had not happened. I shrugged and settled in with Linda for a relaxing poolside weekend. In preparation for an early Monday work call, I tucked in around 9:30 Sunday evening.

I was awakened Monday morning by a call from the second assistant director. "Forget your work pickup time," he said, "it's now a will-notify." I found this mildly disturbing, but not terribly so — funny last-minute changes aren't uncommon in Hollywood. So Linda and I headed down to the pool, where the daily brunch was set out. And when I sat down to eat, I opened a copy of the local paper and saw a picture of one of our producers on the front page — behind bars.

And that's when the fun really began.

We were told by the hotel manager that, under Venezuelan law, we and all those associated with the picture were formally under house arrest until the movie crew had been paid. What's more, if we tried to leave the country without paying a *solvencia,* we would join our producer behind bars.

"Are you serious?" I asked the hotel manager.

"I'm afraid so," the manager replied, seemingly rather embarrassed. "Even your great boxer, Señor Foreman, had to pay a *solvencia* before leaving the country."

Well, this kind of message will get your attention. I couldn't reach the American ambassador, but I got through to Joe Funicello, who knew nothing of our plight. I asked him to check into what George Foreman had had to pay to get out of the country. Joe got back to me shortly with a figure: a half-million American dollars. With the rate of exchange at that time, I guessed I was into the Venezuelan government for about a billion bolivars.

When I finally reached someone from the State Department, he said, "The problem, Mr. Vaughn, is that the man who made the deal with these coproducers, an Italian, was assassinated a couple of weeks ago. So now all bets are off."

"What are we supposed to do?" I demanded.

"This is South America," he replied with an audible shrug. "That's the way the cookie crumbles."

Our day under house arrest turned into night. Then it turned into days, then weeks.

489

Pictures of Linda, Pip, and I appeared in the local papers practically daily. One of the producers, negotiating behind the scenes, offered us a deal: If I wanted to leave, he thought he could get a *solvencia* for me of somewhere between five and fifty thousand dollars. But by this time I was angry and getting angrier. "I'm not paying a penny," I said. "And if you want me to finish this picture anytime in the future, *you* pay the *solvencia*."

Word got to me that a lawyer representing the producers would like me to meet him in his office to see what he could do to help us. I agreed, with the stipulation that I could bring my driver, my stand-in, and my American stuntman, Bobby Herron, with me to the meeting. (Yes, I was nervous.) The lawyer's office agreed, and we traveled in a four-car caravan to the lawyer's office, which was way out in the countryside and literally underground, in a building buried beneath a drive-in movie screen.

Breaking our agreement, the guards at the entrance refused to let my trio enter the building. "The hell with it," I decided, "I'll go in alone." After all, wasn't I Napoleon Solo, fearless international secret agent? Actually, no. I was Bobby Vaughn, in a damned pickle.

The lawyer was a large, menacing, mustachioed figure with a vague resemblance to Marlon Brando in *Viva Zapata.* The room was filled with pictures of dying bulls, and a large *pistola* rested on the desk.

His first words to me were, "I know you *gringos* think we are all savages down here."

I could think of no reasonable answer to that remark, so I remained silent.

The negotiations began. Perhaps *extortion* would be a better word. The upshot was that, if I would pay the lawyer something in the high five figures, he would be able to spring us from the country. I declined, partly because of the unfairness of the situation, partly because I frankly doubted his ability to follow through on his promise. I returned to Linda at the Avila, and our house arrest entered its second month.

Finally, a plan was hatched with the help of our wardrobe lady's daughter, who worked at the airport. If we would agree to dress in native clothes — including our poodle Pip — and wait for the first plane that would take us, no matter where it was going, a day could be set for our departure.

And so it happened. Attired in serapes, sombreros, and carrying numerous shawls and baskets (one of which housed Pip), we got the first available plane to Madrid, where we moved into a four-star hotel on the main drag. We returned to the United States shortly thereafter.

The picture was finally finished in Barcelona on the set Clint Eastwood had used when making *Fistful of Dollars*. I insisted on a provision in my new contract stating that I would be paid in American dollars in cash in a bag before filming began each morning. My driver also had to be on standby, waiting to drive me to the hotel and then on to the airport in case anything went wrong. The movie was finally released the following year with a new title, *Blue Jeans and Dynamite*. I've never seen it.

Shortly after our move to Connecticut from Beverly Hills in 1981, I was called to do a three-month shoot in Yugoslavia of a World War II film, an all-Yugoslavian production. The cast included three other Americans: James Franciscus, Edward Albert (Eddie Albert's son), and Steve Railsback, who'd given a brilliant performance as Charlie Manson in a made-for-TV movie. No other Americans were involved in the production.

I had just one problem with accepting this job: I had a broken ankle at the time. It's a bit ironic. I'd just taken our six-year-old son, Cassidy, for his first skiing lesson, and

I'd pointedly declined to do any skiing myself. "What if I fell and broke my ankle? I'd be out of work for months." The following day, on a bright, sunny day in New Canaan, Connecticut, I stepped off a curb and broke my ankle. But since I'd avoided telling my agent Joe Funicello about the mishap, when the offer came through for the Yugo film, Linda and I decided I should accept. Based on the translated script that we had read, nothing was required of me physically, except riding a horse, which I did as well as most actors — that is, passably.

Between the time I agreed to do the film and my departure for Belgrade, I began to have pain, increasing slightly each day. My doctor suggested that I go ahead with the trip, and if the pain became unbearable, have the pins removed. Simple enough, right? Wrong.

The first evening in Belgrade, I dined with the film's director, a high muckety-muck, I was told, in the Communist-led film industry. (I never got his name or the name of the picture straight.) In perfect English, he dismissed my ankle problem, saying, "We are so proud to have you in the picture, you could do the entire film using a cane or sitting or both."

Then he hit me with the bomb: All the American actors would have to do their dialogue in English *and Serbo-Croatian.* I said, "Well, I hope you have a lot of large cards with the dialogue spelled out phonetically for the U.S. gang, because I'm sure none of them is conversant in the Yugo lingo." That didn't seem to bother the director, and we drank a toast to the picture's success.

The following day, I met Jimmy, Ed, and Steve. "I fear we may have signed on to a gobbler," I told them, and explained what I'd learned. "I've got a feeling there are more surprises yet to come," I added. I was right.

In keeping with Communist ideology, everyone in Yugoslavia, including foreign guests, was ostensibly treated the same — badly. Our main location, a World War II battleground, with thousands of real Yugoslavian soldiers conscripted by the government serving as extras, was one-and-a-half to two hours from our hotel in Novi Sad. This meant that the driving time from base to location was roughly equivalent to driving from Beverly Hills to Palm Springs, and we had to make the trip twice every bloody day. (More about blood later.)

The next problem was eating. Our translator (I'll call him Zuko) explained that our contracts called for us to have a warm noonday meal brought from our hotel in Novi Sad. Unfortunately, it wasn't warm or even edible after the two-hour drive. (As for the director, a man who enjoyed a fine wine and a nice meal, I don't know where he ate because I never saw him once we broke for lunch.)

After two days, we four Americans went on strike and ate at the local restaurant, where the food was so salty we had to wash it down with unlabeled bottled water from our hotel. Fortunately, no Slavic two-step felled us.

Then there were the dressing rooms, and the toilets they contained. Each day, we were told they were on the way, and each day they failed to show up. So Zuko suggested we walk a few dozen meters into the forest. "Select a tree, and I'll make sure your name is attached to the tree you choose." And we did, because we were guys, and guys don't fret about things like that.

We were supposed to be driven back to our (frankly rotten) hotel every night, and usually we were. But on three different occasions, I was left at the location in my World War II Communist partisan garb and had to hitchhike the hundred miles back.

After a few weeks of this, I stopped complaining (except to my agent) and just waited for the ordeal to end. Linda and Cassidy visited for a day, then flew off to Paris and Geneva for some normal vacation time. On several occasions, we four U.S. thesps took the four-hour train ride to Vienna for an unsalted meal — and it was worth every minute.

As for my ankle: I told Zuko that, at some point, if the pain got too bad, I'd like to have a top-of-the-line surgeon remove the pins. I'd even brought my American X-rays with me. When the day came, I was introduced to a very nice English-speaking doctor who had trained in London.

Feeling reasonably confident, I told the doc, "You can use a local anesthetic, since that's the way the pins were inserted." He agreed and cleaned my ankle quite thoroughly with some foul-smelling liquid. Then, over the next half hour, he gave me a series of shots, asking after each one whether I felt sufficiently numb to proceed with the surgery. Finally, although it still seemed my ankle was not completely ready, I told him, "What the hell? Let's go for it."

You've already guessed what happened. When the doctor pulled the largest horizontal pin, I screamed like Olivier in *Oedipus* (often described as "the most terrifying sound ever heard on a stage"). I don't know what it's like to deliver a baby, but I pray it doesn't equal this horrific experience.

Nervously, the doctor finished bandaging the wound. "You'll have to have it rebandaged every few days until it heals," he said. "But I'm going on vacation. I suggest you go to the local emergency hospital for this service.

"By the way," he added. "I wonder if I can ask you a favor?" He gave me the name of an English medical text. "This is a book on current surgical techniques, and I would really like to have it." I blanched a bit when I heard the word *current,* but I assured him I would find the book and send it to him as my gift. He was most appreciative.

A few days later, I had my driver take me to the Novi Sad ER. However, I didn't remain long. As soon as I took my place at the back of the queue, I noticed I was slipping around. Looking down, I saw blood covering the ground all the way to the door of the examination room. Yells filled the air — from two gunshot victims being wheeled past on a gurney and from someone near the front of the line who apparently had been stabbed multiple times.

I hobbled out and gave my driver the

"Let's get out of here" sign. When I explained what was going on, he suggested that his girlfriend — some kind of nurse — could come to the hotel with new bandages. She arrived within minutes and became my private dressings-changer for the rest of my stay. When I paid her in American dollars, she reacted as if I'd given her her weight in emeralds.

I sent the doc his very expensive medical book, but I don't know whether or not he received it, since I never heard back from him. And the picture? I never saw it.

One last on-location experience, this one on top of Machu Picchu, outside of Lima, Peru. The film was titled *Hour of the Assassin,* and the director was Luis Llosa, the brother of one of Peru's most famous writers, the novelist Mario Vargas Llosa.

I wasn't particularly worried about this job until I heard from the American producer that the Maoist guerrillas known as the Shining Path were billeted very near our filming location. Although they'd kidnapped a number of American businessmen, I was assured that the guerrillas understood we were making a movie and that they would not cause us any problems. In response, I said I expected to have twenty-four-hour bodyguards armed with AK-47s at my side at all times. Much to my surprise, a deal to this effect was struck, with the sole proviso that I autograph pictures for the three guards. Sure enough, the guards were with me day and night, either drunk or asleep in the hall outside my suite.

Each day I went up the mountain in a bus with the crew. (A young local boy ran the entire distance alongside the bus and in return received dollars, pesos, and other forms of random loose change from all of us on the bus.) St. Genesius must have smiled on our little picture (he is the patron saint of actors). Other than some gunfire after dark, all went well, although once again I have never seen the finished picture.

I arrived safely back in Beverly Hills, only then telling my wife the circumstances of the shoot.

Linda was not amused. She made me promise that, in the future, before I went anywhere in connection with an acting job, I would find out where I was going to work and how large the budget was, so that I could determine how safe I would be and whether or not my salary would really be paid. Only then would I even read the script.

And that's the way I've done it ever since.

Epilogue

The rest is silence.

I've just reread Robert Brustein's magnificent book, *Letters to a Young Actor.* Former dean of the Yale School of Drama, teacher, actor, director, playwright, critic, and lifelong pillar of the theater, Brustein has supervised well over two hundred theatrical productions. He was the founding artistic director of the Yale Repertory Theatre and Harvard's Tony Award–winning American Repertory Theatre, and the founder of the Institute for Advanced Theatre Training at Harvard. Meryl Streep and Kevin Kline were among the many theater luminaries first mentored by Robert Brustein.

Over the last half-century, I've read hundreds of books about acting and life in the theater. Brustein's is the best. In these final pages, I just want to add a few observations of my own to the wisdom Brustein has to offer — in particular, on the topic of how an actor can create a career for him- or herself.

Whenever aspiring young actors ask me how to get started in our profession, I suggest they consider following the path I took. I've already described it in these pages, but there are several variations possible, all of them good as far as I can see. One way is go to New York, the nation's theatrical hub, and enroll in an outstanding college drama department while pursuing a B.A. in theater arts. Another is to go to Los Angeles to enroll in the theater school at UCLA, USC, or one of the other top-flight West Coast universities. And a third option is to move to the Chicago area and study at one of the many fine schools there (like Northwestern or the Goodman Theatre), and look for opportunities at the local professional theaters, like the Steppenwolf Company.

Where I differ with Brustein is that he advises you to spend all of your early college years fully immersed in academics. I suggest something that is a little different and that is not easy to pull off, which is to combine on- and off-campus acting as much as possible.

When I joined the superb Los Angeles City College Drama Department, I made it clear to Jerry Blunt (the tough, brilliant acting teacher who was the real head of the department, although another chap with a Ph.D. had his name on the stationery) that I was going to be seeking professional acting jobs — work in the "little theater," as we called it back then, that paid Equity wages. I promised Jerry that whenever there was a choice between a school production and a professional job, I would get his permission before taking the paid assignment. And to Jerry's credit, he agreed to my proposal and backed me fully.

In this way, Jerry allowed me to get a fast start on learning about how to audition for roles in Hollywood, both in film and on stage. This enabled me to become a member of the number one professional little theater in Hollywood at that time, the Stage Society, and so get a two-year head start on my fellow students in the real world of theater — the world of ongoing rejection.

Is it still possible to follow this dual path while in school? I think it's certainly harder than it was back in the fifties, and it was hard enough then. But I also think it's worth a try. I know it served me well.

But then there is the larger question: Why should a man or woman devote a lifetime to the craft of make-believe in the first place?

Does the theater (including its electronic offshoots, film and television) offer any real value beyond the purely monetary to the person who practices its arcane crafts or, for that matter, to society as a whole?

Professor Brustein addresses this issue in his chapter on "Anti-Theatrical Prejudice," in which he cites the disdain for actors and acting expressed over 2,500 years ago in Plato's *Republic:*

> The Philosopher cautioned, "Suppose that an individual clever enough to assume any character and give imitations of anything should visit our country and offer to perform. We shall bow down before a being with such miraculous powers . . . crown him with fillets of wool, anoint his head with myrrh, and conduct him to the borders of some other country."

For Plato, the ability of the actor "to assume any character and give imitations of anything" was "miraculous," astounding, admirable — and extremely dangerous. So much so that actors would be banished from the ideal society limned in *The Republic.*

Plato had a problem with actors. He considered their talent for eliciting feeling rather than thought a threat to his well-ordered, perfectly rational republic. The preferable alternative was clear: politics. The active engagement of man's highest powers in pursuit of society's greater good was obviously more desirable than the theater, a world of shadows where everything is possible and nothing is true. By banishing theater from his republic, Plato hoped to encourage those of the greatest intellectual and social talents to devote those skills to worthwhile pursuits rather than the empty, ephemeral pleasures of playacting.

Many centuries later, when theater was making a comeback after its long eclipse in the post-classical medieval world, the French *philosophe* Jean-Jacques Rousseau drew inspiration from Plato. "What!" he said. "Plato banished Homer from his republic and we will tolerate Molière in ours?" And about actors, Rousseau warned:

If they join a bit of art and intrigue to their success, I do not give the state thirty years before they are its arbiters. The candidates for office will be seen intriguing for their favor. The elections will take place in the actresses' dressing rooms, and the leaders of a free people will be the creatures of a band of histrions. The pen falls from the hand at the thought.

Rousseau was joking, but like many of the best jokes, his has a sting in its tail — the sting of truth. Rousseau's nightmare has now become a commonplace reality. Not only do the politicians of today court actors for their favor, they have *become* actors, practicing the crafts of theater in the carefully staged press conference, the art-directed photo op, and the thirty-second commercial. This, in turn, has inspired actors to take up politics, applying to the world of statecraft the talents of *seeming* and *feigning* that Plato and Rousseau found so powerful, so seductive . . . and so destructive.

I think I know more than most about the intersection between politics and theater. I've lived much of my life at that crossroads. More than once I've been accused by adversaries of "meddling" in politics (as if an actor doesn't have the rights afforded to every citizen of free speech and public activism); more than once I've been urged by supporters to throw my hat into the political ring. I've resisted the temptation. I know my strengths and my limitations, my abilities and inclinations — and I know where my personal demons are buried. As a professional, I'm well-suited to exactly the life I've led and relished — a life of thrilling, surprising, amusing, horrifying, moving, and, above all, entertaining audiences on stage and screen. And as a citizen, I'm well-suited to the role I've played in the public arena — a curious and concerned onlooker, an occasional gadfly and critic, a dedicated voter and supporter of the causes I believe in.

Having lived my life among theatrical people, I can say with conviction that I *don't* want to see Rousseau's nightmare come to full fruition, in a world where actors (rather than Plato's philosophers) rule society. Like Plato, I consider the task of making this a better world the noblest human pursuit, and I reserve my highest admiration for the people who've devoted their lives and talents to that task — the Robert F. Kennedys, the Martin Luther Kings, and the Nelson Mandelas of our world.

But unlike Plato, I wouldn't ban actors from my ideal state (and not just for selfish reasons). Plato and Rousseau were right to point out the similarity between the arts of the actor and those of the politician. Both use words, gestures, expressions, and intonations to play on the emotions of an audience. At their most skillful, both are able to evoke intense sympathy from onlookers, even eliciting approval (at least temporarily) for words and deeds all right-thinking people will condemn. This is the power of the demagogue, and a heady brew it is — as I learned decades ago, when I acted the part of the psychopathic yet charismatic Jocko de Paris in *End as a Man.*

But this similarity is no reason to banish the actor from the perfect republic. Just the opposite. Maybe the citizen schooled in the ways of the theater and familiar with the deceptive charms of the thespian is the one best able to recognize and resist the lures of the would-be tyrant.

Maybe if — through some miracle of time travel — the good citizens of Salem had been able to attend a performance of Arthur Miller's *Crucible,* there would never have been a witch hunt.

As Sinatra sang, "Regrets, I had a few" — but very few. There are some great stage roles I wish I'd been able to tackle in the late 1960s, at the height of my powers: Cyrano, Oedipus, Richard III, Professor Henry Higgins, and a handful of others. (Vietnam and the other events of that turbulent era got in the way.) And I wish I'd learned to sing.

But otherwise, as you've just read, I've had a most fortunate life. Thanks for sharing it.

ACKNOWLEDGMENTS

I've come to learn that, like a play, television show, or movie, a book is a collaborative effort. I'm grateful for this opportunity to name and thank some of those who helped bring this book to the light of day.

First, my most sincere and profound thanks to my friend and editor, Karl Weber. It was his confidence, contacts, and curiosity that made this book possible. Without that trifecta, I would have been merely another author in search of a publisher, preferably one who understood that my book wasn't just another Hollywood memoir about "and then I slept with X." After several preliminary meetings in which Karl got to know me and scrutinized some of my primary sources (up to forty years old), he concluded, "This is a trove of material," and "There is definitely a book here." Now I know that Karl was right. His literary taste and sound judgment have contributed enormously to whatever value this book has to offer, and I look forward to working with him on my next project.

I want to thank my diligent and constructive literary agent, Lynne Rabinoff, who not only served me and this book project well but also appreciated my sense of humor. Lynne introduced us to our wonderful publishing team at St. Martin's and helped to ensure that the complex transition from raw manuscript to finished book proceeded smoothly.

At St. Martin's, there are many contributors to mention: Thomas L. Dunne, our publisher, who understood what we were trying to accomplish in these pages and supported us handsomely; Peter Joseph, our editor, who guided us with a deft and sure hand; Mark McCauslin, our skilled copy editor; Meg Drislane, our talented production editor; and the wonderful publicity and marketing team that have made my first foray into full-scale commercial publishing an enjoyable and fascinating experience. Heartfelt thanks to you all.

My warmest plaudits to my very good friend, author and foreign correspondent Peter Evans, who chronicled the life of Aristotle Onassis and, in *Nemesis,* revealed his connection to the murder of Robert F.

Kennedy. My chapters on this tragic event, and my small connection to it, owe much to the diligent research and shrewd insights of Peter Evans.

My thanks to the late Dr. Phillip H. Melanson, whose book *The Robert F. Kennedy Assassination: New Revelations on the Conspiracy and Cover-Up* is one of the finest examinations of that terrible event, and to my friends Dr. Robert Joling, past president of the American Academy of Forensic Science, and Phillip Van Praag, for allowing me to reference *An Open and Shut Case,* their study offering the most recent evidence concerning the RFK assassination.

And special thanks as well to Hélène Gaillet de Neergard, who met with me in late fall of 2007 to discuss what she knew about Aristotle Onassis and the killing of RFK. Historians will be forever in her debt — as will I.

Thanks to Jon Heitland, whose extraordinary *Man from U.N.C.L.E. Book* was my primary guide to an exciting four-year period of my own life. And thanks to Michael Kackman, whose book *Citizen Spy: Television, Espionage, and Cold War Culture* was a wonderful (and useful) reminder of what the fifties and the sixties were like, both on screen and off.

Thanks to Charles Marowitz, author of *The Other Chekhov,* which fleshed out for me many memories of the legendary dramatic theorist Michael Chekhov. And to Tracy Spotteswoode, whose magnificent BBC radio play *Solo Behind the Iron Curtain* captured those harrowing weeks in August 1968, when the Soviet Union destroyed Czechoslovakia's experiment in "socialism with a human face" as if she'd lived through them personally.

My ever-lasting thanks to my schoolmates from Los Angeles City College in the early fifties, Jim Butler and John Hackett. Jim provided the "lion and lamb" imagery and much more that I used in my first antiwar speech in Indianapolis back in 1966. John took my mountain of facts and turned them into a brilliant, moving, and eloquent denunciation of our military presence in Southeast Asia. Without their help, I couldn't have become a spokesperson for the antiwar movement, and I would have missed an important part of my life.

And many, many thanks to my transcriptionist and typist, the patient and always good-humored Phyllis Travell, for deciphering my hand printing on hundreds of legal-tablet pages, the text that finally made up *A Fortunate Life.*

Finally, and most important of all, thanks to my wife, Linda, who, by sharing the adventure of my life, has made it truly worth living. She has been unfailingly supportive of me through all the ups and downs of an actor's career, as well as through these past two years in which work on this book has taken me away from her far too often. Here's hoping that she and I will be able to write many more memorable chapters together in the years to come.

The employees of Thorndike Press hope you have enjoyed this Large Print book. All our Thorndike and Wheeler Large Print titles are designed for easy reading, and all our books are made to last. Other Thorndike Press Large Print books are available at your library, through selected bookstores, or directly from us.

For information about titles, please call:
(800) 223-1244

or visit our Web site at:
http://gale.cengage.com/thorndike

To share your comments, please write:
Publisher
Thorndike Press
295 Kennedy Memorial Drive
Waterville, ME 04901